Records Management

FOR

DUMMIES®

10/13

Records Management
FOR
DUMMIES®

by Blake Richardson

WILEY

John Wiley & Sons, Inc.

Records Management For Dummies®

Published by
John Wiley & Sons, Inc.
111 River Street
Hoboken, NJ 07030-5774
www.wiley.com

Copyright © 2012 by John Wiley & Sons, Inc., Hoboken, New Jersey

Published by John Wiley & Sons, Inc., Hoboken, New Jersey

Published simultaneously in Canada

For general information on our other products and services, please contact our Customer Care Department within the U.S. at 877-762-2974, outside the U.S. at 317-572-3993, or fax 317-572-4002.

For technical support, please visit www.wiley.com/techsupport.

Wiley publishes in a variety of print and electronic formats and by print-on-demand. Some material included with standard print versions of this book may not be included in e-books or in print-on-demand. If this book refers to media such as a CD or DVD that is not included in the version you purchased, you may download this material at http://booksupport.wiley.com. For more information about Wiley products, visit www.wiley.com.

Library of Congress Control Number: 2012948917

ISBN 978-1-118-38808-2 (pbk); ISBN 978-1-118-38809-9 (ebk); ISBN 978-1-118-38810-5 (ebk); ISBN 978-1-118-38812-9 (ebk)

Manufactured in the United States of America

10 9 8 7 6 5 4 3 2 1

WILEY

About the Author

Blake Richardson (Surprise, Arizona) is the author of numerous publications on records and information management. Blake is a Certified Information Professional (CIP) and Certified Records Manager (CRM). He has over 15 years of experience in developing comprehensive Records and Information Management programs with several Fortune 500 companies. Blake frequently conducts presentations on a wide range of Records and Information Management topics.

Dedication

To my wife, Kelli, son, Raleigh, and daughter, Molly.

Acknowledgments

I would like to acknowledge Dr. Mark Langemo, CRM, for instilling in me the passion for records management, Steve Peterson, CRM, for providing his welcomed insight, and my records and information management colleagues for their professionalism and dedication — thank you all!

Publisher's Acknowledgments

We're proud of this book; please send us your comments at http://dummies.custhelp.com. For other comments, please contact our Customer Care Department within the U.S. at 877-762-2974, outside the U.S. at 317-572-3993, or fax 317-572-4002.

Some of the people who helped bring this book to market include the following:

Acquisitions, Editorial

Senior Project Editor: Paul Levesque

Acquisitions Editor: Katie Mohr

Copy Editors: Amanda Graham, John Edwards

Technical Editor: Steven Petersen

Editorial Manager: Leah Michael

Editorial Assistant: Leslie Saxman

Sr. Editorial Assistant: Cherie Case

Cover Photo: © iStockphoto.com/ CTRdesignLLC (background image)

Cartoons: Rich Tennant (www.the5thwave.com)

Project Coordinator: Patrick Redmond

Layout and Graphics: Jennifer Creasey, Timothy C. Detrick, Corrie Niehaus

Proofreader: Bonnie Mikkelson

Indexer: Valerie Haynes Perry

Publishing and Editorial for Technology Dummies

    Richard Swadley, Vice President and Executive Group Publisher

    Andy Cummings, Vice President and Publisher

    Mary Bednarek, Executive Acquisitions Director

    Mary C. Corder, Editorial Director

Publishing for Consumer Dummies

    Kathleen Nebenhaus, Vice President and Executive Publisher

Composition Services

    Debbie Stailey, Director of Composition Services

Contents at a Glance

Table of Contents

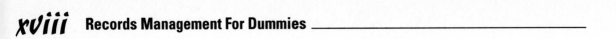

Introduction

· ·

*R*ecords and information management isn't a new concept or discipline. From the moment one cave person grunted to another or scrawled the first picture on the inside of a cave wall, information and recordkeeping was born. That first cave person probably had not been assigned the title of "Records and Information manager" or official scribe for the cave community, but nonetheless felt a need to communicate and keep what we know today to be records.

Over millions of years, the information grunt has grown — not only into structured languages that are spoken, but also into an exponential increase in the documentation and transmission of information. Most of this increase has occurred at a staggering rate over the past 15 years — you guessed it, we have computers, e-mail, and the Internet to thank for our information overload. The reality is that information is a good thing. However, if not managed appropriately, you may never realize its true value, and someday find yourself in a corner curled up in the fetal position mumbling "Delete"!

About This Book

Hold onto to your seat; you're about to enter the riveting world of Records and Information management. Okay, *riveting* may be embellishing a bit, but the truth is whether you're a small-business owner or work for a global corporation, you deal with information on a daily basis — you receive it, you send it, you determine what's relevant, and you make decisions, whether consciously or subconsciously, as to what information to retain. This book is not about information technology (IT); this book is about information management. The goal of the book is to assist you and all companies, regardless of size, number of employees, or annual revenue, in making this entire process more manageable and compliant with applicable laws and regulations.

Records and Information management is an ongoing process and not a one-time project. Depending on the size of your company, it may take a significant up-front investment of time to implement an effective program. However, the up-front investment will help to minimize any back-end debacles. After you have your Records and Information Management program in place, it needs to be maintained. This book provides proven best practices and tips for ensuring that you are successful — and for good measure, I'll throw in a hearty "Good luck!" to start things off.

Conventions Used in This Book

In an effort to avoid any confusion while you are reading this book, I thought I would briefly explain some nuances:

- ✔ Website addresses, known as URLs, are highlighted like this: www.web siteaddress.com.
- ✔ Menu commands are given in the order in which you should select them. For example, Choose File⇨New⇨Folder.

Foolish Assumptions

No offense intended, but I've made some assumptions about you — yes, you over there! I assume that you haven't received a doctoral degree in Records and Information Management or any other formal training in this area. I bet you receive and send information each day, and that you may have trouble finding information later when you need it. Or, you might wish that you had another filing cabinet because the one you have has a No Vacancy sign on it.

I assume that you know how to use a computer — not that you're a computer prodigy, but you know enough to get by. This includes knowing how to use e-mail, document software, and spreadsheet applications, and that you have not used formal Records and Information Management software programs (yet). My apologies for any incorrect assumptions!

How This Book Is Organized

This book is structured in a sequential or step-by-step practical approach that will take you from the beginning of your records and information journey through more advanced, relevant topics and issues facing today's organizations. The book also lends itself to readers who want to focus on particular subjects or just want to refresh their knowledge.

Part I: Setting the Stage

Part I provides instruction and guidance on creating the foundation for your Records and Information Management program. This includes obtaining an understanding of common terms, the benefits you and your organization can realize by implementing a program, and how to get senior management buy-in and their continuing support for the initiative. In addition, Part I provides options and step-by-step instructions for inventorying your records and information to develop an effective retention schedule.

Part II: Filing Made Simple

In Part II, you get to examine different filing methods and equipment and determine which ones best fit your company's needs. You get some guidance on how to create an electronic folder structure, receive tips for naming files, and find out how to prevent electronic repositories such as hard drives and shared network drives from becoming cluttered. In addition, Part II provides instruction on how to effectively manage e-mail in a manual and automated environment.

Part III: Capturing Records

The ongoing management of your records and information is an essential part of the process. In Part III, you discover the purpose and perils of backup tapes and find out how to effectively manage them so that they don't come back to bite you. In addition, you look into the role that records and information play in lawsuits and see what you need to know about document imaging and its benefits, as well as determine how technology can help you manage your records and information.

Part IV: Parking Spaces

Ever wonder what to do when you have too many records and not enough storage space? Part IV to the rescue! Part IV helps you understand how to properly store records onsite as well as offsite with a vendor. I examine storage requirements and compliant destruction methods that will ensure that your records are properly protected and destroyed when the time comes.

Part V: Creating a Plan

What's a Records and Information Management program without policies, audits, and training? Part V guides you through the process of establishing a comprehensive policy, determining what components of records and information management need to be audited, and gives you options that ensure that employees are effectively trained.

Part VI: The Part of Tens

Ten is a nice round number for listing things. In the case of this book, I discuss ten management guidelines and ten emerging trends. The first list provides you with practical tips that, if they become habit, will make managing records and information a lot easier. The second list provides insight into hot Records and Information Management topics and issues that are just now beginning to peek over the business horizon.

Bonus Content: Appendix

In the online appendix, you find helpful tools such as templates, sample forms, vendor information, and Records and Information program assessments. These tools have practical applications that you can use to inventory and appraise your information, as well as forms that provide different retention schedule formats. (To access all bonus content, visit this book's website at www.dummies.com/go/recordsmanagefd.)

The appendix includes a comprehensive listing of Records and Content Management software vendors and assessments of their products. Also provided are ARMA International's Generally Accepted Recordkeeping Principles and Maturity Model for Information Governance, which allow you to determine the current state of your records and information management and what it takes to make it better.

What You're Not to Read

First, you don't have to read this book from front to back, or back to front depending on where you reside. If you want to just get information about a certain topic, you can open this book to any chapter and get the information you need.

The book has been designed to first lay the foundation for managing your records and information and then build upon it. So reading the book from start to finish will work as well!

Icons Used in This Book

One picture is worth . . . well, you know the old saying. That's why *For Dummies* books use icons to give you a visual clue as to what's going on. Essentially, icons call your attention to bits of special information that might very well make your life easier. Following are the icons used in this book.

 Remember icons signal either a pertinent fact that relates to what you're reading at the time (but is also mentioned elsewhere in the book) or a reiteration of a particularly important piece of information that's — well — worth repeating.

 Tips are the Ann Landers of business books. They offer sage advice, a bit more information about a topic under discussion that might be of interest, or ways to do things a bit more effectively.

 Warning icons spell trouble with a capital T. When you see a Warning, read it, because it's trying to tell you that if you're not careful, you might do something at this point that could cause disaster.

Where to Go from Here

By reading this book you will have taken the first step in managing your records and information. Educating yourself on the subject matter is essential. Like every organization, your company has its own operational nuances. However, you will find that the Records and Information Management principles in this book are applicable to all businesses.

So absorb what you read and determine how to apply it to your own situation. I'm not promising that filing records and determining how long to retain information will be the highlight of your day, but putting an effective program in place may help you sleep better at night.

Last but not least, for updates to this edition, check out www.dummies.com/go/recordsmanagementfdupdates.

Part I
Setting the Stage

"I like getting complaint letters by e-mail. It's easier to delete than to shred."

In this part . . .

Part I lays the foundation for managing your records and information by guiding you through the process of identifying and classifying them so that you can develop a retention schedule. Along the way, you'll find out about the benefits of implementing a Records and Information Management program and discover how to get senior management buy-in and support.

Chapter 1

Fundamentally Speaking

● ●

In This Chapter

▶ Defining the terms

▶ Understanding the effect of records and information

▶ Evaluating the role of the records manager

▶ Managing expectations

▶ Trimming your expenses

▶ Seeing how you can improve efficiencies

▶ Reducing risks

▶ Setting up your own support group

▶ Developing a marketing plan

● ●

Congratulations! You're taking the first and necessary step to getting your records and information management house in order. Regardless of whether you've already ventured into the world of overflowing file cabinets, paper cuts, and maxed out computer storage space — it's okay. Just sit back, relax, and we'll take the trip together.

These days, almost every organization needs to develop and implement a records and information management program. From the corner bagel vendor to the multinational conglomerate, and every sized business in between, they all receive and send information. Putting this type of program in place helps you manage your records and information so that you meet your business needs and comply with laws and regulations.

A records and information management program has many components. Before developing and implementing your program, familiarize yourself with the pieces of the puzzle, as well as the jargon associated with the various pieces. This chapter goes over some common terms and also discusses some of the most important program elements.

The Inside Scoop — Terms and Terminologies

Understanding records and information management jargon may sound elementary, but knowing how the terms are actually used is important. These terms have differences and similarities, and some may sound off-puttingly foreign or (misleadingly) self-explanatory. For example, all records constitute information, but not all information is a record.

What is information?

In layman's terms, *business information* is the total volume of — but not limited to — all paper and electronic documents, spreadsheets, recorded telephone conversations, databases, and tacit or *gray matter* knowledge produced by an organization. "Information" is an all-encompassing term and everything else is a subset of information. Most organizations have three categories of information:

- Records
- Business value
- Nonvalue

For the record

A *record* is information created or received by an organization that provides proof of its legal status and business transactions, regardless of whether it's in paper or electronic format. A record can be considered the memory of the organization. Records make up only a small percentage of the information population of a company; however, they're very important to the continuing operation of a business.

In all likelihood, any information you have that serves as evidence of your company's transactions, history, and legal responsibilities, as well as status, is a record. This includes information such as contracts, employee files, invoices, tax returns, and articles of incorporation. Records are *media neutral,* which means that the format doesn't dictate whether something is a record. The records may exist in paper, electronic, or microfiche formats — it's the content that matters!

As important as all records are to your organization, *vital records* are the most important. Vital records are needed to resume your company's operations in the event of a disaster. Vital records are either organizational or operational:

- **Organizational vital records:** Includes articles of incorporation or Board of Directors minutes and bylaws. Vital records of this nature help an organization reestablish its legal status and existence.

- **Operational vital records:** Needed to resume critical business functions and ensure that your revenue stream stays intact. In most cases, you can't resume operations if you're unable to pay your employees, provide your products or services, or collect on accounts receivable.

Chapter 4 provides step-by-step instructions on how to identify and protect vital records — stay tuned!

Business value

Business value information refers to information that's important to a company but doesn't meet the criteria of a record. Think of business value information as referential material — spreadsheets, reports, and presentations — that assist in decision-making, but have a finite purpose and life (such as a sales spreadsheet that you create to show the boss). This type of information has business value but isn't evidence of your organization's business or legal transactions, and also usually has a limited lifespan.

Nonvalue

If something isn't a record, and has no business value — what is it then? Some call it *nonvalue information* (or clutter), which is simply information that has lost its company value. For many organizations, nonvalue content residing in storage boxes, file cabinets, hard drives, network drives, and removable devices (flash drives) comprises the largest population of information they retain — scary huh? Examples of nonvalue information might include old let's-go-to-lunch e-mails, pictures of your toga party, an ancient presentation, and even records that have exceeded their assigned retention period.

The information life cycle

All business information has a *life cycle*. The premise of the life cycle is that records and information become either less important over time or are accessed less frequently as they age (or both). Most records and information begin to lose value after approximately 90 days. For example, an invoice must be accessible during a 30-day period for processing purposes. After the invoice is paid, you may need to access it during the next two months to resolve any payment disputes or inquiries.

Although all records age, not all lose their importance to an organization over time. Records such as deeds, articles of incorporation, and Board of Directors meeting minutes retain their importance and should be kept permanently.

Figure 1-1 makes clear the distinct phases in the life of records and information.

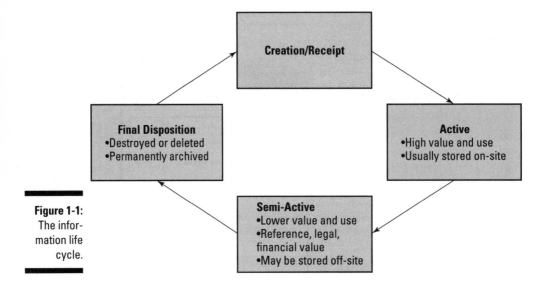

Figure 1-1:
The infor-
mation life
cycle.

To grasp the concepts behind the life cycle diagram you see in Figure 1-1, think of that new toy you received as a kid. When you first got that shiny red fire truck or that new doll, you played with it constantly; you kept it close by so that you didn't have to look for it. However, as time passed, it lost some of its appeal — it might have ultimately been relegated to your closet. A few years later, when mom tells you to clean out your closet, you find the fire truck or the doll, which has no value to you now, and you decide to throw it away; or, if you're sentimental, you keep it.

Grooving with the records (and the information retention schedule)

An important tool you can use to manage the life cycle of records and information is a *retention schedule,* which is a document used to list an organization's records and how long to keep them. Although commonly referred to as a "records retention schedule," records and information management professionals have begun to incorporate items of business value information that are *not* records into the retention schedule.

The primary reason for this change is that organizations are starting to realize that nonrecord content accounts for a significant amount of their total information population, and if left unchecked, will continue to grow out of control. Record and information retention schedules are discussed in depth in Chapter 3.

Hold on!

If a company believes there's a chance it's going to be sued, or chance just flew out the window when the subpoena was served this morning, the company needs to determine what records and other information may be relevant to the lawsuit. After this is determined, the powers-that-be will want to implement an *information hold order.* Organizations may use different names for the hold order, such as *legal hold, records hold order,* or *freeze.* In many cases, information hold orders pertain to legal matters, but can also apply to tax audits, regulatory investigations, and operational issues.

An information hold order doesn't just apply to records; it can apply to nonrecord content as well. When a hold order is enacted, the information must not be altered or destroyed. This topic is covered in depth in Chapter 8.

For now, you've probably absorbed enough terms and definitions for one day, so it's time to move on.

Role Playing

Businesses that effectively manage their records and information perform better. All organizations create and receive information, but some don't capitalize on the opportunity to understand it and properly optimize it.

It's true; if you improperly manage your records and information, it can result in hefty fines, closure of your business, and possibly a chance to get acquainted with other inmates at your local five star federal prison. But enough with the scare tactics.

Information is tangible. It should be viewed and treated as a company asset, just like your inventory, real estate, and equipment. Look at your file cabinets and computer folders as gold mines waiting to be tapped. Yes, there's gold in them thar hills! Just look at companies like Amazon, Google, and Facebook for examples of organizations that capitalize on information as an asset. They know their customers' desires; some may argue that they can even anticipate your needs.

Aside from death and taxes, there is another inevitable: Companies will create (and enter into) new initiatives. A company may be launching a program to increase sales, offering a new product line, purchasing a software system, or opening a new location. Regardless of the nature of the initiative, responsible organizations don't jump haphazardly into the fire without conducting exhaustive research and analysis of available information. In many cases, the needed information isn't available, so they conduct specific studies geared toward providing them with the information they need. Business decisions should be based on timely and accurate information.

And information isn't used only for major business initiatives; it plays a vital role in routine daily business processes such as invoice payments. When you pay an invoice, you don't just take the word of the vendor that you need to pay $25,000 for a box of paper clips (unless it's a very big box of paper clips). You ensure that the product has been received; you check the packing slip and match the invoice to the purchase order. The entire decision process is based on information.

The Records and Information Manager

Time to hit the rewind button: For decades many organizations, even large ones, didn't have an employee with the official title of records manager, much less a records and information manager. Back in simpler times, before personal computers, e-mail, and the onslaught of compliance-related laws, records management consisted of an employee ordering a file, and the file clerk pulling the file from a shelf, providing it for the requestor, and then refiling it when it was returned.

The evolution of the records manager

Today, most public and private organizations realize the need to dedicate a manager and staff to oversee records and information management. Although the phrase *from the basement to the boardroom* may not be applicable to all records and information management operations, the role that records and information management plays within many companies has significantly changed over the past decade.

This change has brought about an evolution in the job description of records and information managers. No longer is the manager responsible only for ensuring that her staff pulls the correct file and refiles it in a timely and accurate manner. Records and information managers are now tasked with many other responsibilities related to an organization's records and information life cycle. In addition — and maybe even more importantly as a sign of the profession's credibility, records and information managers are increasingly serving as consultants to company employees on matters related to records and information.

Records managers now chair and serve on corporate committees, assist senior management, and work in close conjunction with different departments such as legal, risk management, compliance, and IT. They are sought out for their expertise on records– and information management–related topics. So how did this change in the records manager's role come to be?

In the past, the records and information a company possessed were mainly used to facilitate the processing of routine functions such as accounting, payroll, and purchasing. Technologies hadn't been developed to allow organizations to easily *data-mine* — conduct in-depth analysis in areas like customer buying habits or trending. Records were kept in file cabinets; gigabytes of data on personal computers and how to manage it hadn't yet entered into corporate conversations. Regulatory legislation such as Sarbanes-Oxley, the Fair and Accurate Credit Transactions Act (ACTA), and the Health Insurance Portability and Accountability Act (HIPAA) didn't exist.

The big bang!

Thanks in part to Bill Gates, Steve Jobs, Intel, and white collar greed, the role of the records manager began to transform in the '80s and '90s. Not so long ago multiple employees might have shared a lone computer, and no one thought that was inadequate. (Today, if this were still the case, there would be a corporate coup.) Companies didn't ponder the records and information management impact that adding so many computers would create, but instead focused on efficiency and productivity.

And companies weren't negligent by not anticipating the records and information effects caused by the proliferation of desktop computing. Probably only a handful of visionaries could have foreseen these potential issues — which, ironically, created job security for many records and information managers. And that leads you to see how these managers have been able to evolve with the changing tides and obtain the necessary knowledge and skill set to operate in today's records and information management environment.

School is in session

At a young age, many children dream of becoming a firefighter or astronaut. Probably not many aspire to be a records and information manager. Most records and information managers never received formal training, much less a degree in this field. And in many cases, this responsibility was never originally listed on their job description. As it has occurred for many managers, one day the boss calls you into the office and says that in addition to your other responsibilities, you're now in charge of managing the company's records — and don't mess it up! If this has happened to you, probably your first thought was, "I don't remember making the boss mad." And then, "I know nothing about managing records and information."

Today's records and information managers (and staff) need help to stay abreast of a myriad of topics such as compliance laws, document imaging, enterprise content management, information hold orders, discovery, secure shredding, offsite storage, retention scheduling, and the effects of file shares and applications like Microsoft SharePoint (all of which are covered in Chapters 9, 10, 8, 12, and 3, respectively).

So, what's a newly christened records and information manager to do? Some options are more advisable than others. Some managers may decide to travel down the status quo highway, and maintain a mind-set of, "If it ain't broke, don't fix it." The risk assumed with this approach is that as a manager, you might not know what you don't know — meaning the state of records and information management within the organization may be in shambles, but how can you tell?

Another course of action is on-the-job training and self-learning. You may seek to improve your knowledge of records and information management by understanding the current processes and learning from your staff. The possible pitfall here is that when trying to improve the efficiencies of the current operation, you might not know whether fundamental problems are putting the organization at risk.

I can associate with that

The best option is to begin your records and information management education as soon as possible. A great way to make this happen is to seek resources, guidance, and knowledge from reputable sources in the records and information global community. Managers can significantly benefit from the been-there-done-that guidance available from numerous records and information management professionals and associations. Two of the more prominent and recognized associations are ARMA (Association for Information Management) and AIIM (Association for Information and Image Management); these are not-for-profit and nonprofit associations, respectively. Their missions are as follows:

- ✔ **ARMA** (www.arma.org): Educate, advocate, provide resources, and set standards that enable professionals to govern information as a critical element of organizational value.

- ✔ **AIIM** (www.aiim.org): Ensure that information professionals understand the current and future challenges of managing information assets in an era of social, mobile, cloud, and big data. Big data is covered in Chapter 16.

In addition to these two organizations, other records and information management associations focus on specific industries, such as nuclear energy and health and pharmaceuticals. Most records and information management organizations have an international headquarters, with local satellite chapters. A quick Google search for *ARMA Chapters* or *AIIM Chapters* will provide you with information on a chapter in your area.

These organizations offer programs for experienced records and information managers as well as the new kids on the block. In most cases, their membership represents a variety of industries. By attending these educational sessions, you have a great opportunity to learn, share, and network.

Let me see your credentials

Pursuing a designation is a personal choice. You should assess the current and future Records and Information Management direction of your organization and determine whether you need to acquire additional skill sets and education to lead the charge.

Have you ever received an e-mail with cryptic letter combinations after the sender's last name in the signature block? You guessed it — those letters are designations and certifications. Some may call it the "ego alphabet," but in fact, it reflects a person's achievement and expertise in specific disciplines. For many years no formal designations for records and information managers existed. However, in 1975, that changed when the Institute of Certified Records Managers (ICRM) was incorporated.

According to the ICRM website, the goal of the ICRM has been, "to meet the requirement to have a standard by which persons involved in records and information management could be measured, accredited, and recognized according to criteria of experience and capability established by their peers." The folks at ICRM determined that a need existed for accreditation, and they established the Certified Records Manager (CRM) designation, which is still the most recognized designation for records and information managers. To achieve the designation, a person must first be accepted as a candidate. Candidacy is based on a combination of formal education and practical records and information management experience. After acceptance candidates must successfully complete a six-part examination that covers a variety of relevant topics.

Over the past two decades, as technology, laws, and regulations affecting records and information management burst upon the scene, additional designating and certifying bodies have been created that focus on document imaging, privacy, and technology, to name a few topics. Table 1-1 shows some of the prominent designations in the records and information management profession.

Table 1-1   Records and Information Management Certifications

Certification	Certification Name	Certifying Body	Description
CDIA+	Certified Document Imaging Architect	Computing Technology Industry Association (CompTIA)	An internationally recognized credential acknowledging competency and professionalism in the document imaging and document management industry
CIP	Certified Information Professional	Association for Information and Image Management (AIIM)	A certification recognizing the holder as a professional in information management

Certification	Certification Name	Certifying Body	Description
CIPP	Certified Information Privacy Professional	International Association of Privacy Professionals (IAPP)	Demonstrates a strong foundation in privacy laws and regulations
CISSP	Certified Information Systems Security Professional	The International Information Systems Security Certification Consortium, Inc. (ISC)^2	Demonstrates an information assurance professional who defines the architecture, design, management, and controls that assure the security of the business environments
CKM	Certified Knowledge Manager	Knowledge Management Professional Society (KMpro)	Demonstrates the ability to link organizational knowledge to the strategic vision and initiatives of the company
CRM	Certified Records Manager	Institute of Certified Records Managers (ICRM)	An internationally recognized credential acknowledging an individual's proficiency in managing records
ICP	Information Capture Professional	The Association for Work Process Improvement (TAWPI)	Recognizes achievement and dedication of professionals in payment/remittance processing, data capture, imaging operations, and forms processing
PMP	Project Management Professional	Project Management Institute (PMI)	Demonstrates that the holder has the experience, education and competency to lead and direct projects

When you earn a designation like the CRM, you feel a sense of pride and accomplishment. Better still, you stand a good chance of increasing your credibility and marketability. Many employers today looking to hire a records and information manager prefer (or require) the candidate to have the CRM designation.

In 2011, AIIM introduced the Certified Information Professional (CIP) designation, which is a great complement to the CRM designation. The CIP consists of one exam, with no educational or work-related prerequisites required to take the exam. The exam is designed not only to test a person's records management knowledge, but also technical knowledge in a variety of areas, such as master data management, text analytics, and technical architecture.

I've got to do what?!

As if keeping on top of the technical aspects of her job isn't enough, a records and information manager is now expected to do even more. The 21st century records and information manager has to hone skills in additional and essential areas. For example, yesterday's file room manager rarely interacted with other departments' employees on matters of records management, but those days are over. Records and information managers now find themselves responsible for consulting, formulating and implementing organizational policy, training, reviewing contracts, managing vendors, and addressing senior management and other employees through verbal and written communication. Because of these new responsibilities, records and information managers have to become well-rounded professionals prepared to effectively handle many scenarios. The next section addresses the complementary skills records and information managers need to enhance their success.

The written word

Writing is an art, a science, and a skill that records and information managers need to effectively communicate. As with any form of communication, the first step is to know your audience. You wouldn't address the CEO in the same manner as your co-worker in the next cubicle. If you are writing a procedure for a function in your department, it will likely contain extensive details that allow the reader to perform the process. However, in most cases, when composing a document intended for senior management, you won't need to include many of the details. You may be thinking, "But aren't details a good thing?" Yes, in some cases they are vital, but depending on the target audience, it may be the death of your document.

Say hello to the *executive briefing*. Records and information managers in today's corporate environment often have to document proposals — say, an initiative that affects the entire organization, or a recommendation to purchase a software application — for senior management review. As its name implies, keep your executive briefing brief, but provide enough information to get your point across. It's a delicate balancing act. The reality is that most senior managers are very busy (or so they say), and consider yourself lucky if your document commands more than a few minutes of their time. Therefore, you have to make the most of it.

The following tips help you compose an effective business document and should also help you avoid some common writing pitfalls:

- ✔ **Know the subject matter.** Forget winging it. Don't attempt to write about something you don't know the first thing about. Make sure to research the topic and be prepared to respond to questions.

- ✔ **Plan.** Resist the urge to immediately begin drafting a business document. Plan and outline your communication before you begin writing. This allows you an opportunity to organize your thoughts. Thinking of the outline as a table of contents for your document will increase your chance of not forgetting important points.

- ✔ **Less is more.** Don't inundate the reader with unnecessary words or details. Make the reading experience efficient and convenient.

- ✔ **Avoid jargon or slang.** Anyone who has spent time in corporate America has heard phrases such as *boil the ocean*, *bleeding edge*, *bricks and mortar*, and *30,000 foot level*. "Corp-speak" may be okay for water cooler conversations but shouldn't find its way into business documents.

- ✔ **Write once, check twice.** Proofread immediately after you write; then go have lunch, sit back down, and proofread again. Typos and grammatical errors can instantly discredit the communication and the author. Take advantage of the spell-check tool in your word processing app, and have a co-worker review the document before you distribute it.

- ✔ **Pay attention to names, titles, and gender.** You don't want to find out after you send your document to Ms. Jones, the vice president of the Sales department, that she's actually a he (Mr. Johnson), the CEO, and that you demoted him because you didn't know his title. Besides being offended, the reader may feel that you don't pay attention to details. If you're not certain about the spelling of someone's name, job title (and what it means), or gender, check with someone who does know (like an assistant), or use gender-neutral language.

- ✔ **Professional doesn't necessarily mean formal.** Business documents shouldn't require the reader to have a dictionary and thesaurus to interpret your communication. Many readers will immediately detect when an author is trying to impress them with extravagant language rather than substance.

- ✔ **Remember the five Ws (and one H).** Your business document should answer all the questions relevant to the reader — who, what, when, where, why, and how. For example, who is this communication relevant to, what should they know, when and where will it apply, why is it important, and how should they use this information?

✓ **Include a call to action.** Most business communication is intended to achieve a purpose. So, make sure that your document contains a *call to action* — something the reader is supposed to do. Don't leave it to the reader to decide what to do with the information you provide.

✓ **Don't provide too many choices.** If you know what you want, ask for it and instruct the reader (diplomatically) to follow the needed course of action. Most senior managers don't like to receive mandates; therefore, present options and choices to the reader, but not too many. Ensure that the options you present in your document don't dilute your objective. For example, say you submit a proposal to the CFO requesting to purchase and implement an electronic records management software application. You prefer to buy all the modules at one time, but another option is to buy the modules incrementally as needed. If either option is approved, you succeeded.

✓ **Convey what's in it for the reader.** This is one of the most important aspects of business writing. Benefits engage the reader. Why should I take time to read something that provides no benefit to me? As the author, construct and tailor your communication so that it's not all about your wants and needs, but how it benefits the reader or the organization.

If you need assistance with your writing skills, many large organizations have online training classes designed to help employees with their development in areas such as business writing. Another option is to find a mentor. If you have a co-worker whose writing you admire, ask him for help.

Professionally speaking

It's not all about writing. You likely have to speak to an audience, whether one person, entry-level employees, or senior management. For many people the mere thought of public speaking invokes anxiety and physical distress. Most of the writing tips discussed in the last section are applicable to oral communication, too, so rely on them: Know your subject matter, plan your communication, less is more — you get the picture.

Still, no matter how well some people know the subject matter, plan their communication, or picture the audience in their underwear, they still fear speaking in front of others. If you fall into this category, you're definitely not alone. There is no substitute for practice and experience (whether good or bad). Find associations dedicated to public speaking, such as Toastmasters (www.toastmasters.org). Look up one of its local chapters and see what kinds of resources it can offer in terms of public speaking and leadership skills.

I'm Excited — Why Aren't You?

Here's a fundamental truism: An overwhelming percentage of employees don't find records and information management to be a riveting topic or task. To put it bluntly, they don't like it! Employees find filing documents, boxing records for storage, or cleaning up electronic files a distraction. Chances are that most employees aren't evaluated on their annual performance review by how well they boxed up records or maintained their network folders and files. The sooner the records and information manager and staff accept this reality, the less frustrated they will be.

Core function junction

Employees don't consider managing records and information part of their core business functions (even though for the records and information manager it clearly is). Remember this when developing a records and information management program. Keep it as simple and convenient as possible for the masses without compromising the integrity of the program.

Depending on the size of your organization (assuming that you're not a sole proprietor), you need help in managing the company's records and information. You can't accomplish your objectives by yourself. In this case, it does take a village — okay, maybe other employees — to help manage the organization's records and information.

The best way to get employees to buy into records and information management is to demonstrate how it will benefit them in their daily functions. (See Chapter 2 for more on that particular topic.) Make your requirement a process and not an end-of-month -or-year project. That way, you change the records and information culture of the organization and the employees' perception. Done right, you can transform records and information management from a necessary evil and distraction to a tangible benefit.

Show me the benefits!

Showing the benefits a new company program or initiative will bring to an organization greatly increases its chances of approval and support by senior management and acceptance by its employees. Administrative and support functions — such as accounting; payroll; facilities management; and yes, records and information management — are usually considered cost centers and not profit centers. Demonstrating the benefits of an initiative in these types of areas can sometimes be difficult.

Although records and information management may be a support or administrative function, an effectively designed and implemented program reduces organizational expense, improves efficiency, and ensures that your company is in compliance with laws and government regulations, decreasing the potential for fines. The benefits of a records and management program range from short- and long-term reductions in expense to improving the processing of routine functions.

Know how to market and communicate the organizational benefits of records and information management. A bit later in this chapter you have a chance to look over some proven techniques for developing a marketing plan and how to communicate it to senior management and other company employees.

Trimming expenses

Office space is expensive, and file cabinets aren't cheap nor should be used to store information that's infrequently accessed or not needed at all. Although the cost of computer storage has significantly decreased over the past ten years, the costs associated with *maintaining* electronic storage isn't. My experience over the years has been that the majority of the records and information retained by organizations contains no business value and can legally and operationally be destroyed. This can have a positive impact for all types of businesses.

Effectively managing organizational records and information will prevent your company from appearing on an episode of *Corporate Hoarders*. The storage of each unneeded document and electronic file has a price tag that's taking away from the bottom line of your organization.

As eager as you might be to reduce your company's records and information expenses, don't just dive in and start throwing things away! You have to be certain that the retention periods for the records have expired and that those records aren't needed for any potential lawsuits or inquiries.

Reducing the company's volume of paper records and information decreases the number of file cabinets you need to purchase and use, which results in more space for productive purposes. The less junk you have in a file cabinet, the easier it is to find what you really need.

To make space for the upcoming year, many companies periodically (typically, annually) purge their files from cabinets, place them in a box, and then send them to onsite or offsite storage (usually with a records storage vendor).

The costs related to storing a box of records or adding a gigabyte of electronic storage are minimal. The inexpensive nature of storage is a contributing factor to many legal, risk, records, and information management problems — such as continuing to retain information (that is eligible to be destroyed) that may be a liability to a company in a lawsuit or adding electronic storage rather than deleting files that are no longer needed. If the question is "If storage is so cheap, why not keep everything forever?" the answer should be "Because the cost of storage is just the tip of the iceberg." For example, every gigabyte of storage results in additional expense — *total cost of ownership (TCO)* — which represents a variety of expenses that affect storage, including

- ✔ Electricity
- ✔ Service
- ✔ Engineering and installation
- ✔ Power equipment
- ✔ Cooling equipment
- ✔ Space
- ✔ Racking
- ✔ System monitoring
- ✔ Backups and redundancy

Studies indicate that the price of storage represents less than 20 percent of the TCO (source: Hitachi 2011 White Paper, "Four Principles for Reducing Total Cost of Ownership"). Eliminating unneeded electronic information reduces your storage dependencies, thereby reducing your TCO.

In addition, keeping everything forever because the organization can purchase inexpensive storage can actually increase the company's risk and liability. In decades past, most organizations believed they needed to keep everything to defend themselves in lawsuits. However, over the past decade, many companies have come to realize that keeping information the company no longer needs and that should've been destroyed in accordance with established retention schedules can actually put them in a worse legal position by retaining information that can prove to be a liability during a lawsuit.

In most companies, computers are abundant. What's not abundant are policies, procedures, and employee training on how to manage electronic information. The absence of these requirements and controls promotes a do-nothing approach. Think of a file cabinet or the box of records under a desk that's used as a footstool. And an out-of-sight, out-of-mind mentality with electronic information is worse. Your boss will probably tell you to clean up the files and boxes in the department but won't mention anything about the mess on the computers.

When considering cost-cutting measures, management seldom addresses the need to spring-clean hard drives and network drives. Many companies don't realize the monetary benefit to purging nonvalue information from the organization's computers. For example, every time an employee has to sift through the digital jungle of junk to find what she really needs, an unneeded labor expense is incurred.

Effectively managing organizational records and information can help reduce this cost by maintaining a focus on how to properly name electronic folders and files as well as how to effectively police and purge nonvalue information.

Improving efficiencies

Smart management of your records and information increases efficiencies within your organization. A records and information management program enhances customer service, staff productivity, and decision- making. Increasing your company's efficiencies doesn't involve any magic — just planning, support, and technology.

A records and information management program allows you to achieve efficiency by using the *Right principle:*

> The right information to the right person at the right time

This may sound like an attempt to reach a corporate state of nirvana, but it's actually attainable. You know you've reached this level of enlightenment when your company is able to quickly locate information, reduce storage costs, and make office space available for productive purposes.

After all, we live and operate in an age of convenience — "I want it now!" Yes, Veruca, your clients and customers not only want "it" now, they expect "it" now, too. Clients and customers expect their problems or needs to be resolved or met during a brief phone call or through an intuitive, uncomplicated website experience.

That expectation means you should avoid having to tell customers that you have to order a file, or that you need to transfer him to another department in order to take care of his issue. Similarly, customers will likely become frustrated if your customer service website isn't efficiently designed — requiring excessive mouse clicks, for example — or doesn't provide interactive functionality. You run the risk of losing customers and revenue if you can't provide timely and accurate information.

A records and information management program, in conjunction with the right technology for your company, allows you to index customer information by category, such as personal data, previous purchases or sales, invoices, remittances, and comments. Indexing is the process of applying *metadata,* or information about information.

A good example of this process involves *document imaging.* After receiving a paper document (say, an address change) from the customer, you scan it. You then apply index values to the image, like customer name, customer account number, and form type (address change). After completing the indexing process, you send or release the image to another software application for quick retrieval. (For a more in-depth discussion of document imaging, see Chapter 9.)

Increasing staff productivity

A records and information management program provides employees with the tools to do their job more accurately and productively. Increased staff productivity is one of the biggest and most noticeable benefits of the program. Employees at every level of an organization file, retrieve, and refile information every day. Giving employees the right environment, guidance, and technology to work smarter and faster makes for more satisfied employees, more satisfied customers — and as a result, a more satisfied organization.

Creating efficiencies starts with knowing what types of records and information you have, including paper and electronic information. You have to understand how this information is currently stored and what it's used for. After you have an understanding of your company records and information — and how long you need to keep them — you can take steps to streamline filing and retrieval. You might revamp your paper filing systems or create effective folder structures on your computers so that employees can better use filing systems that meet their operational needs.

Filing systems can significantly benefit organizational efficiency and profitability. The following filing concept represents two extremes:

Instant filing, forever retrieval — forever filing, instant retrieval

The premise of this concept is if you create the proper paper and electronic filing system, you increase efficiencies and decrease company costs.

Take the first half of the preceding axiom: "instant filing, forever retrieval." Picture opening up a file cabinet that contains all your company's personnel files with only one hanging folder (yes, a very large hanging folder). All

500 employee files are located in the one hanging folder but aren't alphabetized or in employee ID order. When you file new employee documents, you just dump them in the folder — instant filing! How much better can it get? Of course, the result is not being able to retrieve a specific document. The efficiencies you gain by instant filing are now negated by the significant time spent going through every piece of paper in the mega-hanging folder.

The second half of the axiom: "forever filing, instant retrieval" — is the extreme opposite. If you're not careful, you can create such a complex filing system that it takes forever to file anything. (Small upshot: When you go to retrieve, you can eventually pinpoint what you need.)

Both approaches decrease staff productivity and increase labor costs. So what's the answer? The solution lies somewhere in the middle based on your organizational needs.

When you take the guesswork out of your job, you become more productive and less stressed. A records and information management program helps you do both. Employees want to do the right thing, but sometimes they just don't know what the right thing is. This is especially true when it comes to dealing with the records and information in their departments. Employees don't intend to keep all information forever or dispose of records before the retention has expired, but in the absence of records and information management guidance and policy, these eventualities do occur. Employees spend unnecessary time determining what to do.

Efficiencies gained through records and information management also benefit the corporate decision-making process. Whether related to routine processing or senior-level initiatives, accessing relevant information in a timely manner can mean the difference between success and lost opportunities or profit or loss. By applying the approaches and principles discussed in this book, companies increase their potential to make better-informed decisions.

Risky business

Organizations face many types of risks. Risks — some expected and some completely unforeseen — come in many shapes and sizes: lawsuits, work stoppages, government inquires, disasters, public relations issues, fines, and penalties. Although an effective records and information management program may not prevent all adverse events, it can eliminate some and reduce others, and ensure that your business is prepared to face the rest.

Whether you're a small-business owner or the CEO of a global corporation, you're exposed to risks. It would be great if you could predict when bad things were going to happen; then you would be prepared. We all know that this is impossible — but wait, is it really? Even though you may not be a soothsayer, you can still be prepared to deal with certain risk-related issues. Consider records and information as a form of risk insurance.

Organizations have the information they need to anticipate and respond to lawsuits, inquiries, disasters, and other risk-related issues. The problem is they may not even know they have it or they aren't appropriately managing or using it. A benefit of a records and information management program is that this type of information is accounted for, classified, retrievable, and retained as needed.

Creating your support group

A records management program without the proper support will fail. Therefore, get the right support in your corner: people who can further the cause of records and information management, and who have a stake in its success. The following list of corporate departments represents key players in your quest for support:

- ✔ Senior management
- ✔ Compliance
- ✔ Information technology (IT)
- ✔ Risk management
- ✔ Internal audit
- ✔ Legal

The senior class

Senior management support (or lack thereof) will determine the fate of your program. All other support hinges on their membership. Keep in mind that by implementing a records and information management program, you're going to be asking departmental management and employees to do things they haven't done before — things they don't consider part of their core group of functions. And they likely aren't going to get on board if the only person requiring them to do so is the records and information manager. Throw in a dash of senior management backing, though, and you have the recipe for cooperation. It's funny how quickly people cooperate when they know you have the CEO's blessing.

Mandating employee cooperation is not the only benefit of having senior-level support. Although you may be the organizational driver for a records and information management program, you may need passengers on your journey in the form of a staff to help you. For example, chances are that you aren't authorized to hire new employees without additional approval, but senior management can provide the approval you need.

In many cases, you might need to purchase software to help manage your records and information, requiring extensive evaluation by the IT department as well as the business sponsor. And records and information software isn't cheap. Senior management can ensure that you receive the cooperation you need from other departments, as well as the funds to acquire the software. After you secure approval from senior management, you have the organizational commission you need to proceed.

The key to compliance

After obtaining support from senior management, knock on the Compliance department's door. If your company has a Compliance department, you quickly discover that it has clout and can be a great ally in your push for a Records and Information Management program.

Small- and medium-sized businesses may not have a Compliance department. If this is the case, your accountant or attorney can be a great advocate for your Records and Information Management program.

The Chief Compliance Officer (CCO) and staff's role in an organization is to ensure that employees are aware of and comply with bylaws and regulations that impact the company. The CCO acts as a consultant to senior management to ensure that the organization isn't conducting business in a manner that violates any laws or regulations.

Your initiative is an essential complement to their efforts. Most compliance laws and regulations have a records and information management component that involves making sure that certain information is readily accessible and retained for the specified length of time.

Techie talk

If your program vision includes a records and information management software application, you need the services of your IT department, who are the resident experts on evaluating and supporting software systems. Most business users of technology know what they want an application to do, but aren't trained to know whether the system is compatible with the organization's current technical infrastructure. IT folks know, though. They have experience in talking with software vendors and asking the right questions.

Before you begin searching for a records and information management software system, document your requirements into a list of mandatory functionality that the application must have. After you compose your list, give it to IT and let those folks conduct the initial screening of vendors. If IT determines that a vendor's system meets your requirements, they will hand it off to you for review. Having their support in this area saves you the time and trouble of having to do a lot of spadework on your own.

Risk reward

A company's risk management department is responsible for the identification, assessment, and prioritization of risks the company is (or may be) exposed to, and finds ways to eliminate or manage them. Risks come in a variety of shapes and sizes: For a grocery store, it may be a customer slip and fall; for a manufacturer it could be a product that has harmed a consumer; for an airline it could be maintenance and safety issues — records and information management to the rescue! Although a good records and information management program won't keep a customer from slipping on a grape in the produce aisle, it will help to ensure that store floor-sweeping logs are maintained and accessible to show evidence that the aisle was properly maintained at the time of the incident. Corporate risk management departments rely heavily on records and information to ensure that risks can be eliminated and mitigated.

Partnering with the risk management folks provides a benefit to them as well as to you. Risk management is a hot topic in every organization. Just like the Compliance department, risk management has the ear of senior-level employees. Garnering their support will help you in your program endeavors.

Take a hike down the audit trail

Most employees cringe at the thought of a visit by the internal audit department. However, as an employee who is trying to get support for a records and information management program, you should welcome them with open arms (figuratively, not literally).

An organization's internal audit department is designed to provide an independent and objective analysis of the company's operations by following a systematic and disciplined approach. Internal audit reviews establish procedures for different company functions to determine whether they're appropriate, and also whether they're being followed. The internal audit department also assesses company business processes and makes recommendations for improvements.

Internal audit fits into your support group because they have needs that you can help fill. For example, they rely on records and information to do their job. Prior to starting a scheduled audit engagement, internal audit needs access to review specific department records such as policies and procedures. After the audit is underway, it needs to evaluate transactional records like invoices to ensure that they were processed correctly. A records and information management program can ensure that this information is readily accessible, allowing internal audit to be more efficient.

Internal audit can help you because it usually reports directly to senior management, giving itself the ability to advance your cause with the right people — a win-win for everyone involved.

The tax man

The tax department takes a vested interest in how the organization's records and information are managed. These folks are required to produce large volumes of information for federal, state, and municipality requirements. In many cases, tax-related inquiries can last for years, which require the organization to retain information — resulting in information hold orders.

Organizations place a significant amount of emphasis on tax records. The inability to properly manage tax records can result in hefty fines and penalties. Most companies retain tax records permanently. A Records and Information Management program can benefit the tax department by ensuring that the information life cycle is appropriately managed and readily accessible for governmental inquires.

The legal beagles

The last — but certainly not the least — important addition to your support group is the legal department. Aside from senior management, this one group of employees may be able to provide you more support than all the other departments combined (and vice versa). It's not uncommon for large companies, depending on the industry in which they operate, to deal with multiple lawsuits at one time. The core of each lawsuit involves information — in most cases lots of information. Whether information can or cannot be found may mean the difference between winning a lawsuit and paying millions of dollars in judgments.

In the past decade, e-mails have played a huge role in litigation. However, due to the massive volume of e-mails that a company receives daily, coupled with the absence of effective e-mail management policies and technology, e-mails prove to be one of the most difficult information types to manage. Here's your chance to shine.

Organizations spend millions of dollars annually just finding and reviewing information that is potentially relevant to lawsuits. The sad part is that the majority of information they collect and evaluate turns out to not be pertinent. One lawsuit may require the review of gigabytes of e-mails and other electronic file content as well as paper documents.

A comprehensive records and information management program allows the legal department to reduce the amount of irrelevant information they have to review by ensuring that information is identified, classified, accessible, and retained for the appropriate length of time. In addition, a well-designed program includes e-mail usage and management policies, and the ability to place information hold orders to ensure that information pertaining to lawsuits is not altered or destroyed.

Marketing Your Program

One of the biggest hurdles in obtaining support for a records and information management initiative is the organization's lack of awareness and understanding of its importance and the benefits it provides. Senior management knows that managing company information is a good thing, but they are so removed from the details of the process that they don't know what resources it actually takes to create and implement an effective records and information management program. It's your job to educate them.

When a company develops a new consumer product, it markets and advertises it. Think of your records and information management program as a new internal company product. It may not reduce wrinkles and make you look younger, but it can definitely reduce stress.

As you prepare to market your initiative, remember that all members of your support group have different needs. Although an effective records and information management program addresses the needs of the corporate masses by its very nature, you need to tailor your marketing message so it focuses on their specific issues and concerns. The more you can emphasize what's in it for them, the more successful you'll be.

A basketball team that never practices — just walks on the court at game time and plays its opponent — would probably lose the game. Practice is the key to winning. However, before you start to practice, you need to know what you're going to work on. Say hello to the game plan.

To improve their team's chance of success, coaches develop game plans based on information about the opponent: their likes, dislikes, tendencies,

and patterns. Coaches use this information to determine where they can expose the opponent's weaknesses and capitalize on their own strengths. Then coaches formulate a game plan as the basis for how their team plays their opponent.

The more knowledgeable you are about each department, the better equipped you are to win them over.

Before you begin showing up on the doorstep of all the departments in your organization to discuss records and information management, ask yourself the following questions:

✔ Who are my internal customers?

✔ What organizational functions do my customers perform?

✔ What are my customers' needs and pain-points?

✔ What do I have to offer my customers?

✔ How will a records and information management program benefit my customers?

✔ How will I bring awareness of the program benefits to my customers?

✔ How will I market the product to my customers?

✔ What price or effort does the customer have to pay or expend to use the product?

✔ How will I roll out the product to my customers?

Chapter 2

Appraising

*T*he process of determining the value of records and information is known as the *appraisal.* The appraisal involves identifying, documenting, and evaluating the legal, fiscal, historical, and operational significance of company records and information for disposition purposes. The appraisal provides details such as name, description, media format, whether the records and information are vital, and how they're used.

The objective of the appraisal is to provide a mechanism for companies to identify the records and information they possess to know how long to keep them as well as how to manage them during their life cycle. The absence of an appraisal creates an ad hoc and decentralized environment in which employees, out of necessity, make individual or departmental decisions regarding the management of their records and information.

Different appraisal methodologies and options produce different results, so it's important to understand the premise and nature of each alternative to determine which approach best fits your organizational objectives. This chapter provides the information you need to make the appropriate decision.

Preparing for the Appraisal

Whether you're a small-business owner or work for a large corporation, if the decision has been made to appraise your records and information, you will need to properly prepare. Several major appraisal elements need to be considered, such as the underlying methodology for an appraisal, its degree of comprehensiveness, communicating the appraisal plan to management, and its scheduling.

Push for the purge

Regardless of the appraisal approach you choose, the organization will have to dedicate time, resources, and planning to make it a success. Each appraisal approach requires evaluating a significant amount of information. The less information you have to evaluate, the quicker the process can be completed.

One way to reduce the amount of information that needs to be evaluated is to pare it down prior to the appraisal. It is estimated that more than 50 percent of the paper and electronic information that organizations currently store doesn't have any business value and can be immediately discarded. You can eliminate what you no longer need by conducting a *preliminary file purge* (purge).

Prior to conducting a purge, it's extremely important to clearly communicate to everyone who is participating not to destroy information that could possibly be records during the event. The purge should focus on cleaning out unneeded duplicate copies of information, supplies, and items that should not be in the filing system. You shouldn't purge any information that is part of an active or potential lawsuit or government inquiry. The primary types of information that should be discarded during the purge are copies of records and nonrecords that are no longer needed, nonrecord information that no longer has any business value, and content that never had business value — junk.

A purge is conducted to eliminate unneeded nonrecord content in preparation for an appraisal. A purge may be conducted on a company-wide basis or department by department, based on your appraisal schedule. A purge will help reduce the amount of content that has to be appraised, and also provides a benefit to the company by reducing storage needs and costs, allowing employees to find the information they need in a more efficient manner.

If you decide upon a comprehensive appraisal approach (which is recommended), the purge should include the destruction and deletion of both paper documents and electronic files. This includes paper documents in all file cabinets and electronic files on all computers.

In preparation for the purge, it's a good idea to reach out to the management staff of the participating departments to discuss the process — be sure to highlight what they can expect and provide an opportunity for them to ask questions. During the discussion, you may want to make the recommendation that they assign a departmental "point person" who can be your liaison during the purge itself. This approach provides a knowledgeable person who can funnel all departmental purge questions to you.

Paper documents disposed of during the purge event shouldn't be placed in recycle bins or trash containers. Although the content you are getting rid of may no longer have any organizational business value, it may contain information of a personal, confidential, or competitive nature. In preparation for purging paper documents, you need to arrange for a secure document-shredding vendor to provide you with locking shred bins to properly dispose of the content.

Don't forget the hard drives

The objective of purging electronic content is the same as for paper — get rid of what you know longer need. However, how you accomplish this is significantly different. Purging electronic content requires employees to review electronic folders and files on hard drives and network drives as well as information residing on portable media such as CDs, USB drives, and so on. The following types of electronic information are examples of items that need to be reviewed during the purge process:

- ✔ E-mails
- ✔ Word, Excel, and PowerPoint documents
- ✔ Collaboration site content (for example, Microsoft SharePoint)
- ✔ PDF files
- ✔ All graphics files, such as TIFFs, JPEGs, PNGs, and BMPs
- ✔ Audio and video files

Note: The electronic information listed here represents *unstructured* information. Appraising *structured* (software system data) information is covered in Chapter 16.

Although the volume of electronic content belonging to a department may dwarf what they have in their file cabinets, computers can provide assistance to help manage that content. When you access a particular drive, your computer provides a Date Modified column. (See Figure 2-1.) *Modified* here means the last time any changes were made to the file and then saved. Computers allow you to sort folders and files in this column by date. **Note:** The Date Modified field of some file types such as .mdb (Microsoft Access Database) files may change upon viewing instead of when actually modified by the user.

Name	Size	Type	Date Modified ▼
2011 Landscape.ppt	309 KB	Microsoft Office Po...	1/19/2011 3:58 PM
Approaches.doc	22 KB	Microsoft Office Wo...	1/5/2011 10:31 AM
IBM eDiscovery Houston ARMA.zip	3,795 KB	Compressed (zippe...	3/20/2009 10:29 AM
RIM Fundamentals Series II.ppt	2,705 KB	Microsoft Office Po...	3/16/2009 4:40 PM
Survey Questions.doc	35 KB	Microsoft Office Wo...	1/15/2009 4:14 PM
RECORDS MANAGEMENT POLICY FUNDAMENTALS.ppt	670 KB	Microsoft Office Po...	1/8/2009 10:23 AM
RECORDS MANAGEMENT POLICIES.doc	40 KB	Microsoft Office Wo...	12/5/2008 3:23 PM
Building a Foundation.ppt	238 KB	Microsoft Office Po...	9/17/2008 9:28 AM

Figure 2-1:
Date
modified.

Date Modified is a great starting point for determining whether electronic information is still relevant. If you sort by most recent date first, this information probably still needs to be retained. On the flip side, if you haven't modified your oldest files in several years, an increased probability exists that the file is eligible to be deleted. However, neither scenario is a guarantee. Employees still need to review all files to ensure their status.

Another strategy in helping employees make a decision to either retain or delete a file involves examining the Created date and/or Accessed date of a file. The *Created* date provides the creation date of the file. The *Accessed* date indicates the last time anyone accessed or reviewed the file. If you right-click the file you want to review, the contextual menu shown in Figure 2-2 appears.

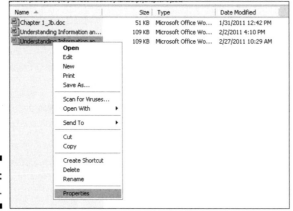

Figure 2-2:
Properties.

Select Properties from the contextual menu to review the Created and Accessed date, as shown in Figure 2-3.

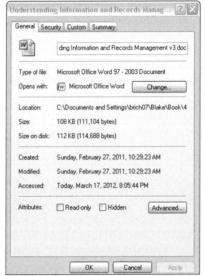

Figure 2-3:
Created and
Accessed
date.

Choosing an Appraisal Method

Yes, you have options. Two primary appraisal methods are in practice today. One is traditional, and the other is a relative newcomer to records and information management, but is gaining substantial traction in the governmental sector.

The appraisal method you choose will lay the foundation for the organization's records and information retention schedule and overall program. Therefore, it's extremely important to prepare for the appraisal process and research the options.

A method to the madness

You find two main appraisal concepts — *departmental* and *functional.* Each approach has upsides and issues to consider. The record series method represents the traditional approach used by many organizations. The functional method is a relatively new concept now in use by many governmental agencies and gaining momentum in private industry:

✔ **Departmental:** The focus of the record series appraisal method primarily concentrates on each record series type that a department possesses, with minimal concern as to how the record types are used or what department functions they help facilitate. The record series method ultimately results in each record type being listed individually, by department, on the organization's record retention schedule.

✔ **Functional:** The functional appraisal approach focuses on appraising departmental functions rather than appraising individual record or document types. This method is based on the premise that each record series is part of a function. In this case, all record types that support an individual process will be grouped together for retention purposes.

For example, the Accounts Payable department is responsible for paying vendor invoices. The process involves several different record types — purchase orders, packing lists, invoices, and remittances, for example. The record series appraisal method looks at each of these records in an individual manner. Each will be appraised separately and each listed on the organization's record retention schedule under Accounts Payable.

The functional appraisal approach views these records in a macro or conglomerate fashion. All the records support the Accounts Payable function. Therefore, the retention schedule will reflect the function, such as "payables," not the individual records.

The good and the . . . good

Both appraisal methods should be researched before choosing which one to incorporate into your company. The research and decision process should be a group effort, including at a minimum the department that owns the information, as well as the Legal, Compliance, and Tax departments. The following is a guide to help you understand how each approach may impact your company:

✔ **Departmental:**

- The appraisal will take more time to complete because you are evaluating each record series.

- Will increase the number of entries on the record retention schedule because you are accounting for each record series.

- Provides the organization with the ability to manage the life cycle of individual records.

- Provides the ability to place information hold orders on a specific record series instead of placing a hold on a group of records that possibly aren't relevant to the matter, causing records to be held that may otherwise be eligible to be destroyed or deleted.

- Can provide a better and quicker understanding of the individual record types a department possesses, versus all records that are applicable to a function being labeled with a function name such as "payables."

- The process of approving records and information for destruction or deletion may take longer due to the approvers having to review individual records rather than groups of related records.

- Subsequent filing and retrieval of records and information may take longer due to having to file at the individual record series level instead of filing at the functional level.

✔ **Functional:**

- Expedites the appraisal process by eliminating the need to evaluate individual record types and allowing you to focus instead on the records that are part of a function *as a group.*

- Will ultimately reduce the time spent by employees deciding how to classify, file, and retrieve records and information because they are accounted for at the aggregate level.

- When grouping records that are part of a function together for retention purposes, the possibility increases that you will keep some function-related records longer than they need to be retained. For example, an invoice needs to be retained for seven years; however, the packing slip related to the Accounts Payable process may only need to be kept for one year.

- Without additional available documentation, it can reduce the organization's ability to identify specific record types that departments have and use because the records are not individually listed on the retention schedule.

- Allows the company to obtain a better understanding of what records facilitate the processing of functions.

- Expedites the destruction and deletion approval process because the approvers don't have to review individual record and information types.

- Reduces the number of line items on the retention schedule, making it more efficient to use.

- Information hold orders have to be placed on a group of functional records rather than at an individual record series level, resulting in the possibility of retaining some related records longer than they are needed.

During the appraisal method evaluation, it's a good idea to determine whether any internal or external factors may impact which approach you should take. Some factors that may have a bearing on which appraisal method to use are as follows:

- ✔ **Volume:** Although volume shouldn't necessarily be a deciding factor in the method you choose, realistically it does play a part. Some companies have started out to complete a departmental appraisal, but found they became bogged down in the process due to the extremely large amount of information they had to appraise. The rationale to move to the functional approach was based on the fact that even though they wanted to account for every record series individually rather than functionally, they were concerned that the process would stall and resources would dry up and leave them with an incomplete appraisal.

- ✔ **Regulatory requirements:** If your organization operates in a highly regulated industry such as nuclear energy, pharmaceuticals, or tobacco, you need to determine whether any regulatory requirements would prevent or dissuade your company from using either appraisal approach. Organizations operating in a highly regulated industry may prefer to conduct a departmental appraisal, which allows them to manage the record life cycle at the departmental level, even if they have a significant amount of volume to appraise.

- ✔ **Litigation:** It is recommended that your legal department or attorneys issue an opinion on which appraisal method they feel provides the best defensible legal position for the organization. For example, a functional approach lumps records related to the same function together and may ultimately result in less information being captured about individual record types and some records being retained longer than required by law or regulatory entities. A functional appraisal may make it difficult during a lawsuit to determine what specific records may be involved. In addition, during a lawsuit, audit, or governmental inquiry, you may have to produce information that should already have been destroyed that proves damaging. If an organization feels that the legal risks are too great, it may decide to pursue the departmental appraisal approach, even if it has a significant amount of volume to appraise.

Conducting the Appraisal

After your organization has decided which appraisal method to use, it's time to plan the process. Planning is the key to a successful appraisal. It includes items such as determining how the information will be captured, letting all participating parties know what it is expected of them, conducting preappraisal department visits, and figuring out what to do with the information after you have it.

The following sections provide you with the knowledge and tools you need to conduct the appraisal. You find out what options exist for capturing appraisal information and see an example of forms that can be used to document the process.

Capturing appraisal information

Once again you have options! You have three primary methods to choose from for capturing appraisal information:

- ✔ Inventory
- ✔ Interview
- ✔ Questionnaire

Each option can be used to capture appraisal information regardless of the appraisal method (departmental or functional) that your organization is pursuing. However, each approach has distinct advantages and disadvantages that need to be considered before proceeding with the appraisal.

Taking inventory

The *inventory* appraisal method is the most time consuming (for the department, you, and your staff) and labor intensive of the options, but it provides the most accurate results. This approach requires an in-depth review of a department's records and information.

If you are conducting a departmental appraisal, this approach involves opening every file cabinet and desk drawer, as well as accessing employees' computers. During the process, your goal is to document a department's content at the folder level, not the document level.

The following list provides guidance on how to inventory paper and electronic information at the folder level:

- ✔ For example, if you open a file cabinet drawer and see a lot of hanging folders, you can assume that each document in the same folder is related. You don't have to account for every document, but you do need to note the hanging folder and the type of information it contains.
- ✔ The same is true for electronic content — not each file, but each main computer folder. If a computer folder is labeled Invoices, you don't have to go through it to make sure that all the items in the folder are in fact invoices.

If you are conducting a functional appraisal, the method is different. Instead of focusing your initial efforts on documenting the department's individual record types, you start by obtaining an understanding of the department's functions and documenting their processes and workflows. After you have captured this information, you work backward to identify the record types used to support each function.

An effective functional appraisal is comprised of the following items:

- ✔ For example, you first want to sit down with management and employees from the department you are appraising and ask them to list and describe the functions they are responsible for performing.

- ✔ After the list is complete, you work with departmental employees to determine what individual record types are part of a functional series.

Have a knowledgeable employee from each department tag along with you while you're evaluating the department's records and information. This helps in case you have questions about the department's content.

Going through with an interview

The *interview* appraisal method involves meeting with management and knowledgeable employees from each department and asking them a series of questions in an effort to appraise their records and information. This approach doesn't require you to open file cabinet drawers and computer folders, resulting in a quicker but less accurate and detailed appraisal. However, with proper planning, the interview option can still be effective, and it will allow you to account for most of your company's records, information, and functions.

Your challenge during the interview is to get employees to think about the *total population* of their records and information — to make sure that you capture as much of it as possible during the appraisal process. Get them to think about the out-of-sight, out-of-mind records and information. This may take some gentle prodding. File cabinets full of documents are easy targets. It's the paper records they have boxed up and sent to storage, and the thousands of computer files on their hard drives and network drives, that employees don't think about during the interview process.

If you are conducting a functional appraisal, you need to focus your initial interview questions on the department's functions. Then move on to questions about the records and information used to process the functions. A lack of understanding of a department's processes will make it difficult to identify the records that are part of the function.

Quizzing with a questionnaire

The questionnaire method takes the least amount of time to complete, but it is the least comprehensive of the appraisal options. When using the questionnaire method, you provide managers with a set of questions and simply rely on them (or their staff) to document their record and information types and functions and how they interact. Unlike the inventory and interview methods, you'll not be in the department to assist in the gathering of the information.

Although the questionnaire method is not as accurate or comprehensive as the other approaches, a well-designed questionnaire form can increase your odds of achieving acceptable results. The questionnaire you develop should be easy for management and their staff to understand and fill out. You may want to attach a separate definitions-and-instructions page to guide them along.

Documenting the appraisal

After you decide how the appraisal will be conducted, you have to determine how to document your findings. Appraisal forms are used to capture pertinent information. The form format and questions will vary depending on the appraisal method — departmental or functional.

When conducting a departmental appraisal, the same form can be used for inventory, interview, and questionnaire approaches. The form should be constructed so that it's easy to understand and complete regardless of who is filling it out. When using the questionnaire approach, it's recommended that you create an instruction page that provides guidance on completing the form.

Prior to conducting the appraisal, you should have a kickoff meeting with the department employees to communicate what will be involved in the process and what their roles and responsibilities will be. The meeting can give employees an opportunity to ask questions and raise concerns.

The form for the functional appraisal is different from the form used for departmental appraisals. The functional appraisal form leaves room for the listing of functions and their related records. When conducting the functional appraisal, the same form can be used for the inventory, interview, and questionnaire approaches. Again, when using the questionnaire approach, it's recommended that you create an instruction page that provides guidance on completing the form.

Figures 2-4, 2-5, and 2-6 show examples of appraisal forms that you can use for the departmental and functional methods, as well as an example of a questionnaire instruction page.

INSTRUCTIONS - Type or print a separate form for each new record series.	ABC COMPANY RECORD & INFORMATION APPRAISAL FORM	Page ___ of ___
1. Division	2. Department	3. Unit
4. Record Series Title		
5. Record Series Description		
6. Record Series Format (Check all applicable) Paper ____ Electronic ____ Microfilm ____ Other ____	7. Is the Record Series Considered Vital No ____ Yes ____	8. Current Retention Period Number ____ (Check One) Month(s) ____ Year(s) ____
9. Record Series Becomes Inactive After Number ____ (Check One) Month(s) ____ Year(s) ____	10. Do Duplicates Exist No ____ Yes ____ If Yes, Where?	11. Regulatory Requirements No ____ Yes ____ If Yes, Please List
Name and Title of Preparer	Telephone Number	Date

Figure 2-4: Departmental appraisal form.

Figure 2-4 is an example of a departmental appraisal form. The form focuses on the individual record series and their characteristics such as the format (paper or electronic) and whether they are considered vital and are governed by any regulations.

The functional appraisal form focuses on the departmental function or process first, including a description of the function, and then focuses on what records are used to perform the function.

If the organization has made the decision to proceed with a questionnaire appraisal, the following instruction page example (record series appraisal) can provide the guidance needed to ensure that it's accurately filled out by departmental or agency personnel. The same approach can be used for the functional appraisal. The questionnaire is designed to be convenient and easy to understand and complete.

INSTRUCTIONS - Type or print a separate form for each new function.

ABC Company
Record & Information
Appraisal Form

Page ____ of ____

1. Division	2. Department	3. Unit

4. Function name

5. Function description

6. List all record types used to support this function and their current retention period

7. Active period of function

Number _____

(Check One)

Month(s) _____

Year(s) _____

8. List format for each record types used to support function

Record Name _____ Format (P, E, B) _____

Record Name _____ Format (P, E, B) _____

Record Name _____ Format (P, E, B) _____

Record Name _____ Format (P, E, B) _____

9. List software used to support function	10. Is the function Considered Vital No _____ Yes _____	11. Regulatory requirements related to function No _____ Yes _____ If Yes, Please List

12. Do the record types support any other functions (list other functions) Function 1 _____ Function 1 _____ Function 1 _____ Function 1 _____	13. Do duplicates of record types exists No _____ Yes _____ If Yes, Where?	14. Additional comments
Name and Title of Preparer	**Telephone Number**	**Date**

Figure 2-5: Functional appraisal form.

Questionnaire Appraisal - Completion Instructions:
(A separate form is to be completed for each record series)

Field #	Field Name	Completion Instructions
1.	Division	List division name (if applicable)
2.	Department	List department (if applicable)
3.	Unit	List unit (if applicable)
4.	Record Series Title	List name of record series or title, e.g. "Invoices"
5.	Record Series Description	Provide a general description of the record type and any other terms or names used for this record. This may include abbreviations used by the department to refer to the record series.
6.	Record Series Format	Please indicate the media format in which the record series resides. If the record series resides in multiple formats please list all that are applicable.
7.	Is the Record Series Considered Vital	Is the record series used to support any functions considered vital to the organization business resumption efforts in the event of a disaster?
8.	Current Retention Period	Currently how long is the record series retained before it's destroyed or deleted?
9.	Record Series Become Inactive After	When does the record series lose its need to be frequently accessed for processing or inquiry purposes?
10.	Do Duplicates Exist	Are copies of the record series store elsewhere in the Division/Department/Unit or in any other Area of the organization? Is so list the area(s).
11.	Regulatory Requirements	Is the management and retention of the record series governed or mandated by any outside entities, laws or regulations?

If you have any questions regarding the completion of this form, please contact the Records and Information Management Department at ext. ####. Please submit completed forms to the Records and Information Management Department.

Figure 2-6: Questionnaire appraisal instruction form (departmental).

Processing the appraisal results

After the appraisals have been completed, the fun starts! The appraisals need to be reviewed for errors and omissions. During this time, follow-up visits or phone calls may need to take place with departments to ensure that the appraisal information is as accurate and comprehensive as possible. The next step is to begin conducting research of the appraisal information to develop the organization's retention schedules. In the next chapter, I tackle everything associated with creating and implementing a records retention schedule.

Chapter 3

Scheduling

· ·

In This Chapter

▶ Examining scheduling options

▶ Researching retention periods

▶ Obtaining retention period approvals

▶ Creating the retention schedule document

▶ Implementing the retention schedule

▶ Maintaining the schedule

· ·

A *retention schedule* is a document that provides an organization with direction on how long to keep their records and information, but you need to keep in mind that having a retention schedule is more than just knowing when it's okay to get rid of something. An organization that implements a well-designed and researched retention schedule can also benefit from better compliance to regulations, use of office space and computer storage, response to legal and audit matters, and record and information life cycle management.

Traditionally, retention schedules have focused on official company records. However, due to the corporate explosion of information, many organizations are realizing that they have huge amounts of electronic data residing on computers and servers that aren't official company records, but have business value. Companies are now taking action to manage the life cycle of this type of information by accounting for it on the retention schedule.

A big part of developing a retention schedule is determining how long to keep the different types of records and information that were documented during the appraisal. This chapter provides guidance on how to research and determine the correct retention periods for your records and information, along with determining what type of retention schedule to use, how to implement the schedule, and how to give it a tuneup.

Keeping Your Options Open

The retention schedule is the most important and frequently accessed records and information management document within an organization. Therefore, it is vital to ensure that the schedule is developed in a manner that meets the company's legal and compliance needs as well as the processing needs of employees. A well-designed and formatted retention schedule provides employees with clear instructions on how to classify and retain their records and information.

Completing the appraisal is the first step in developing a retention schedule. The next step is choosing a schedule format. In most cases, the appraisal method you used (*departmental* or *functional;* see Chapter 2 for more on the distinction) will be a factor in how you construct the retention schedule.

You find three primary retention schedule formats:

- ✔ Departmental
- ✔ Functional
- ✔ Big Bucket (sometimes referred to as a *flexible* schedule)

The following sections provide examples of the different schedule formats, their benefits, as well as any issues that need to be considered. This information should be carefully examined by organizations to ensure that the retention schedule option chosen meets their legal, regulatory, and operational needs.

Note: The retention schedule examples covered in the next four sections only represent the different formats. Later in this chapter, I go over all the components related to retention schedules. In addition, the retention periods used in the following format examples are only for representation purposes. Later, this chapter covers how to determine the appropriate retention periods for your organization.

Working with the Departmental retention schedule

The Departmental retention schedule is the most prominent of the schedule formats, and it provides your organization with the most detail. (See Figure 3-1.) The Departmental retention schedule — as its name implies — individually lists all record series or types that are assigned to a particular department.

Figure 3-1:
Depart-
mental
retention
schedule
(depart-
ment,
record
series, and
retention
period only).

Department: Human Resources	Retention Period (Years)
Affirmative Action Plans	5
Applications	3
Background Checks	3
Drug Testing - Negative	3
Drug Testing - Positive	10
EEOC Complaints	5
Employee Files - Active	10
Employee Files - Temporary	5
Employee Files - Terminated	10
Employee Investigations	5
Employment Verification Forms	3
Job Descriptions	3
Policy and Procedures	10
Resumes	3

The Departmental retention schedule is favored by many organizations because it's the one option that provides them with a comprehensive listing of *all* official company records. Doing it that way helps to provide the following benefits:

✔ **Retention applied to individual records:** The Departmental retention schedule allows each record type to be assigned a retention period. This ensures that records are only kept as long as they're required. The other retention schedule options assign retention to functions made up of individual records or apply retention to individual record types based on a limited category of retention periods. Such approaches create the potential of keeping records too long.

✔ **Litigation, audit, and inquiry response:** In the event of litigation, audits, or governmental inquiries, a Departmental retention schedule allows specific records relevant to the event to be easily identified and collected. The other retention schedule options require employees to know which records are part of a particular function. This may increase the chance that some records get overlooked.

✔ **Easy to understand:** Listing individual record types by department makes it easier for employees to understand how long they need to retain specific records versus individual records being lumped under a function.

✔ **More effective life cycle management:** The Departmental retention schedule approach allows companies to more effectively manage the entire life cycle of individual record types. By assigning retention periods to each record, an organization is able to move records to offsite storage or migrate them to less expensive electronic storage on an individual basis, and dispose of specific record types when their retention period has expired instead of managing multiple record types as one large group because they are related to a single function.

Compared to the Functional and Big Bucket retention schedule formats, the departmental approach has potential downsides:

- ✔ **More line items:** Listing each department's individual record series causes the retention schedule to become very lengthy.

- ✔ **Redundant entries:** Multiple departments may have the same record series name listed on their portion of the retention schedule. For example, the Benefits department and Public Affairs department may both have a record series of "Correspondence" listed under their area. This creates duplicate entries and increases the length of the schedule.

- ✔ **Conflicting retention periods:** Different departments may have different retention periods for the same record series. For example, one department may retain "Policies and Procedure" records for five years, while another department retains them for seven years. This results in inconsistencies in retention periods.

- ✔ **Harder to maintain:** The additional line items on a retention schedule results in more effort in updating changes to the record series (changes in retention periods or deletions of an inactive record type, for example).

Scheduling based on function

Functional retention schedules group together common records series that are part of an organizational function, regardless of the department where the records are created or maintained. Instead of listing individual departments and their respective records, the Functional retention schedule lists major functional categories and the subfunctions that support it, as shown in Figure 3-2.

Figure 3-2:
A Functional retention schedule showing the major function category, related functions, and retention period only.

Financial Management Functional Schedule	Retention Period (Years)
Accounts Payable	7
Accounts Receivable	7
General Ledgers and Journals	10
Gifts Donations and Other Revenue	7
Public Assistance Accounts	5
Tax Receipt and Disbursement	7
Auditing	5
Banking	7
Bonds Management	10
Budgeting	5
Cash Receipt Management	7
Escrow Accounts Management	10
Grants Administration	7
Investments Management	10

The Functional retention schedule lumps related functions under a functional category. In the example shown in Figure 3-2, all the functions listed have one thing in common — they are part of the Financial Management function. A specific function such as Accounts Payable may have a different retention period from the others. For example, Accounts Payable–related records may need to be retained for seven years, while Budgeting records may only need to be retained for three years.

Following are some of the issues that should be considered before adopting the Functional retention schedule approach:

✔ **Requires a thorough knowledge of business processes:** Creating a Functional retention schedule requires you to have an understanding of the organization's business processes and the records that are part of the functions, resulting in increased development time.

✔ **Demands a significant culture change:** The Functional retention schedule approach requires a shift in employee thinking. Most employees instinctively relate their records to the work they perform; for them, seeing their records as being part of a bigger organizational process can be a stretch. The focus should not be on who owns the work, but rather on how the work is processed.

Some organizations create a separate reference document that provides details about each individual record series listed on their Functional retention schedule. Figure 3-3 gives an example of what that would look like.

Figure 3-3:
A functional reference document.

Accounting-Accounts Payable (Retention Period 7 Years)
Tracking of funds owed by ABC Company
Accounts Payable Transaction Journals and Special Handling Reports
Cash Requirements and Create Payment Control Group Reports
Daily Balance Reports
Internal Revenue Service (IRS) Registers and Forms
Travel and Training Expense Files
Voucher and Payment Files

The Functional retention schedule provides the following benefits:

✔ **Ensures a concise retention schedule:** The Functional retention schedule has fewer line items than a standard Departmental schedule. This approach makes classifying records and information convenient for employees. Employees don't have to classify individual record types; they are able to apply aggregate classifications to all records related to a function.

✔ **Calls for fewer record series to maintain:** Having fewer individual record types listed on the schedule makes it easier for the organization to update the schedule.

✔ **Eliminates duplicate record series:** Unlike the Departmental retention schedule, the Functional retention schedule does not contain duplicate record types, which also promotes retention period consistency.

✔ **Reflects actual business processes:** The Functional retention schedule is designed to mirror the organization's business processes. This approach provides the ability to quickly identify company functions.

✔ **Promotes standard naming conventions:** Organizations that use a Departmental retention schedule may have identical record series assigned to multiple departments. Although each record type is identical, departments may refer to them differently. For example, the Customer Care department may refer to correspondence as customer communication, while another department refers to it as correspondence. The Functional retention schedule lists the record type once, using a standardized name and description.

Bring out the big buckets

The Big Bucket retention method is the newcomer to the retention schedule format family. The National Archives and Records Administration (NARA) is credited for being the early adopter of this approach, introducing the concept back in 2004.

Like any new concept that bucks traditional thinking, big buckets have been the topic of heated debates in the records and information management community. Although the Big Bucket approach has not been widely adopted at this point, it is gaining momentum as organizations struggle to find a convenient (but compliant) method to manage their growing population of records and information.

The issue that organizations face today is that they are stuck with way too many categories of records, a state of affairs that can make it difficult for employees to properly classify them. The Big Bucket concept is meant to remedy this. It takes the Functional retention schedule a big step farther by creating a set of retention buckets: — 3, 5, 7, 10, and 50 years, for example. This approach assigns individual records to an aggregate function (like the Functional retention schedule). The function is then grouped with similar functions to create a major function. The major function category is then assigned a retention period. Figure 3-4 illustrates the principles behind the Big Bucket concept.

Figure 3-4:
The Big
Bucket
retention
schedule,
showingindi-
vidualrecord
series,
department
function,
and major
Big Bucket
category
only.

Department (Functions)	Record Series	Retention Period (Years)
Accounts Payable		**7**
	Invoices	7
	Journal Entries	7
	Packing Slips	1
	Purchase Orders	2
Accounts Receivable		**7**
	Collections	7
	Credit applications	3
	Journal Entries	7
	Ledgers	7
Accounting		**7**
	Bank Statements	7
	Income Statements	7
	General Ledger	7
	Journal Entries	7
GENERAL ACCOUNTING (Big Bucket)		**7**

The example shown in Figure 3-4 represents an organization that has decided (for classification and record-retention purposes) to consolidate three separate accounting-related departments into one major function — General Accounting. The decision in this case was made to use the Big Bucket approach for the organization's accounting functions and assign a retention period of seven years to this particular "bucket," even though some individual record series may have a retention period of less than seven years and some may have periods of more than seven years.

The following are advantages to adopting the Big Bucket retention approach:

✔ **It simplifies classification.** The Big Bucket retention schedule approach makes it easier for employees to classify records by reducing the number of classification choices. The Big Bucket approach makes classification of records faster, thus helping to reduce classification backlogs.

✔ **It promotes consistency.** Because the Big Bucket retention schedule method lists only major processing functions, it significantly increases the consistency and accuracy of classification and retention.

✔ **It's easier to maintain.** The status of individual records series sometimes changes. This may be due to a retention period modification, the fact that the record is no longer created or received by the organization, or by a change of the record's name. In most cases, the Big Bucket retention schedule can take such modifications in stride because its schedule accounts for major functions instead of focusing on individual records types.

The following issues are considered potential disadvantages to using big buckets:

✔ **It can lead to increased retention.** Because the Big Bucket retention method lumps related functions into one major function, the potential exists for some individual record types that support these functions to be retained longer than required. The Big Bucket category for General Accounting, for example, may be assigned a seven-year retention period. Imagine, however, that the purchase order records that support the Accounts Payable function, which falls under General Accounting, may only be required to be retained for two years. The decision to retain records longer than required is usually based on risks and costs.

✔ **It can result in a decrease in descriptive data.** Because the Big Bucket retention method lists only major processing functions, it significantly reduces the amount of descriptive data related to individual records than would be available on a Departmental retention schedule. Records and information managers, attorneys, and tax department employees rely heavily on descriptive data to search for records and information to respond to lawsuits, audits, and inquiries.

✔ **It can render event-driven retention impossible to manage.** Some records are assigned *event-driven* retention periods. This means that the retention clock doesn't begin to tick until an event occurs. Employee personnel files, for example, may be assigned a retention period of ACT + 10 years. "Active" in this case refers to duration of employment. The ten-year retention period starts when the employee leaves the company. If an employee works for a company for 5 years, the total retention period for the employee's personnel file will be 15 years. Big Bucket retention schedules don't allow event-driven situations. This issue is commonly resolved by adding conditional retention buckets to handle these types of records.

Deciding on a retention schedule format for your organization is a very important process that impacts the future of the company's records and information management program. The decision-making process should be a group effort, including the Records and Information manager and the Legal, Risk Management, Tax, and Compliance departments (if applicable). This approach allows each group to carefully examine the formats and determine which method best meets the organization's needs.

Conducting the Investigation

Now that you have decided upon a retention schedule format, you need to put on your research cap. Whether you choose to use the Departmental, Functional, or Big Bucket retention schedule approach, you need to determine what retention periods to assign to your records and information.

Determining appropriate retention periods involves the consideration of federal and state regulatory requirements, contractual obligations, intellectual property requirements, and statutes of limitations, as well as administrative needs specific to the industry in which you operate. If you operate in a heavily regulated industry such as nuclear energy, petroleum, insurance, or pharmaceuticals, for example, the respective industry's governing bodies or governmental legislation may have already established the retention period of some of your records.

It only takes a simple search of the Internet to find a multitude of sites telling you how long to keep your records and information — but be sure to take such information with a grain of salt. Retention periods found on the Internet may provide you with retention food for thought, but the authors of these sites don't know the intricacies of your business. For the majority of organizational records and information, no absolute retention rules exist. Each organization has its own needs and nuances. One organization may keep a record series for a certain length of time, while another company retains the same record series differently. Therefore, retention recommendations found on the Internet shouldn't be used to formulate the retention of your records and information.

Considering the value

Retention periods aren't arbitrarily assigned. They are determined by appraising a records value to an organization. As part of that appraisal process, you need to evaluate four primary record value categories:

- ✔ **Administrative:** The majority of records kept by an organization are assigned retention periods based on administrative or operational need instead of by applying a retention period based on requirements mandated by outside regulatory entities. In this context, you're retaining records because you need them to conduct your business — nothing more and nothing less. Examples of records retained for administrative purposes may include policies and procedures, correspondence, and budgets.

- ✔ **Legal and regulatory:** In this context, records should be appraised for their legal and regulatory value. Doing so ensures that the records are retained for the appropriate length of time to ensure that organizations are positioned to meet and respond to their legal and regulatory compliance obligations.

- ✔ **Fiscal:** A fiscal appraisal determines the usefulness of a record in serving as documentation of the organization's financial transactions.

- ✔ **Historical:** A historical appraisal involves assigning retention periods to records that document organizational history. This includes records such as company photographs, newsletters, and press releases.

Researching retention periods

The credibility of your organization's Records and Information Management program is gauged in large part by the accuracy of its retention schedule — more specifically by the retention periods you assign to your records and information. The best way to ensure retention period accuracy is to research laws and regulations that impact your company, as well as its operational needs.

The retention of most organizational records is determined by administrative or operational needs. This means that the retention period is not mandated by an outside entity such as the federal government, but by how long records and information serve their intended business purpose. An example of an administrative record is budgets. Budgets are formulated at a specific time of year for the upcoming fiscal period. The document is needed during its respective budget year and is used as a planning tool for the next year. After that point, the budget document likely serves no business purpose to the organization and can be destroyed.

However, the retention period of records such as financial statements, private health information (PHI), and customer payment card data is mandated by federal law or industry compliance standards. In some cases, laws and regulations are vague and don't provide specific retention periods for records. In these cases, the appropriate organizational employees have to examine the issue and determine retention periods to assign that can help to ensure compliance and reduce risks to the company.

Regardless of whether your records are of an administrative nature or are governed by outside entities, you will still need to conduct research. Using the value categories as your guide, you can begin to categorize your records and information in preparation for researching, determining, and applying retention periods. The retention schedule method you decide to use (Departmental, Functional, or Big Bucket) will have an impact on your research. If you use the Departmental approach, you have to research and determine the correct retention period for individual records. If you use a Functional retention schedule, you need to assign the appropriate retention to each function. If you use a Big Bucket approach, you have to determine the correct retention period for the major functions of the organization.

Researching record retention periods takes teamwork. Normally, it involves the Records and Information Management, Legal, Tax, and Risk Management departments, along with department owners of the records and information. The Records and Information Management department should take the lead, conducting the initial research, making recommendations, and coordinating communications with the other departments.

Understanding your industry, departmental functions, and supporting records and information is the key to starting your retention period research. Becoming familiar with the function of a department can help you understand how to direct your research. The appraisal forms I describe in Chapter 2 — the ones I told you to use when inventorying your organization's records and information — are a great starting point. An effectively designed appraisal form provides the ability for you to gain insight on departmental functions, how records are used to support the functions, and how long the department is currently retaining the records.

To assist you in starting your research, I want to highlight some record types paired with the retention periods traditionally assigned to them. For example, accounting-related records are usually assigned a seven-year retention period for tax purposes. Figure 3-5 lists some of these record types and their corresponding retention periods. *Note:* This information should only serve as a guide. You should check with your attorney or tax accountant before implementing any record retention periods.

Figure 3-5:
Common
record types
and their
commonly
assigned
retention
periods.

Record Type	Retention Period (Years)
Accident Reports and Claims (settled)	7
Accounts Payable	7
Accounts Receivable	7
Annual Reports	Permanent
Articles of Incorporation	Permanent
Board of Director's (all records)	Permanent
Budgets	3
Bylaws	Permanent
Contracts (after expiration)	7
Correspondence	3
Employee Files (after separation)	7
Expense Reports	7
Financial Statements (Annual)	Permanent

Mining your natural resources

You have a number of different options when it comes to conducting retention period research. Although the Internet *can* be a great resource for finding out how different laws and regulations may impact your retention strategy, make sure that you only access the appropriate federal, state, or municipality websites to get information. Third-party sites that boast about how they can "clarify" federal, state, or local laws may be offering (unfounded) opinions and interpretations of a law or regulation.

As you are conducting research into laws and regulations that impact your record retention, you should document the specific citation that provides information regarding record retention. Documenting the citations you're using as the basis for your retention approach adds credibility and defensibility to your organization's Records and Information Management program. In addition, it can be a great help to the other departments that need to review and approve the retention schedule. The following is an example of how a citation impacting record retention might look:

Securities and Exchange Commission (SEC) 17 CFR Part 210

In addition to the Internet, retention research software applications offered by some Records and Information Management vendors are a good option for medium to large organizations, as well as those companies that operate in highly regulated environments with multiple geographical locations. In most cases, you purchase the software and licenses and then subscribe (for a fee) to periodic updates, which include new federal and state laws or changes to existing laws. Two of the leading vendors in the United States providing retention research software are as follows:

✔ **Information Requirements Clearinghouse,** at www.irch.com

✔ **Zasio,** at www.zasio.com

Another resource to consider when developing your records and information retention schedule is a consultant. You can find many qualified and reputable Records and Information Management consultants who specialize in record appraisals and record retention schedule development. If you decide that this is a good option for your organization, it is important to do your homework and find a vendor that has experience with paper and electronic records and legal and regulatory research, as well as a client reference list. It's recommended that the records management consultant you choose have been awarded the Certified Records Manager (CRM) certificate from the Institute of Certified Records Managers. The certification provides assurance that the consultant has adequate knowledge of the record retention schedule process. Consulting services can be expensive. However, if you don't have the necessary experience in-house, or do not have the time to conduct proper research, the investment is well worth the peace of mind of knowing that you have a legally defensible schedule.

For smaller organizations, you can utilize a CPA or attorney to develop your records and information retention schedule. In most cases, this will prove more economical than hiring a consultant.

As you continue your research journey and begin to assign retention periods to record series and functions, you can use the chart depicted in Figure 3-6 to see whether you are in the retention "norm" of a cross section of industries. The chart provides ranges of retention periods and what percent of organizational records are assigned to each range. *Note:* This chart is only for reference purposes to help you determine whether you are possibly assigning too many records to a specific retention period range. Depending on your organization and industry, your retention period allocations may conform to these guidelines or may vary to some degree.

Figure 3-6:
Retention
period
ranges and
record per-
centages.

Retention Range	% of Total Records
Less than 1 year	2-5
1-3 years	10-20
4-5 years	20-30
6-7 years	20-30
8-10 years	10-20
11-20 years	5-10
Permanent	2-5

When conducting research and assigning retention periods to departmental records, you most likely will encounter duplicate records among departments, such as correspondence, budgets, and policies and procedures. In this case, unless a specific departmental need exists, it's recommended that you assign the same retention period to like record types for the sake of program consistency. (This is not an issue if you are creating a Functional or Big Bucket retention schedule because you are assigning retention periods to functions rather than to individual record series.)

Assigning retention periods to nonrecord information

The volume of nonrecord information in an organization is much greater than the population of official company records. In this context, *nonrecord information* doesn't meet the criteria of a record and may include content such as spreadsheets, presentations, and other referential material. The retention of nonrecord or business-value information is not determined or governed by any outside entities. Nonrecord information should *only* be retained for the length of time it serves a business purpose — after that, it should be discarded.

Most companies that come up with retention periods for business-value information are doing so by assigning blanket retention periods. The retention period assigned, however, usually varies by department. A department (and the information it creates or receives) is evaluated for risk and sensitivity. For example, the nature of information in the Legal or Compliance department may be deemed to present more risks or be more sensitive than information received or created by the Facilities Management department, resulting in a longer retention period.

Such an approach would lead one to determine that, for the Legal department (to take that example), all business-value information is to be destroyed after three years from the date it was created. The rationale behind such a directive is that the Legal department's nonrecord information shouldn't be of value to the organization after three years. (Note that, if after three years, certain business-value information is still considered important, the information should be reevaluated to determine whether it needs to be classified as a company record.)

Looking for Approval

Obtaining retention period approvals is an important step in the development of the retention schedule. Retention periods shouldn't be developed in a vacuum by any one employee or department. Although the Records and Information manager (and staff) drives the initial retention research process and documents retention periods and applicable citations, approval should be a team effort.

In most companies, the approval team consists of department management (owners of the records and information), the Records and Information manager, and a representative from the Tax and Legal departments. This approach provides a comprehensive and expert review of the retention periods, and can help spot any issues that may result in adjustments to how long the records and information need to be kept.

Department management

Department management and their staff are the owners and users of the records and information. They have the most knowledge of how long records need to be retained to support the processing of departmental functions. In addition, they can provide important insight into the *active period* of their records. This is the period that the records need to be readily accessible for processing. Understanding the active period allows you to assist the department in moving the records to an inactive storage location, which helps eliminate clutter in the department.

Paying a visit to the Tax department

Your Tax department or tax accountant should review the retention periods you have developed to ensure that they adequately meet the organization's tax-reporting obligations. The Tax department can provide you with information regarding tax retention periods related to routine functions as well as tax audit requirements.

Legalizing your retention

The Legal department plays a vital role in the review of the records and information that will be listed on the retention schedule and the assigned retention periods. A legal review helps to ensure that organizational records and information are retained in a manner that improves the company's defensibility, reduces risks, and provides credibility.

The Legal department understands the types of organizational functions that are prone to litigation and risks and knows how long the records that support the functions should be retained to improve the company's position.

Creating the Retention Schedule Document

After you receive the necessary retention period approvals, you are ready to begin constructing the retention schedule document — that crucial piece of paper (either real or virtual) that will be distributed throughout the organization to provide employees with the direction they need to manage the life cycle of their records and information.

Some organizations, especially those that use the Big Bucket retention schedule approach, may only have one retention schedule that is used throughout the company, while other organizations that use either Departmental or Functional retention schedules may deploy multiple retention schedules. Usually companies that use multiple retention schedules do so because they have different operations with distinct functions.

An effective retention schedule is designed to provide information in addition to just retention periods. The following sections list the different components of a retention schedule and describe how they benefit the organization.

The pieces to the retention schedule puzzle

Although the retention period assigned to a record may be considered the single, most important piece of information on the schedule, other parts of the schedule are also important in managing its life cycle.

When choosing the components to be included as part of the retention schedule, remember that a schedule's primary purpose is to help employees *manage their records,* so keep it as simple and easy to read as possible. Cluttering the retention schedule with things that have no meaning to employees will reduce adherence. Some organizations create separate schedules for employee use and Records and Information Management department use. The former schedule is simplified and only contains items that are relevant to departmental employees, while the latter schedule provides more detail that can be useful in the event of an information hold order or audit.

The following is a list of commonly used retention schedule categories. The list contains information that is specific to the Departmental retention schedule format. However, some of the categories are common across all retention schedule formats (Departmental, Functional, and Big Bucket). Common categories are denoted with a *C.*

- ✔ **Record series name:** This is the official name of the record. Avoid using nicknames or abbreviations.

- ✔ **Record series description:** This section is used to provide details about the record, such as departmental nicknames or abbreviations used to refer to the record. In addition, this section should be used to provide information about how the record is used in support of a function.

- ✔ **Record series code:** The *record series code* is a unique identifier for the record series. This type of code is used primarily in conjunction with a records management or Enterprise Content Management (ECM) software application. It allows the system to track activity related to a specific record type. The identifier is usually comprised of an alphanumeric code such as FIN0001. This represents the first record series in the Finance department.

- ✔ **File plans:** A *file plan* is a classification scheme describing the different types of organizational files and records. The file plan document is separate from the retention schedule and provides additional information about a record. Some organizations opt to not use a file plan in lieu of an effectively developed retention schedule. (File plans often make use of record series codes.)

- ✔ **Start code:** A *start code* tells you when the retention clock should start ticking. You find several common start codes, such as Current Month (CMO), Active (ACT), and Permanent (PERM). Some organizations also use a start code of Tax (TAX). Start codes are used in conjunction with retention periods, such as CMO + 3 years.

  For example, a start code of CMO means that the retention period starts in the month that the record was received or created. A start code of ACT means that an active period exists prior to starting the retention period. An employee personnel file may have a retention period of

ACT + 5 years. The active period is the duration of employment, whereas the five-year retention period begins when the employee separates from the company. The next one is self-explanatory — PERM means that it is retained forever. The start code, TAX, indicates that the retention clock starts ticking in the current corporate tax year.

✔ **Trigger event:** A *trigger event* is an occurrence that starts the retention period of a record. A trigger event pertains specifically to the ACT start code. Every record series that is assigned an ACT start code has a trigger event. This includes records such as contracts, employee files, and policies and procedures.

In the case of a contract, the trigger event is when the contract expires. An employee file experiences a trigger event when an employee separates from the company. The trigger event for policies and procedures occurs when they are updated or superseded.

✔ **Retention period (C):** The retention period represents how long the record series or records related to a process or function need to be kept before they can be destroyed. One option to the standard Total Retention Period section is to break it out into two additional sections — an Active retention period and an Inactive retention period.

The Active period represents the time frame that the record series is frequently accessed and needs to be stored in the department or on online storage (electronic records) for quick retrieval. The Inactive period is the period of time in which the record series is no longer frequently accessed, but still must be retained for tax, legal, or regulatory purposes. Records that have reached their inactive period can be taken out of file cabinets and placed in box storage. Inactive electronic records can be migrated to near-line or offline storage.

✔ **Retention rules (C):** Retention rules provide information to departments on what to do with a record or groups of related records after the retention period has expired. For example, retention rules could specify which records will be destroyed and which will be forwarded to the Records and Information Management department for permanent archival.

✔ **Media format (C):** *Media format* pertains to whether a record series or groups of records are in paper or electronic format or both. (An example of both would include Accounts Payable invoices.) An organization may receive paper invoices from one vendor and electronic invoices from another.

Retention periods apply to record series (or, in the case of a Functional or Big Bucket retention schedule, related groups of records), regardless of their media format. In addition, during a lawsuit, audit, or inquiry, a Media Format section in the retention schedule allows the person searching for relevant records to know that the information is in multiple formats and that he may have to search file cabinets as well as electronic applications.

✔ **Vital (C):** This section of the retention schedule alerts employees to what record series or groups of related records are vital to the organization in the event of a disaster. By indicating on the retention schedule which records are vital, employees can know at a glance which records have been earmarked for special protection so that they can be accessed quickly to assist in business resumption efforts. When using the Functional or Big Bucket retention schedule format, you should provide information about specific records that are considered to be vital to a function.

✔ **Citation (C):** This area of the schedule provides information on what laws and regulations govern the retention period of a record series or function. This information allows organizations to respond to questions from outside parties in the case of lawsuits, audits, or inquires as to why certain records are still retained or have been destroyed. When using the Functional or Big Bucket retention schedule format, you should indicate laws and regulations that apply to specific functions.

Organizations using a Functional retention schedule may use all or some of the previous "common" categories, plus the following categories:

✔ **Departmental category:** This section lists the departments of the organization, such as Accounts Payable, Facilities Management, and Legal.

✔ **Record group:** This category provides further description of the record types assigned to the department.

✔ **Process description:** This section provides information regarding the department's processes and the records that support departmental functions.

Big Bucket retention schedules may use all or some of the "common" sections in addition to the following:

✔ **Functional category:** A functional category is comprised of multiple departments. The functional category General Accounting may be comprised of Accounts Payable, Accounts Receivable, and General Ledger.

✔ **Departmental category:** This section lists the departments assigned to the Functional category.

✔ **Functional description:** The description provides details about the function and related processes.

Use Figure 3-7 as a quick reference tool to determine which record retention schedule components are assigned to each schedule format.

Component	Schedule Format		
	Departmental	Functional	Big Bucket
Record series name	√		
Record series description	√		
Record series code	√		
Start code	√		
Trigger event	√		
Retention period	√	√	√
Retention rules	√	√	√
Media format	√	√	√
Vital	√	√	√
Citation	√	√	√
Departmental category		√	√
Record group		√	
Process description		√	
Functional category			√
Functional description			√

Figure 3-7:
Retention
schedule
components.

Sampling retention schedule forms

Many options exist for documenting your record retention schedule. Some organizations use a form format, while others prefer to use a narrative format — both methods are acceptable. In this section, I have you take a look at both approaches so that you can determine which format works best for your company.

Form formats

Organizations that use a form format may choose to do so because they feel it is an easier read — just like how scanning bullet points can be easier on the eyes than reading a document that is full of paragraphs. The form option lists the categories in a logical sequence, regardless of whether you are using a Departmental, Functional, or Big Bucket retention schedule. Figures 3-8, 3-9, and 3-10 provide examples of the different retention schedule formats using the form option. *Note:* Additional retention schedule form examples are provided in Appendix A, available online at www.dummies.com/go/records managefd.

Department: General Ledger								
Record Series Name	Record Series Description	Record Series Code	Start Code	Trigger Event	Retention Period (Years)	Media Format	Vital	Citation
Annual Statements	Comprehensive yearly report of company activities.	GEN0001	PERM	-	-	Paper, electronic	Yes	Sox 404
Balance Sheet	Statement of assets, liabilities and capital.	GEN0002	TAX	-	6	Electronic	Yes	
Journal Entries	Recording of financial transactions from journal vouchers.	GEN0003	CMO	-	10	Paper	No	
Policies and Procedures	Policies and procedures for all General Ledger functions	GEN0004	ACT	Superceded	7	Electronic	No	

Figure 3-8:
Depart-
mental
retention
schedule
(form option).

Figure 3-9:
Functional
retention
schedule
(formoption).

Department	Record Category	Start Code	Retention Period (Years)	Media Format	Vital	Citation
Accounts Payable	Purchase orders, invoices, check registers, vendor files	CMO	7	Paper, electronic	No	IRS 1234
Accounts Receivable	Deposits, collection notifications, adjustments	CMO	7	Paper, electronic	Yes	IRS 1234
Merchandise Accounting	Invoices, freight claims, vendor correspondence, adjustments	CMO	7	Electronic	No	IRS 1234

Figure 3-10:
Big Bucket
retention
schedule
(formoption).

Function	Departments	Start Code	Retention Period (Years)	Media Format	Vital	Citation
General Accounting	Accounts Payable, Accounts Receivable, General Ledger	CMO	7	Paper, electronic	No	IRS 1234
Administration	Facilities Management, Mail Services, Records Management	CMO	6	Paper, electronic	No	OSHA 1234
Human Resources	Benefits, Human Resources, Relocation, Training	CMO	10	Paper, electronic	No	EEOC 1234

Narrative formats

This approach conveys what is usually found in the form format without the form structure. The narrative option can be used for all retention schedule formats. Figure 3-11 represents a Functional retention schedule using the narrative approach.

Figure 3-11:
Functional
retention
schedule
(narrative
format).

Audit Records

Records document the unit's response to internal and independent management, operations, and fiscal audits. This series may include but is not limited to audit reports; written responses showing how recommended changes will be implemented; and related documentation and correspondence.

Retention: (a) audit reports for 20 years, destroy (b) 7 years for work papers, drafts, and all other records, destroy.

Implementing the Retention Schedule

Now that your retention schedule document is complete, you need to decide the most effective way to implement it across your organization. Employees are looking for Records and Information Management guidance. The retention schedule provides what they need. It is the most accessed program document. Therefore, it is important to select a distribution method that can get the document on the monitors of the masses.

Keeping it electronic

The retention schedule should be distributed electronically. In addition, employees should be instructed not to print the retention schedule or download it to a hard drive or network drive. Departmental retention schedules are usually updated several times annually. Functional and Big Bucket schedules are modified less frequently. If employees are printing or downloading the schedule, they may not have the most current version, which can lead to records and information not being retained appropriately.

The ideal distribution outlet is the company's intranet. By developing an intranet website where employees can access the retention schedule, your company can help ensure that its employees are applying the correct retention periods. If your company doesn't have an intranet, you can place the retention schedule in a designated folder on your network that is accessible by all employees. Small businesses that do not have an intranet or company network can print the retention schedule as needed and inform employees when updates have occurred.

Providing direction

When introducing the retention schedule to the organization, it's a good idea to create an accompanying "directions" document of some kind. Such a document can help employees understand how to read and use the schedule. The document should provide information on each retention schedule category as it appears on the schedule.

Although the retention schedule is somewhat self-explanatory, some Departmental retention schedule categories are traditionally a point of confusion for employees — such as record series codes, start codes, trigger events, media formats, and vital. Providing additional information and directions on how to interpret these categories can help employees feel at ease with the schedule.

Updating the Retention Schedule

Retention schedules are dynamic — they change, some types more than others. Retention schedules are developed based on business functions, legalities, regulations, and administrative needs. Chances are that if changes occur in any of these areas, they will result in a change to the retention schedule.

Modifications to the retention schedule may include a change to the retention period of an existing record, the addition of a new record, or the deletion of a record no longer in use. The Departmental retention schedule is the most susceptible to change, while the Functional and Big Bucket formats are the most immune.

For example, if the federal government enacts a change to a healthcare privacy and protection law, such a change may impact the retention of one or more record series on the departmental schedule. In this scenario, a Functional or Big Bucket retention schedule needs to be reviewed to determine whether the retention period assigned to functions (and supporting records) is adequate to comply with the changes in the law.

In many cases, you may not be aware of a change in a law, regulation, or business process that impacts the retention period of a record. Therefore, it's recommended that you create a mechanism that allows employees to submit a *change request form* to the retention schedule.

Creating a template or web form that can be made available on the company's intranet is an ideal way to allow employees to submit their changes. A template form (see Figure 3-12) ensures that you are provided the required information that you need to start the change process. If your company does not have an intranet, an e-mail template form can be created for the same purpose.

In addition to processing periodic retention schedule changes, it is recommended that a comprehensive review of the organization's retention schedule be conducted on an annual basis. A review of this type helps to ensure that the retention schedule is staying current with organizational changes. The following list describes some areas to target during the review:

✔ **Acquisitions or divestitures:** Has the organization acquired any companies during the past year? Most acquisitions result in new operations, functions, and records being added to the organization. In addition, has the organization divested itself of any operations? If so, the retention schedule needs to be updated to reflect the change.

Figure 3-12:
Retention
Schedule
Change
Request
Form
(departmen-
tal).

Record Retention Schedule Change Request Form		
Name		
Location		
Department		
Extension		
Date		
Addition		
Record Name	Record Description	Proposed Retention Period
Vital (Y/N)	Citation	Media Format
Deletion		
Record Series Code	Reason for Deletion	
Active Record		
Record Series Code	Nature of Change	

✔ **New or defunct departments:** Has the organization created any new departments not listed on the current retention schedule, or deactivated any departments that were listed on the retention schedule?

✔ **Consolidation of departments:** Have any departments combined operations? If so, their functions and records may need to be combined on the retention schedule.

Part II
Filing Made Simple

The 5th Wave   By Rich Tennant

"I'm not sure it's appropriate to send a digital resume to a paper stock company looking for a sales rep."

In this part . . .

*H*ere's where you find out about the different methods for filing paper records and see what equipment options will make the process more efficient. You'll also look at the best approaches for filing electronic information so that you can find what you need when you need it and prevent your hard drive and network drives from becoming digital graveyards.

Chapter 4

I Know It's Here Somewhere

*O*rganization breeds efficiency — in most cases, this familiar phrase is accurate. However, in some cases, it doesn't quite hold true. Implementing a filing system that doesn't meet your company's needs is an example of an organization that creates inefficiencies. You can organize your information and place it in folders, but if you can't find what you need when you need it, it may be time for a filing makeover.

The goal of this chapter is to help you understand document filing options to help you select the approach that works best for your company. This includes an analysis of methods for filing paper and electronic information, as well as a look at filing equipment and supplies.

Filing Methods

Prior to implementing your filing system, you'll want to spend some time reviewing commonly used methods. Obtaining an understanding of how each method works can help you make the correct choice (or choices). Most companies use more than one filing system. The types of records you create and receive are going to determine the right method.

When reviewing the following filing methods, keep your own records in mind and think about which methods seem like a good fit. A rule of thumb is to focus on retrieval and not filing. Filing is the easy part; it's finding what you need, when you need it, that causes the headaches. In addition, think about how your current filing needs may change in the future. This may include events like acquisitions, selling a division, or changes in administrative methods. Having to retrofit an established filing system that contains thousands of folders is a large undertaking. The more factors you consider now, the less paper cuts you'll have to endure in the future.

The following sections detail three of the most commonly used filing methods:

✔ Alphabetical

✔ Straight-numeric

✔ Alphanumeric

The next sections take a look at each method in a bit more detail.

The alpha file

The most common filing method is alphabetical. Alphabetical filing may seem like a no-brainer; you probably discovered how to alphabetize in first grade. However, a little more is involved than just placing the file starting with a *B* after the *A* — enough to warrant a 36-page alphabetical filing standard issued in 1995 by the American National Standards Institute (ANSI) and the Association for Information Management (ARMA). The standard provides guidance on a variety of alphabetical filing scenarios.

Alphabetical filing is an easy and effective filing method if you plan ahead and take steps to ensure consistency and quality. In most cases, it's not the letters of the alphabet that pose issues for employees filing alphabetically. It's understanding how to handle items such as names with multiple words, plural words, punctuation, Roman numerals, acronyms, prefixes, and abbreviations.

To help simplify the process and increase filing accuracy, you can implement the *unit* approach. Units serve as an alphabetical filing guide. Units segregate each word of a name — including prefixes, titles, and suffixes — and provide direction on how to handle punctuation. Figures 4-1 and 4-2 illustrate how you can use the unit approach to alphabetize proper and company names.

Figure 4-1:
Alphabetical
filing units
(proper
names).

Name	Unit 1	Unit 2	Unit 3	Unit 4
Becky A. Smith, M.D.	Smith	Becky	A	MD
Becky A. Smith, Mayor	Smith	Becky	A	Mayor
Bill A. Smith	Smith	Bill	A	
Col. Bill A. Smith	Smith	Bill	A	Col
Mr. Bobby A. Smith	Smith	Bobby	A	Mr
Mrs. Bobby A. Smith	Smith	Bobby	A	Mrs
Ms. Bobby-Anne A. Smith	Smith	BobbyAnne	A	Ms

Figure 4-2:
Alphabetical
filing units
(company
names).

Name	Unit 1	Unit 2	Unit 3	Unit 4
ABC Supplies	A	B	C	Supplies
Beef-N-Shake	Beef	N	Shake	
East-City Freight	East	City	Freight	
Earl's Self-Storage	Earls	Self	Storage	
Gulf-Union Railway	GulfUnion	Railway		

The numbers don't lie

Numeric filing is typically the fastest and most accurate filing method. Although different variations of numeric filing exist, the primary method used by most organizations is *straight numeric*. Straight numeric filing involves filing information from lowest to highest number.

Straight numeric filing has its advantages: It's simple, requires minimal employee training, and allows you to easily purge records that are no longer required to be retained. It's easier for employees to file information numerically than alphanumerically because they only have to remember one concept — lowest to highest number in order, rather than an alpha and a numeric order approach. Privacy is another advantage of using straight numeric filing. In many cases, a folder that's alphabetically filed may contain a person's name on the folder label. It's easier for someone with malicious intent to find her target by name versus her employee identification or account number.

Straight numeric filing is typically used in large filing operations. Unlike alphabetical filing, straight numeric filing requires *cross referencing* (sometimes referred to as *indirect access*). This refers to the need to have a reference that allows you to know what file number you need. For example, if you need to retrieve a medical file for a patient, you first have to access his or her account in your administration software to determine the patient's medical record number.

Before implementing a straight numeric filing system, you need to determine what number is unique to the record you are filing. The number type you come up with should reflect your specific situation and needs, but just for the sake of comparison, I list a few of the more commonly used number types here:

- ✔ Vendor number
- ✔ Account number
- ✔ Medical record number
- ✔ Employee identification number

Before you actually implement your straight numeric filing system, you need to decide whether you'll use the entire number string for your number type or settle for a subset of that string. For example, a client or vendor account number may be comprised of 12 numbers. However, placing all 12 numbers on a folder label for filing purposes may be overkill. You may determine that you can effectively design a straight numeric filing system by only using the first or last six digits of the account number. This approach, especially when using color-coded labels (see Figure 4-3), makes the labeling, filing, and retrieval process easier by creating a visual reference. If you know that you are looking for a file beginning with the number 6, it will have a specific color (green). So, to retrieve or file the folder, you proceed directly to the section starting with green. The same approach is used for the subsequent numbers and their corresponding colors. Truncating the amount of numbers and their corresponding folder label colors allows you to efficiently retrieve and file without having to account for every number. In addition, you can save money on ink cartridges if you don't print every number.

Filing alphanumerically

Alphanumeric filing consists of related letters and numbers. This method provides filing flexibility not provided with alphabetical or straight numeric filing. Alphanumeric filing allows both a name (alpha) and a subject (numeric) reference. For example, a telecommunications company may file projects by state and work order number. In this case, the first two characters of the file folder label may contain the abbreviation of the state in which the project took place — TN (Tennessee). The last four characters may represent the work order number — 1234. Like straight numeric filing, a cross-reference tool needs to be used to retrieve the file.

A disadvantage of alphanumeric filing is that it requires more employee training. Alphanumeric filing is not as straightforward as alphabetical or straight numeric filing. Because it uses a combination of both methods, it is sometimes harder for employees to learn, which may result in an increase in misfiles.

Figure 4-3:
Straight
numeric fil-
ing (side-tab
color-coded
folders).

Evaluating Filing Equipment and Supplies

To some, filing may seem like a straightforward process: Buy a file cabinet and some folders and start filing, or open an electronic folder and click Save. Making such assumptions — "Hey, this stuff is so easy even a kindergartner can do it" — is not recommended if your intent is to actually find what you're looking for. Thanks to our filing forefathers and mothers, filing methods and equipment have been analyzed, updated, and refined over the years to make the process more accurate and efficient.

Understanding what options exist is the first step in determining what will and won't work for your organization. The following sections provide you with the insight that you need to evaluate filing equipment, methods, and supplies.

The right equipment makes a difference

The age of the paperless office first predicted in 1975 hasn't come to fruition — yet. So, as long as companies receive and create paper documents, they'll still probably need file cabinets. Now, as to how those file cabinets actually look and function, an evolution has occurred over the decades. If you look at this particular slice of history a bit more closely, you can see that this evolution has been driven by three primary concepts: efficiency, increased capacity, and footprint reduction.

As the cost of office space continues to increase, organizational space planners are constantly trying to optimize square footage to accommodate more employees and office equipment into smaller spaces. File cabinets are a factor in this equation.

Vertically challenged

For many years, the traditional vertical file cabinet was a fixture in company offices. (Figure 4-4 shows a few specimens in all their glory.) However, their numbers have dwindled over the past two decades, as more-efficient and better-engineered models replace them.

The vertical file cabinet is considered to be the least efficient and most costly file cabinet option. The excessive cost isn't attributable to the file cabinet's price tag, but to its operational inefficiencies.

Photo courtesy of The Smead Manufacturing Company © 2012

Figure 4-4:
Vertical file
cabinets.

The following is a list of the disadvantages of using vertical file cabinets:

- ✔ **Page size:** Separate vertical file cabinets have to be used to file different paper sizes such as *letter* (8½" x 11") and *legal* (8½" x 14").

- ✔ **Less capacity:** Vertical file cabinets provide up to one-third less capacity than other types of equipment.

- ✔ **Space requirements:** Vertical file cabinets require a substantial amount of clearance when the drawers are open.

- ✔ **Filing method:** Vertical file cabinets require the user to file and retrieve from front to back, which requires more time than other methods such as side to side.

- ✔ **Limited use of visual aids:** The front-to-back filing method reduces the ability to effectively use color-coded side-tab folders. (You find out more about color-coded side-tab folders later in this chapter.)

Vertical file cabinets may be a good choice for smaller businesses or for organizational departments that don't have to file or retrieve a significant amount of paper documents. If that sounds like you, that's fine. If it doesn't sound like you, you may want to look into the other options I cover in the upcoming sections. Before purchasing and implementing vertical file cabinets, you should carefully evaluate your needs to determine whether vertical file cabinets are an appropriate fit for your company. (Remember: You do have other options!)

Taking a lateral approach

As vertical file cabinets have been making their corporate exit, lateral file cabinets have been making their entrance. Lateral file cabinets are today's file cabinet of choice for most organizations.

Currently, lateral file cabinets are available in two primary models: pull-drawer models and flip-top models. Lateral file cabinets with pull drawers (see Figure 4-5) are used for top-tab folders that are placed in hanging folders, while lateral file cabinets with flip tops (see Figure 4-6) use side-tab folders. (Folder types are reviewed in the next section.)

Top-tab folders are usually manila folders with a labeling tab located at the top of the folder, while a side-tab folder contains a labeling tab on the side (or end) of the folder.

Figure 4-5:
Lateral file cabinet (pull drawers).

Figure 4-6:
Lateral file cabinets (flip top).

Lateral file cabinets are ideal for offices that (a) process significant volumes of paper that need to be frequently retrieved and (b) need to optimize their space. In addition, lateral file cabinets provide the following benefits:

- ✔ **Efficiency:** Lateral file cabinets allow folders to be filed side by side. This approach provides employees with the ability to conduct a quick visual scan of the contents of the file drawer, whether side- or top-tab folders are used. This approach allows the use of color-coded tab folders, which speeds filing and retrieval.

- ✔ **Versatility:** One lateral file cabinet can be configured to house different paper sizes, such as letter and legal, in different drawers.

- ✔ **Less space:** Although lateral file cabinets are wider than vertical file cabinets, they aren't as deep, which positively impacts the space needed for aisles.

- ✔ **More capacity:** Lateral file cabinets are designed to hold up to one-third more volume than vertical file cabinets.

Keeping an open mind

Open-face shelving is an ideal equipment option for organizations that have a large number of files that are frequently retrieved, as in the case of medical facilities or insurance companies. Open-face shelving consists of levels of open shelves (see Figure 4-7) that use side-tab folders that are assigned color-coded labels based on criteria such as policy or account number, as well as last name.

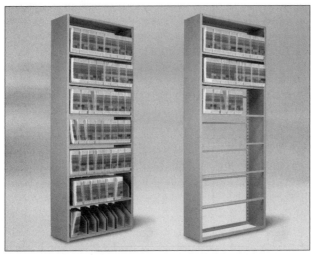

Figure 4-7:
Open-face
shelving.

Copyright © 2012, TAB Products Co LLC

Open-face shelving is considered to be a specialized or niche filing-equipment option. It's most often used in centralized file rooms or in areas with a high volume of filing and retrieval. Open-face shelving provides the following benefits:

✔ **Easy access:** Open-face shelving does not contain drawers, making the file folders accessible at all times.

✔ **Visual:** Of all the filing-equipment options, open-face shelving provides you with the most optimal view of files. By using color-coded side-tab folders, an employee can proceed directly to the shelving section containing the file that he or she needs.

✔ **Filing accuracy:** By using color-coded side-tab folders, it's easier for an employee to determine where to file a folder. It also makes it easier to detect folders that have been misfiled — a red folder in the midst of a sea of green stands out like a sore thumb.

Open-face shelving is typically used in an office environment that experiences frequent filing and retrieval, such as a medical office housing patient medical records or a law office with client case files.

If you use open-face shelving, it's recommended that the shelving units and information reside in an area that can be secured and only accessed by authorized employees. Unlike vertical and lateral file cabinets, open-face shelving can't be closed and locked.

Making the most of it

Necessity — or the lack of office space — is the mother of invention. Mobile shelving — often used in the same business environments as open-face shelving — allows companies to maximize "dead" office space.

Mobile shelving operates on floor tracks that allow the shelving units to collapse or expand. They are either motorized or are equipped with handles that allow you to operate them manually. In addition to saving office space, mobile shelving provides the same benefits as open-face shelving.

You have two primary mobile shelving types to choose from:

✔ **Compacting:** This approach allows the shelving units to collapse or expand, creating an aisle between each unit. (Figure 4-8 gives an example.)

✔ **Lateral slide:** This method arranges the shelving units one behind the other, or in a "stacked" approach. Each unit moves to the side, allowing you to access the unit you need. (Figure 4-9 gives you a sense of how this approach works.)

Figure 4-8:
Mobile
shelving
(compact-
ing).

Figure 4-9:
Mobile
shelving
(lateral
slide).

File folders under "important"

Discussing the different types of file folders may seem very elementary. However, along with file cabinets, file folders have a big impact on employee efficiency and operational effectiveness.

Each type of file folder serves a unique purpose. You can choose from three primary folder types, and all three come in different sizes, colors, weights, and styles. In terms of folder type, your choices are

- Top-tab
- Side-tab
- Hanging

The next few sections take a closer look at each option.

Top-tab

Top-tab folders (see Figure 4-10) or manila folders contain a labeling tab on the top of the folder that allows you to identify the contents. They continue to be widely used by companies due to their lower costs and employee familiarity. Top-tab folders are most effective when the folder is stored in file cabinet drawers and the filing system is small. Despite their popularity, they do come with a few downsides that you should consider before using this type of folder:

- **Additional support required:** Top-tab folders are designed to be placed in vertical and lateral (pull-drawer) file cabinets. They work best when they're inserted in a hanging folder, which increases costs. If they aren't placed in a hanging folder, they may shift, making filing and retrieval more difficult.

- **Trouble detecting misfiles:** Viewing folders from the top does not provide a good visual reference for spotting misfiles, compared to a side view.

Figure 4-10:
A top-tab
folder.

Side-tab

Side-tab folders (see Figure 4-11) or manila folders have a labeling tab on the side (or end) of the folder that allows you to identify the contents. Side-tab folders are primarily used in open-face or pull-drawer lateral file cabinets. They are a good option for frequently retrieved medical and client files. Side-tab folders allow employees to easily scan from a side view the label identifier on the side of the folder, instead of having to look in a front-to-back approach with top-tab folders. However, side-tab folders have become more popular in recent years with many other types of companies due to their functionality. The following list spells out some of that functionality:

✔ **Easier visual reference:** Side-tab folders allow employees to view the file-tab label (indicator) while standing in front of the file cabinet. This increases filing and retrieval efficiency.

✔ **More appropriate for file rooms:** Side-tab folders are the preferred choice for large filing operations or for file rooms with significant filing and retrieval activity due to the visual reference (see the previous point) efficiencies created by the use of side-tab folders.

✔ **More styles:** Side-tab folders offer more choices of styles than other folder options, allowing an organization to tailor its filing.

✔ **Better suited for floor space optimization plans:** Side-tab folders are appropriate for use in conjunction with the kinds of lateral file cabinets (flip-top), open-face, and mobile shelving, which require less office space.

Figure 4-11:
A side-tab folder with a color-coded label.

Hanging with the hanging folder

Hanging folders are equipped with metal strips with hooks on each end that hang from rails in vertical and pull-drawer lateral file cabinets (see Figure 4-12). Hanging folders come in a variety of thicknesses and quality. Because hanging folders are commonly used to house other folders (for example, manila top-tab folders), it's important to ensure that you use good-quality hanging folders. Hanging folders are used in two ways. Some people start by labeling the hanging folders, using the provided plastic tab covers and then simply placing loose documents directly into the folder, while others stick with the labeling but then place top-tab folders inside the hanging folder. The first approach usually limits the contents of the hanging folder to one subject or classification of documents.

The second approach allows you to label each top-tab folder so that multiple folders related to a document type can be filed in one hanging folder. For example, you could label the hanging folder Tax Returns, and then place within it top-tab folders labeled 2009, 2010, and 2011.

Figure 4-12:
A hanging folder.

Copyright © 2012, TAB Products Co LLC

Folder labeling

How you label a folder impacts how quickly you're able to file and retrieve a document. As was the case with file cabinets and folders, you have tons of labeling options. A quick check of any office supply website will immediately overload you with choices — you'll be awash in different sizes, different colors, permanent adhesive labels, or labels that can be removed so that folders can be reused. In addition to the different label types, you also have the option of computer-generating your labels. Several vendors offer software applications that you install or access online to produce standard or custom labels.

I recommend computer-generating your labels whenever possible — and those label sheets that you can pick up at any office supply store makes it easy. Hand-written labels can be illegible, resulting in inefficient filing and retrieval as well as misfiles. In addition, software- or template-generated labels offer the following advantages:

- ✔ **Consistency:** Using label software or templates provides format consistency, which allows employees to become familiar with the label style. Familiarity with the label format speeds filing and retrieval.

- ✔ **Color-coding:** Printed or computer-generated labels allow you to create custom color-coded labels to fit your organization's specific needs.

- ✔ **Bar codes:** Label software often lets you generate bar codes for your labels. This feature is a great option for larger filing operations. Label bar codes can be scanned with a hand-held bar-code scanner whenever folders are removed from a shelf, delivered to an employee, or placed backed on a shelf. Used in conjunction with spreadsheet, database, or records management software, bar codes can allow you to know the location or status of a file.

Selecting a Filing Method

In the previous sections, you had a chance to review the components needed to establish a filing system — filing methods, equipment, and folders. Now it's time to decide which of the options will work best for your company. The first step in selecting your filing options is to understand the organization's processes and records; then select an approach that best supports these functions.

Selecting the right filing method can enhance employee efficiency, customer service, and compliance with laws and regulations. Implementing the wrong filing system can lead to lost records, misfiles, increased labor costs, and frustration. I'll work hard in the following sections to ensure that you have the information you need to make the right selection.

Creating a records profile

In this section, you start off with identifying the characteristics of your records. The objective is to develop a comprehensive understanding of how your records operate within your department or company. You have two primary areas to evaluate:

- ✔ **How records are requested:** Understanding how records will be requested is essential in determining how they need to be filed. How do employees reference the records — by name, subject, number, or by a combination? If files are requested by name only, an alphabetical filing system is appropriate. If files are requested by number, such as an employee identification or customer number, you should use straight numeric filing. If records are requested by a combination of name and number, they should be filed alphanumerically.

- ✔ **The volume of records involved:** If the volume of records is low (hundreds), an alphabetical filing system is usually adequate. However, if the number of files is large (over 5,000), it's recommended that you consider implementing an option that is more expandable and flexible, such as straight numeric.

Unless you have a very small number of files or you store your files in your desk, you should avoid filing your records in vertical file cabinets with top-tab folders. Using side-tab folders in lateral (flip-top) or open-face shelving can maximize your filing efficiencies by requiring less floor space and providing you with the best view of your files.

Growing, growing — gone!

Another important factor to evaluate when implementing a filing system is the need to account for growth. When implementing a filing system, you should forecast how many new records you receive or create and at what frequency. Predicting file growth can help you determine the appropriate filing method and how much equipment and floor space you will need.

Not allowing for future growth can have negative effects on your organization. It can, in some cases, result in having to forgo your current filing method for one that is more suitable to your volume of records. In addition, it can mean that you don't have enough room to file your records, impact your budget — hey, buying more file cabinets costs money — and lead to a decrease in employee productivity because of overstuffed filing equipment.

Evaluating the current state of affairs

If you already have a filing system in place, it's a good idea to periodically evaluate the system to determine how well it's working for you. The following is a list of common symptoms that may indicate you are in need of a filing makeover:

- ✔ Overstuffed file drawers and folders
- ✔ Difficulty finding what you need
- ✔ Lost files
- ✔ Having to regularly expand your file system capacity

If you are encountering any one (or a combination) of these issues, your current filing system is probably not operating properly. You should conduct an analysis to determine the cause.

In many cases, these symptoms are caused and can be alleviated by managing the life cycle of the records. Regardless of the type of record, each has an active and inactive period (life cycle phase). When file cabinets and shelves become crowded, it's usually due to inactive records not being removed from active filing equipment. Therefore, part of implementing a good filing system is identifying a record's active time frame and sending it to inactive storage after it is no longer frequently accessed. Taking this approach may eliminate the need to purchase additional filing equipment.

Creating a Digital Filing System

The volume of electronic files in most organizations far outweighs that of their paper counterparts. It's extremely important to understand how to effectively design and implement a computer filing system to find what you need, when you need it, and to keep computer drives from growing out of control.

Drawing the parallels

The first step in designing and implementing a computer filing system is to understand that the basic concept for filing paper records is the same as for electronic records — it all comes down to knowing how the records will be referenced and retrieved. Just as you create paper folders labeled with names and file them alphabetically, the same holds true for electronic folders. Think of your computer folders as an electronic file cabinet. Although this sounds logical, most people do not draw the parallels between paper and electronic filing.

Electronic filing *does* offer more filing flexibility. It's easier to create folders and subfolders, add additional identifying information, and then retrieve information. Although this is an advantage, it can become a filing and records management challenge. Think it through: A paper filing system is an established and controlled process; you can see the files in the file cabinets. It would be obvious if an employee decided to purchase a new file cabinet and began to file a department's records by using a new and unapproved method.

It's not that obvious with electronic filing. In most organizations, employees have the ability to create ad hoc folders and subfolders, either on their hard drive or on a network drive, and file information in them as they see fit. This may occur for a prolonged period of time before it's discovered — if it ever *is* discovered.

Because of the ease with which folders can be created, guidance and accountability have to be imposed from above when it comes to electronic filing systems. This includes guidelines on how to name folders and files (I review these items later in this chapter).

When creating an electronic filing system, it's important that you determine where your records are to be filed. For organizations with a *local-area network (LAN),* departments are usually assigned a specific drive for their use. After this has been determined, the next step is deciding on the main folders you need to establish.

The main folders you create need to encompass the primary record types, functions, or processes of the department. Think of the main folder as the highest-level category. For example, the Human Resources department may create a main folder structure that mirrors what you see in Figure 4-13.

Figure 4-13:
Main folder
structure.

401k Terminations
Affirmative Action
Alcohol & Drug Testing
Applications & Resumes
Background Checks
COBRA
EEO
Employee Files
FMLA
Job Postings
Leave of Absences
Performance Appraisals
Testing
Training

In addition to establishing a department's main folders, electronic filing allows you to easily create subfolders related to each main topic, as shown in Figure 4-14. This provides the ability to refine the filing and retrieval process.

Figure 4-14:
Electronic subfolders.

Always make sure that each file gets assigned to a folder. That means whenever you open a main folder, you generally never see individual files, but rather subfolders. (Refer to Figure 4-14.) The one exception here is those cases where the main folder is really all there is — no additional subfolder refinement needs to take place. Figure 4-15 illustrates what you want to avoid when opening a main folder or high-level subfolder.

Figure 4-15:
Uh-oh. Individual files haven't been assigned to separate subfolders.

In the scenario shown in Figure 4-15, you see a bunch of individual files that represent a bewildering variety of topics. Instead of throwing them all into one pot, it would be better to group them in related subfolders for organizational purposes. Files saved in this manner will increase retrieval time due to lack of organization.

Establishing a predefined folder structure — one that encompasses the main functions of your department, plus additional subfolders that you can use to refine filing and retrieval — helps to ensure that employees don't create their own folder structures, which can reduce filing and retrieval efficiencies for other employees.

After the filing structure has been developed and implemented, employees should be made aware that no new folders should be added (or existing folders deleted) without appropriate approval. In addition, you should let your employees know that you expect them to store any business-related records or information of business value on the local network rather than on their (individual) hard drives. Saving records and information on hard drives prevents others from having access to content that may be needed for processing or decision-making.

When creating computer folders and subfolders, be aware of the following concept:

"Instant filing, forever retrieval — Forever filing, instant retrieval"

This means that you can create an electronic filing structure so simplistic that it allows you to immediately file a document. Picture a paper file cabinet drawer with one super-sized hanging folder. Regardless of the record type you're dealing with, you stick that document in the hanging folder — instant filing. However, when it comes time to retrieve the document, you may have to sift through the entire contents of the hanging folder to locate what you need — forever retrieval.

The same issue can happen with electronic filing. If you have a significant amount of electronic documents — documents of very different record types to boot — and yet create only the one folder for all that you have, yes, you can save the documents very quickly, but you'll spend ages retrieving what you've saved. Conversely, you can create an electronic filing structure with so many subfolders that it takes too long to file, but you can immediately pinpoint its location for retrieval. The ideal electronic filing solution is a balance of simplicity and good organization.

Naming folders and files

An electronic filing system should only be considered effective if employees can efficiently use it to file and retrieve information. To increase the effectiveness of your system, you need to ensure that folders and files are properly named. When naming your folders and files, you should avoid the following common pitfalls:

✔ **Abbreviations and acronyms:** Although departmental employees may be very familiar with abbreviations and acronyms commonly used in their department, employees in other departments that have a need to access the information may not be familiar with them, potentially resulting in not finding the information they need.

✔ **Vagueness:** Avoid using nondescript names such as Jane's Files, Bob's Desk Files, or 2012 Misc. In most cases, this type of labeling doesn't provide adequate detail and will increase retrieval times. Instead, use meaningful labels such as July 2012 ABC Company Executed Contract.

I think it's safe to say that, at least once in your working career, you have managed to save a file on your computer by using a filename you thought made perfect sense at the time, only to discover the following week when you attempted to retrieve the file that you had no idea what you named it. Don't worry; you aren't alone. It happens every day in every organization. It's a result of not implementing standard naming conventions for folders and files.

The goal is to keep folder names and filenames short, but as informative as possible. A person looking for information should be able to tell what the file is about without having to open it. Developing standard naming conventions can help you achieve this goal and significantly reduce the "filename made sense last week" syndrome. Following are a few standard naming convention recommendations:

✔ **Date:** If you start your filename with the current date, you should be able to track it down much faster. If you're attempting to retrieve a document that you know was from the prior month, you can immediately dismiss any files that have a more recent date.

✔ **Version:** Applying a version number to a filename allows you to know whether you are accessing the most current version of a document.

✔ **Consistency:** Be consistent in the way you name your files. If you made the decision to file by using a naming order of current date, last name, and first name, stick to that pattern. Inconsistency increases retrieval time.

✔ **Structure:** Each operation should agree upon a standard structure for naming files. For customer complaints, this may include the date (6-23-2012) last name, first name, and division.

Chapter 5

Drives Can Drive You Crazy

• •

In This Chapter
▶ Managing the risks
▶ Cleaning up your drives
▶ Keeping your drives humming

• •

*O*ver the past decade, we have witnessed an explosion of digital volume. The growth rate of electronic content is staggering, and it has impacted every organization. Industry experts project that digital information doubles every 18 months. Much of this electronic information finds its way onto your company's personal (hard) and network drives.

Regardless of the size of your organization, if you receive and create electronic information, you have to store it somewhere. Just like paper information, digital content also has a life cycle that needs to be managed. In this chapter, I analyze how organizations are negatively impacted by unmanaged electronic information residing on hard drives and network drives and then move on to showing you how you can manage the electronic information life cycle, as well as how to maintain your drives going forward.

At-Risk Drivers

Even with the growing adoption by organizations of electronic records and Enterprise Content Management (ECM) software applications used for storing, retrieving, and managing electronic information (covered in great detail in Chapter 10), many organizations have not made the move to discontinue the use of their hard drives and shared network drives or use their ECM system in lieu of drives. Therefore, drives are still heavily used by employees to store digital content.

Employees perceive drives to be convenient and easy to use. However, a number of risks and limitations are associated with drives that most organizations aren't aware of or aren't prepared to resolve. These issues have appropriately led to drives being nicknamed the Wild West of computing.

Out of sight — out of mind

Most of the records and information that your company creates and receives ends up being stored on employee hard drives or network drives and, in many cases, to both. With paper file cabinets, your folders, records, and information are visible. You have to take action when you continue to receive new records and information but your file cabinets or shelves can no longer accommodate the volume. This isn't (usually) the case with electronic records and information.

Over the past decade, the cost of computer storage has continued to decrease. Most organizations have opted to regularly increase the storage capacity of their network drives rather than implement processes to clean up information that is no longer needed. This approach has led to an electronic out-of-sight, out-of-mind mentality. After files are saved to a drive, they tend to stay there. Organizations that continue to increase storage capacity may be unknowingly masking the fact that they're not properly managing their information.

Driving up the costs

Although computer storage may not be as expensive as it once was, the cost of not properly managing records and information is on the rise. As organizations create and receive more electronic content, but fail to manage storage repositories such as hard drives and network drives, it can negatively impact the organizations' bottom lines.

The problem with the out-of-sight — out-of-mind mentality with regard to electronic content is compounded by unmanaged computer drives. Hard drives and shared network drives are becoming *digital graveyards.* Files are being saved to hard drives and network drives and then promptly forgotten. For organizations that aren't addressing this issue, their employees aren't motivated to ensure that drives are appropriately used, cleaned up, and maintained.

This lack of company acknowledgment and action of hard and network drive issues typically results in gigabytes (or even terabytes) of poorly named electronic files, folders with no structure, and the continuous addition of server storage, causing employees to have to search through massive amounts of information to find the file they need. But wait, isn't electronic retrieval supposed to be faster than getting up from your desk, walking to the file cabinet, and finding a folder? The answer is yes — theoretically. However, if files and repositories (drives) aren't managed properly, it will take employees longer to retrieve electronic files, which equates to increased labor costs.

Driving down function lane

Having to search through massive amounts of information on hard drives and network shared drives not only increases labor costs, but it also negatively impacts an organization's ability to effectively support its functions. This includes the ability to rapidly retrieve information for processing work, decision-making, customer service, and responding to regulatory inquiries and lawsuits.

All information is potentially discoverable in a lawsuit. This means that in the event of a lawsuit, the plaintiff's attorney can request an organization to produce any information that he or she believes to be relevant. The massive amounts of information on your hard drives and shared network drives are fair game during legal discovery. It can take a considerable amount of effort and expense to cull through the volume of files on corporate shared network drives. Therefore, it's recommended that this issue serve as justification for appropriately managing drives.

In most cases, the inability of hard drives and shared network drives to adequately support business functions is due to the absence of effective folder structures, which results in a lack of organization. Many companies find their important business-related documents filed with pictures of the company luau, old spreadsheets, and other electronic content that may or may not have been useful at some point. Information that is no longer serving a business purpose typically makes up the majority of the files on your hard drives and shared network drives, and acts as noise and clutter that reduce the overall effectiveness and efficiency of employees and organizations.

Cleaning Up Your Driving Record

The explosion of electronic content on company drives didn't happen overnight. If it had, you would've seen employee rebellions around the globe. The increase in volume has occurred over a span of years, resulting in employees unknowingly adapting to and accepting the growth. Many employees and organizations still don't realize the extent and impact of the issues related to drives.

Regardless of the problems a company is experiencing with its hard drives and shared network drives, chances are that the issues are attributable to the fact that organizations did not anticipate the unbridled growth of electronic files, and how to manage that growth. The following sections help you understand the steps for getting hard drives and shared network drives under control.

Taking time to know your drives

Hard drives and shared network drives serve as convenient repositories for electronic files. However, they have inherent characteristics and limitations that can quickly negate their convenience. The first step in getting your drives under control is to understand these issues:

- ✔ **Duplication:** As implied by the name *shared* network drives, multiple employees have the ability to save files to the same drive. Although this is a good feature, over time, if different employees are saving the same files to different drive folders, it won't take long for the drive to contain a significant amount of duplicated content. In some cases, different employees may be saving the same file to the same folder, but are required to assign the file a unique name. Even though the files have different names, the content is still the same.

- ✔ **Versioning:** Duplication of files also leads to the issue of *versioning*. When duplication exists, you may not know whether you are viewing the most current version of a document. An employee may modify a duplicated file, but another instance of the duplicated file may be accessed and incorrectly acted upon.

- ✔ **Folder structure:** Although hard drive and shared network drive folders can be organized and named in a structured manner to meet the needs of an employee, department, or operation; over time, new unapproved folders can be created by employees and files can be placed in the folders if the proper controls are not in place. This undermines the integrity of the filing and retrieval process.

- ✔ **Naming:** Hard drives and shared network drives allow employees to assign a naming convention of their choosing to folders and files. This promotes filing inconsistencies and inefficient file retrieval. One employee may refer to a topic or file differently from another employee.

- ✔ **Metadata:** Hard drives and shared network drives don't allow employees to assign metadata. *Metadata* is defined as data about data. This means that, aside from the filename, you are unable to assign additional descriptive information about the file's contents. For example, if you are saving a contract to a shared network drive, you don't have the ability to apply associated metadata such as the contract type, execution date, and contract duration.

- ✔ **Searching:** The absence of file metadata prevents effective searching. You must either rely on *full-text* searching (searching the text of the file) or on a filename search. In addition, employees in one department may not have authorization to search or access files on another department's shared network drives. To top things off, hard drive content often isn't located on the company's network, but rather resides on individual computers, limiting the accessibility to information.

Mapping a course of action

Now that you understand the characteristics and limitations of hard drives and shared network drives, you can begin to take steps to manage them. It is recommended that the cleanup be a company-wide initiative supported by senior management. The effort to clean up the existing content on organizational drives can be significant due to years of file accumulation, and will need management's support to ensure cooperation and compliance. However, cleaning up drives can also be initiated at the individual department level.

As you begin the cleanup process, it's important to remember that computer hard drives shouldn't be used to store official company records or information that has business value. Ideally this information should be stored in a records management or content management software system. (For more information on such software systems, see Chapter 10.) If your company does not have this type of software application, the information should be stored on the organization's shared network drives to ensure that the content is regularly backed up, searchable, and retrievable. For small businesses that may not have a computer network, this information should be stored in logically named folders on a hard drive. If you must store important business documents on a hard drive, ensure that you conduct regular backups.

Some organizations begin the cleanup process by diving right in and deleting files that no longer have any business value. Although this is an important part of the process, a more effective approach is to begin by developing a project team to organize and drive the initiative. The project team should consist of a minimal number of employees (4–6) from key areas of the organization. Limiting the number of team members allows adequate input, but helps to eliminate decision-making gridlocks. A typical project team should include (if applicable) representation from the Records Management, IT, Legal, and Operational departments.

Planning is an essential component of the drive cleanup process, regardless of the size of your business. The project team should include a cleanup plan that encompasses the following items:

- ✔ **Strategy:** Before reviewing or deleting any hard drive or network shared drive files, the project team should establish an information strategy that will be a road map for how the organization plans to clean up, use, and maintain its shared network drives. A strategy can help determine whether content such as databases and program files should be segregated and assigned to separate dedicated drives or servers, what information to retain and delete, a plan for developing folder structures, and when to perform routine drive maintenance.

- ✔ **Communication:** The project team should develop an employee communication plan that encompasses the reason for the cleanup, a schedule of events, the expected benefits, and an overview of the process.

✔ **Deletion:** The project team should consult with the appropriate organizational representatives from areas such as the Legal and Tax departments to determine what approvals, if any, need to be obtained before files can be deleted. This applies primarily to official company records listed on the company's record retention schedule. However, both records and nonrecord information may be relevant to pending or active lawsuits or governmental inquiries. It's recommended that the Legal and Tax departments (and any other applicable departments) provide a list to the project team of record types and nonrecord information that should be retained. This information should be distributed to the departments participating in the drive cleanup.

✔ **Execution:** This phase of the plan should include details of how to execute the cleanup. This involves how to create departmental folder structures, what folders should be created, how to rename individual files, distribution of the company's retention schedule, employee procedures, and guidance and monitoring of the cleanup.

Creating a folder structure

To ensure that the cleanup initiative is a success, departments need to create folders that capture the department's primary functions and needs (refer to Chapter 4 to see how to create a folder structure). This step should occur prior to deleting, renaming, or moving any files. The steps for creating folders and subfolders in Windows are as follows.

Creating a folder:

1. **Choose File⇨New.**

   The New submenu appears, as shown in Figure 5-1.

2. **Select Folder from the New submenu.**

3. **In the new blank folder that appears, type a name for the new folder.**

Creating a subfolder:

1. **Double-click the new folder that you just created.**

2. **Choose File⇨ New.**

   The New submenu appears. (Again, see Figure 5-1.)

3. **Select Folder from the New submenu.**

4. **In the new blank folder that appears, type a name for the new folder.**

When creating your folders and subfolders, it's critical that you name them appropriately. Folders should be named in a manner that allows anyone to reasonably determine their contents. Keep in mind that a department's folders may be viewable by employees in other departments. Therefore, avoid using abbreviations or cryptic naming conventions that may only be familiar to certain employees.

Developing the folder structure first allows employees to place files that still need to be retained in appropriate folders during the file review process. Figure 5-2 shows how a departmental folder structure for a Human Resources department might look.

If the cleanup is a company-wide initiative, it's important to understand that some folders may be common across departments. For example, many departments in an organization retain the same types of records and information specific to their operation, such as policies and procedures, correspondence, and budgets. During the planning phase, these categories of information should be identified in an effort to expedite the folder-creation process.

During the folder-creation process, it's important to analyze and scrutinize requests from departments for the same folder types. Although a valid need may exist, it can also be an indicator that multiple departments are storing duplicate information. If this is the case, you should work with the departments to determine who should be considered the owner of the information. In some situations, operational needs justify duplicate information being retained in different departments. However, departments that are not considered the official owner or *department of record* should delete the information as soon as it no longer serves a useful business purpose.

Creating a new folder

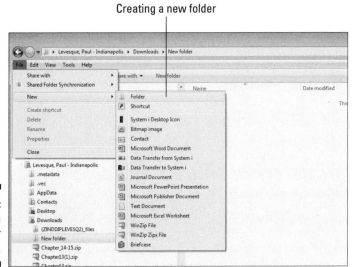

Figure 5-1:
Creating a new folder or subfolder.

Figure 5-2:
Human
Resources
departmen-
tal folder
structure.

To help determine when electronic records and information should be deleted, you can assign a retention suffix to the folder name when creating your departmental folder structure, as shown in Figure 5-3. This process makes it convenient for employees to subsequently manage shared network drives.

Figure 5-3:
Folder
names,
including
the retention
period
suffix.

Name ▲
Applications and Resumes - 3 Years
Background Checks - 5 Years
Employee Files - Active + 5 Years
Equal Employment Opportunity Commission - Active + 5 Years

Administering shared drives

As you begin the process of creating departmental folders on your shared drives, it's recommended that a primary and secondary employee be appointed drive or department administrator. It is the responsibility of the administrator to ensure that the network drive or department folder structure is maintained. (Additional information on maintaining shared drives is covered in detail in the section "Maintaining Your Drives," later in this chapter.)

One important aspect of the administrator's job is to assign security and rights to the drive or department folders.

Assigning security to a drive or folder ensures that only authorized employees are able to access files. For example, the Accounting department may share a drive with the Human Resources department. However, the Accounting department shouldn't be able to access Human Resources folders. When it comes to assigning security to an entire drive, it's recommended that you consult your IT department. In addition, IT is usually responsible for assigning users and user groups to a network drive. However, some organizations allow drive administrators (non-IT employees) to assign user or user group permissions to a drive and folders. In fact, Windows even allows you to determine the extent of what user groups are able to do after they have accessed your folder. Table 5-1 lists the various permission categories available to you.

Table 5-1	Permission Types
Type	*Permission*
Full Control	View filenames and subfolders
	Navigate to subfolders
	View data in the folder's files
	Add files and subfolders to the folder
	Change the folder's files
	Delete the folder and its files
	Change permissions
	Take ownership of the folder and its files
Modify	View the filenames and subfolders
	Navigate to subfolders
	View data in the folder's files
	Add files and subfolders to the folder
	Change the folder's files
	Delete the folder and its files
Read & Execute	View filenames and subfolder names
	Navigate to subfolders
	View data in the folder's files
	Add files and subfolders to the folder

(continued)

Table 5-1 *(continued)*

Type	Permission
List Folder Contents	View the filenames and subfolders
	Navigate to subfolders
	View folders
	Doesn't allow access to the folder's files
Read	View the filenames and subfolders
	Navigate to subfolders
	Run applications
	Open files
	Copy and view data in the folder's files
Write	Create folders
	Add new files
	Open and modify files
	Delete files

To assign user group or user permissions to a folder, follow these steps:

1. **Right-click the folder you are interested in.**

2. **On the contextual menu that appears, choose Properties.**

   The Properties dialog box for the folder appears.

3. **Click the dialog box's Security tab to select it.**

   The options for the Security tab appear, as shown in Figure 5-4.

4. **Click to select either the Allow or Deny check box for the listed tasks and then click OK.**

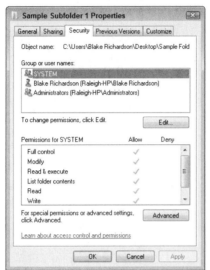

Figure 5-4:
Permission
assignments.

Planning the file review

Knowing how to create your folders and apply security is great prep work, but it's still only prep work. At some point, you have to get your hands dirty and start reviewing files currently stored on hard drives and shared network drives. It's recommended that the cleanup project team provide file review procedures to employees to ensure that the process is correctly followed. The procedures should cover the following topics:

✔ **Retention schedule:** Before any files are reviewed, moved, or deleted, employees should be provided a current version of the organization's records and information retention schedule. This allows employees to know whether a file is eligible to be deleted. Employees should be instructed that if they're unsure about whether a file should be deleted, they should retain it until they receive further guidance from their management team or the records manager. (For more on retention schedules, see Chapter 12.)

✔ **Hard drive usage:** This part of the procedure should communicate to employees that they need to move all records and information still of business value from their own hard drives to their shared network drive.

✔ **Naming files:** The procedure should instruct employees to review the names of files currently on their hard drives and shared network drives for appropriateness, and to modify the names if needed.

✔ **Assigning files to folders:** The procedure should provide guidance on what to do if they have files that don't seem to fit anywhere in the new folder structure. If this occurs, the employee should consult with his or her management team or the records manager. Employees should be advised not to move a file to a folder if it's not a logical fit. The management team should review all files that don't have a good folder fit to determine whether additional folders should be added to the structure.

Reviewing files

Now that you are ready to begin reviewing files, you should take advantage of all the information that your computer and network can provide so that the task is as easy as possible. The General tab of the Properties dialog box for each electronic file you have stored on your hard drive or a shared network drive contains the date the file was created, and when it was last modified and accessed. (See Figure 5-5.) This information will be helpful when determining whether a file is eligible to be deleted based on your organization's record retention schedule.

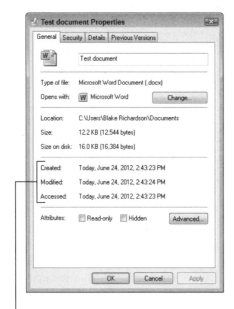

Figure 5-5:
File review
dates.

File review dates

As mentioned in the "Mapping a course of action" section, earlier in this chapter, you need to determine whether approvals will need to be obtained prior to deleting any files.

Each employee should first review her hard drive and move files that still need to be retained to her department folder structure on the shared network drive. Files that are no longer needed should be deleted. As a reminder, no official company records or information of business value should remain on the hard drive upon completion. Files that are deleted from a hard drive are automatically moved to the computer's Recycle Bin. *Note:* The administrator can change the properties of the Recycle Bin so that deleted files are immediately removed (not sent to the Recycle Bin).

As a double-check, after all files have either been moved to a network drive or deleted, it's recommended that each employee review the contents of his or her Recycle Bin to ensure that the files that have been placed there should be deleted. If so, the employee should take the following steps to empty the Recycle Bin. (Remember that when the Recycle Bin is emptied, the files are no longer recoverable.)

To empty the Recycle Bin, follow these steps (see Figure 5-6):

1. **Go to the desktop screen.**

2. **Right-click the Recycle Bin icon.**

3. **Choose Empty Recycle Bin from the contextual menu that appears.**

4. **In the confirmation dialog box that appears, click Yes.**

   All files contained in the Recycle Bin are permanently deleted.

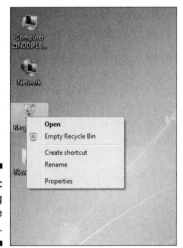

Figure 5-6:
Emptying
the Recycle
Bin.

After everyone has reviewed his or her individual hard drives, it's time to tackle the files currently stored on the shared network drive. The shared network drive file review process is basically the same as the hard drive review. Files that need to be retained should be moved to an appropriate folder and the balance deleted, pending any required approvals.

Cleaning up with software

In recent years, a new category of software referred to as *classification management* has emerged on the records and information management scene. This type of software was developed in response to the significant growth of information stored on network drives and was meant to assist organizations that need to migrate information from network drives to enterprise content management (ECM) applications — applications that allow companies to share information and manage the life cycle of content throughout the organization. Classification management software provides functionality that is helpful during a shared network drive cleanup. The software is capable of inventorying all information stored on the organization's network drives and then providing information regarding files such as size, date, author, insight into the file (phrases and words), and instances of content duplication.

In addition, the software can be loaded with the organization's records and information retention rules and can provide electronic reporting on content that's eligible for deletion. This approach eliminates the need for departmental employees to manually review each file to determine whether it should be deleted. Chapter 10 provides a thorough review of software functionality. You can reference the appendix, available online at `www.dummies.com/go/ recordsmanagefd`, for a comprehensive list of records, document, and enterprise content management vendors.

Maintaining Your Drives

After you have completed the hard drive and shared network drive cleanup, you want to ensure that all your hard work doesn't go to waste. The cleanup initiative can be considered a *project*, but maintaining the company's shared network drives should become an ongoing *process*, and the responsibility of every employee.

Amazing things can happen when a process becomes habit. To transform the process into habit, employees need guidance. The following sections assist you in developing and implementing a usage policy and options for maintaining your drives.

Creating a usage policy

Setting expectations and providing instructions to employees on the use of the organization's shared network drives are essential for ensuring the ongoing management of your drives. The guidance should be clear, concise, and as convenient as possible. A *usage policy* is an effective way to accomplish this objective.

The shared network drive usage policy should cover the major areas that are susceptible to mismanagement. This includes the following topics:

- **Attachments:** Sending e-mails with attachments is a primary cause of information duplication. Instead of sending an attachment via e-mail, place the file on the shared network drive and provide the recipients with a link to the file. However, keep in mind that this only works if the recipients have access to the shared drive. Chapter 15 provides step-by-step instructions on how to create a link to a file.

- **Folders:** After department folder structures have been developed, employees shouldn't create additional folders or delete or modify existing folders without proper approval. Employees should be provided with a mechanism for requesting changes to the established folder structures.

- **Naming:** The usage policy should provide employees with guidance on how to properly name folders and files. They should avoid using abbreviations, numbers, and acronyms that may not be understood by other company employees. In addition, if approved by your organization, the retention period can be incorporated into the name of folders.

- **Retention and deletion:** Employees should ensure that the files stored on the shared drive are retained in accordance with the company's record retention schedule. After a file's retention period has expired, it should be deleted in a timely manner. An exception to this directive exists when it has been determined that a file or information is related to an active or anticipated lawsuit or governmental inquiry (see Chapter 8 for more information). In this case, you must ensure that the file isn't deleted until the matter has been resolved.

Relying on the administrator

Smaller to medium-sized organizations can assign the task of shared network drive maintenance to an administrator. Depending on the size of your organization, one administrator may be assigned to monitor compliance usage on all shared network drives, or it may be necessary to appoint one administrator per drive. The role of the administrator is to ensure that department folders remain intact and that appropriate naming conventions of folders and files are being followed.

Assigning an administrator to oversee all network drives or one administrator per drive usually isn't practical for large organizations. This is due to the large number of departments and volume of folders and files. In this case, the role of administrator is assigned to an employee within each department. The employee who is selected should be very knowledgeable of the department's functions and information. The department administrator should periodically review his shared network drive and report compliance issues to his manager.

Using software to maintain your drives

Earlier in this chapter, I talk about the emergence of classification management software. These types of applications can also help with the continuing maintenance of your shared network drives. The software can be loaded with the company's record and information retention schedule rules to assist you with files that are eligible to be deleted, as well as to electronically report on departmental folder structures and files. The reporting information that these applications can provide helps to monitor compliance to your shared drive usage policy.

Chapter 6

A Message about E-Mail

*T*wenty years ago, most companies couldn't have imagined the impact that e-mail would have on their business. In fact, e-mail now serves as the main contributor to the explosive growth of electronic information. With the growth of e-mail has come the challenge of how to manage it. Due to the volume of e-mail and its management challenges, it can pose significant risks to organizations. It's important to understand these risks and to know how to reduce them.

Trying to manage e-mail may seem like an overwhelming task, but solutions to the dilemma exist — from employee awareness and education to e-mail management software applications. This chapter walks you through the various solutions so that you can determine which one fits your particular situation.

The Anatomy of an E-Mail

The first step in managing your e-mail is to understand its anatomy. The primary reason e-mail is a management challenge is that many employees don't know how to properly evaluate or process e-mails. Understanding what e-mails are — and aren't — can make it easier for employees to manage them.

The following sections provide you with an understanding of e-mail components and show you how to evaluate their contents and the risks of e-mail mismanagement.

Determining the value of the message

At some point each day, you make the trek to your mailbox to see what the postal service delivered. As you review the mail, you are making decisions to keep some items and discard others. In many cases, you can immediately determine the nature of the contents by the envelope and sender, whether it is junk mail or your monthly electric bill. In other cases, you have to open the envelope and analyze the contents to make a decision.

The same concept applies to e-mail. E-mail is an electronic envelope that delivers digital content. Just like a paper envelope contains information such as a postmark (date sent) as well as the sender's and recipient's name, an e-mail envelope contains important information (metadata), some of which is readily visible, like sender, recipients, date and subject, and other information that is embedded in its properties.

Although e-mail metadata is important (more on this topic later in the chapter), it's the message or content delivered by the e-mail that employees need to evaluate. Some e-mails contain information of business importance and should be retained, while others are of no value and should be deleted immediately.

As reviewed in Chapter 1, three categories of information exist: Records, business value information and nonvalue information. The same concept applies to e-mail messages. Information evaluation is not a concept exclusive to e-mail; we were doing it long before e-mail was ever conceived. Drawing the parallel between assessing the contents of a paper document and an e-mail message helps employees grasp the evaluation process.

Microsoft estimates that the average inbox will receive 14,600 e-mail messages in 2012; that equates to over 40 e-mails per day that need to be evaluated by each employee. This doesn't include the e-mails that you draft and send. If the sole responsibility of an employee was to evaluate e-mail, this would not be a big deal. However, employees have other duties and tasks they are required to accomplish each day. Therefore, it's important that the evaluation process be structured, quick, and accurate.

Prior to e-mail, many of us can remember the inbox that sat on our desk. If not managed, it could quickly fill up. The same holds true for our e-mail inbox. It's essential to have a plan for dealing with incoming messages. Your inbox should not be used for storage or viewed as your "to-do" list; rather, think of it as a temporary processing location. After you have read an e-mail message you should take the "4D" approach — delete it, do it, delegate it, or defer it:

✔ **Delete:** Determine whether the message is spam or of any nature that allows you to immediately delete it. Many times, you can determine whether to immediately delete an e-mail by the sender's name or subject line. It is recommended that you explore the built-in spam-blocking features of your e-mail client software. If they seem skimpy, you may want to invest in third-party software applications from vendors such as Norton or Barracuda to help reduce the inbox burden.

✔ **Do:** If the message requires action, take the necessary steps to process it if time currently permits. The rule of thumb is if the action can be completed in two minutes or less, go ahead and do it. This may include processing a function or filing the e-mail for future needs.

✔ **Delegate:** Determine whether another employee should act upon the message. If so, forward the e-mail to the employee and delete your copy, if applicable.

✔ **Defer:** If you believe the task will take longer than the time you currently have available, defer it. The message should stay in your inbox and be flagged for prompt processing.

Each part of the 4D approach can help you manage your inbox, but the one that will have the biggest impact on your ability to control e-mail volume is Delete. However, many employees find it extremely difficult to press the Delete key. Over the years, employees have fallen victim to the "save everything forever" syndrome. The symptoms include an overwhelming urge to hold on to information because of the remote chance it will be asked for in ten years, or that it will help them prove they weren't at fault in a matter that will probably never resurface. The cure usually requires intervention in the form of policies and audits.

It's time for everyone — managers, supervisors, team leaders, and employees — to face facts: The digital age has forced us all to handle and process more information than we ever thought possible, much of which is spam, duplications, and files that have outlived their usefulness. We are being required to do things differently than we did a decade ago. This includes routinely deleting content that provides no value to our organizations.

Scheduling time for e-mail

If you aren't careful, you can find yourself behind your computer for hours at a time *working* e-mail. Typically, most people take two approaches to processing e-mail — continuous and (the more disciplined) scheduled.

It is easy to get caught in the trap of monitoring your inbox continuously throughout the day: You hear the familiar "ding" and know you have a new e-mail and immediately click to view it. This approach can quickly become the "great momentum breaker." For example, if you're working on a project and regularly stop to view your new e-mail, you'll constantly be losing your train of thought and getting nowhere fast.

Another approach is to schedule dedicated time (20–30 minutes) during the day to evaluate and respond to e-mail. Depending on your job responsibilities, you may need to schedule several review sessions. This method allows you to stay productive and not lose track of time.

The rising risks of e-mail

It's hard to remember when e-mail didn't exist. It's now a staple of business communication. As much as we lament its impact on our inbox, most of us find it an essential part of our workday. Many experts consider e-mail the number one information management challenge that organizations face. The issue here is that most companies don't know how to manage e-mail — and often are not even aware of the negative impact that not managing it can have on their business.

The extent of most organizations' attempts to manage e-mail consists of an *e-mail usage policy,* which typically instructs employees not to send offensive or harassing messages. Although this is important, it doesn't adequately address the numerous risks created by not managing e-mail. Such risks include the following:

- ✔ **Operational:** Allowing e-mail to go unmanaged can create significant losses in employee productivity. Most employees rely heavily on e-mail and must sift through large numbers of messages and attachments to find what they need. This can delay processing and decision-making. If an organization doesn't use software to filter junk (spam) e-mail, the burden is increased.

- ✔ **Legal:** Two primary types of legal risks are associated with e-mail — employee conduct and eDiscovery (producing information for a lawsuit; see Chapter 8 for additional information on eDiscovery). Employers are typically held responsible for the acts of their employees — and this includes e-mail. In addition, unmanaged e-mails make it extremely difficult and costly when attempting to produce e-mail messages and attachments in the event of litigation. (Additional information on this matter is covered in Chapter 8.)

> ✔ **Compliance:** Federal regulations and compliance rules now exist that govern how organizations should maintain electronic information (including e-mails) to prove evidence of transactions and prevent breaches of confidential information. The mismanagement of e-mail can lead to penalties, fines, and public relations nightmares.

The following sections of this chapter provide you with the information you need to manage e-mail, which can assist you in reducing organizational risks.

Managing quotas

Most e-mail users have experienced the dreaded message — "Your inbox is over its size limit." After the message is received, a mad scramble ensues to delete messages and attachments, or for employees with a Delete Key phobia, a phone call is made to IT to justify their need for more e-mail storage space. Welcome to the world of e-mail quotas!

An *e-mail quota* is the amount of spaced reserved on a server for your e-mail messages. The quotas established by organizations vary greatly from megabytes to gigabytes. Regardless of the quota size, if e-mail is not properly managed, the quota will likely be exceeded.

The primary culprit that causes you to exceed your quota is attachments. The size of the average e-mail without an attachment is 40KB. Including an attachment can easily quadruple the size of the e-mail. It's important to note that it's not just the e-mail messages and attachments in your inbox that impact your quota, but also information in other folders such as Sent, Deleted, Drafts, and Junk E-Mail. In addition, Microsoft Outlook functions such as Calendar, Contacts, and Tasks are also a contributor to your overall space consumption.

E-mail maintenance should be a process and not a project. Cleaning up your e-mail after you receive the message that you've exceeded your size limit can lead to potentially deleting items that should be retained. The goal is to focus on applying records and information management to the issue rather than trying to keep your storage size below the quota. A good practice is to regularly schedule (once per quarter) time to review your e-mail messages, folders, and calendar items and delete information that is no longer needed. As with any review of this type, you should consult your organization's record retention schedule if you are unsure whether an item is eligible to be deleted. (For more on what retention schedules are and the crucial role they play in an organization, see Chapter 3.)

Filing the Message

Knowing what to do with e-mail messages that need to be retained can help you be more productive and reduce risks to the company. The following sections analyze methods for filing, naming, and retaining e-mail messages. This includes reviewing e-mail management functionality offered in applications such as Microsoft Outlook and determining how it can benefit your organization, as well as using shared network drives and enterprise content management systems to manage e-mail messages.

PSSST! What you need to know about PST folders

E-mail messages (including attachments) that need to be retained should be properly filed in an established folder structure. Most users file e-mail in *Personal Storage Table (PST)* folders. PST is a file extension format controlled by Microsoft and used in its Outlook e-mail application.

PST folders are visible in your Mail Folders pane in Outlook, as shown in Figure 6-1. Additional PST subfolders can be added to any of the default folders such as Deleted Items, Inbox, Drafts, and Sent Items, as shown in Figure 6-2.

PST folders can be created and structured to meet a user's filing needs similar to the folder functionality that's available with shared network drives and hard drives (as detailed in Chapter 5). After your PST folder structure has been developed, it allows you to conveniently click an e-mail and "drag and drop" it into a PST folder.

You'll soon encounter one major drawback to using PST folders: They typically store all information on your computer's hard drive. Content located on a hard drive is only accessible if you have access to that specific computer. In addition, most hard drives do not have automatic backup capability, increasing the potential for lost information.

Work-arounds are available to the hard drive dilemma. PST files can be shared and accessed via your organization's network drives. However, Microsoft has officially stated that it doesn't support this approach due to the potential for the files to become corrupted. In addition, if you share your PST files, only one user at a time can access the information.

Figure 6-1:
Microsoft
Outlook PST
folder.

If you are concerned about backing up your PST files, you can download a Microsoft add-in that makes a copy of your PST files and saves them to a network drive. The download link is available at `www.microsoft.com/en-us/ download/details.aspx?id=9003`.

Before you download the Personal Folders Backup add-in, you should consider the impact of this approach. Whenever you create copies of information, it means that you have more content that you're required to manage.

Some organizational IT departments promote the use of PST folders because it reduces the amount of information on the e-mail server, and it allows employees to store more messages. However, in many cases, this methodology can be detrimental to your records and information management efforts. You should consider other e-mail message filing options in lieu of PST folders, as you discover in the next sections.

Figure 6-2:
PST sub-
folders.

Subfolders

MSG can be good for your informational health

This section isn't about food additives; it's about a good option for filing e-mail messages. Another Microsoft file format is *MSG*. As you probably guessed, MSG stands for *message*. Most e-mail systems are configured (by default) to save e-mail messages to a hard drive or network drives as HTML (Hypertext Markup Language) files. In addition, this approach requires you to save any attachments separately. Using the MSG file extension allows you to save messages (plus attachments) as an e-mail to folders on hard drives and network drives.

You find several benefits to using the MSG file extension:

- ✔ **Visibility:** Applying the MSG extension to a message and saving it to a shared network drive allow other employees to search, retrieve, and view the e-mail. This promotes organizational knowledge sharing. In addition, it provides visibility to the subject matter in the event of a lawsuit or governmental inquiry.

- ✔ **File backup:** Saving e-mail messages by using the MSG file extension to a shared network drive ensures that the file is regularly backed up.

- ✔ **Native format:** When you retrieve an e-mail saved with an MSG file extension, it automatically invokes Microsoft Outlook, allowing you to work directly in the e-mail application. Messages saved with an MSG file extension keep the e-mail in its Microsoft Outlook format, retaining all the e-mail's original metadata. This is important in the event that an e-mail has to be produced for a lawsuit or governmental inquiry.

Although using the MSG file extension approach does not provide drag-and-drop convenience, it does create consistency in the way that employees save electronic content. Saving a message by using the MSG extension is similar to saving a Microsoft Word document by using the DOC extension or a Microsoft Excel spreadsheet by using the XLS extension. Follow these steps to save an e-mail by using the MSG file extension:

1. **Click the e-mail that you want to save.**

   Doing so highlights the e-mail.

2. **Click the File tab and then select Save As.**

   The Save As screen appears.

3. **Using the top panes of the Save As screen, select the network drive location where you want to save the file.**

4. **Click in the Save as Type drop-down menu.**

   The available file format types appear.

5. **Choose the Outlook Message Format (*.msg) option from the Save as Type drop-down menu, as shown in Figure 6-3.**

6. **(Optional) Change the filename for the e-mail message in the File Name field, if desired.**

7. **Click Save.**

   Your e-mail message is saved in its new location in the new `.msg` format.

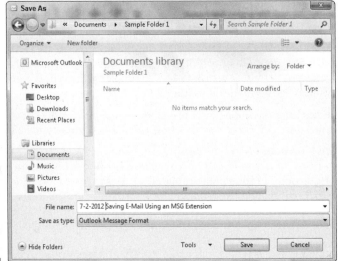

Figure 6-3:
Using the
MSG file
extension to
save e-mail.

Naming e-mail

E-mail messages and attachments should be named as you would any other electronic file you save — meaning that you should follow naming conventions designed so that you (or other employees) are able to retrieve the file at a moment's notice without any fuss and bother. To ensure that e-mails can be quickly retrieved, it's important to name the e-mail in a manner that allows its contents to be readily identified.

If you use PST folders to file your e-mail, the Subject line serves as your filename. However, sometimes the wording in the Subject line can be vague or cryptic, preventing you from easily identifying the e-mail's contents. Microsoft Outlook allows you to easily edit the Subject line. Just follow these steps:

1. **Open the e-mail whose Subject line you want to change, as shown in Figure 6-4.**

2. **Click the e-mail's Subject line.**

   This highlights the current subject.

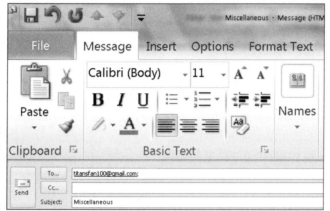

Figure 6-4: Highlighting the old Subject line.

3. **Type the new subject in the highlighted Subject field.**

   The new subject overwrites the existing subject, as shown in Figure 6-5.

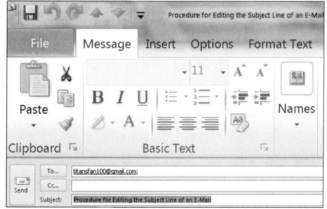

Figure 6-5: Coming up with a more informative Subject line.

4. **Click the File tab and then select Close.**

   You can also click the X in the upper-right corner of the message window to save the change to the subject instead of clicking File and Close.

   A message appears asking whether you want to save the change to the subject.

5. **Click Yes.**

   Your e-mail has a new (and improved) Subject line.

If you're saving files to a shared network drive by using an MSG extension, you have the ability to rename the file as you save it. Just do the following:

1. **Click the e-mail that you want to save.**

   Doing so highlights the e-mail.

2. **Click the File tab and then select Save As.**

   The Save As screen appears with the File Name box (containing the current name) highlighted.

3. **Type in the new name of the file.**

   Figure 6-6 gives an example of a more informative filename.

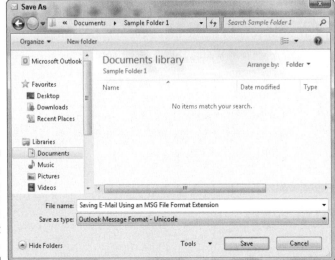

Figure 6-6:
Naming
files with
an MSG
file format
extension.

4. **Using the top panes of the Save As screen, select the network drive location where you want to save the file.**

5. **Click in the Save as Type drop-down menu.**

   The available file format types appear.

6. **Choose the Outlook Message Format (*.msg) option from the Save as Type drop-down menu.**

7. **Click Save.**

Using Software to Manage E-Mail

E-mail volume has increased at a staggering rate over the past decade and will continue to grow exponentially. It's the number one information management challenge for most organizations. As the volume continues to increase, so does our need for finding more-effective ways to manage e-mail. The days where you could just use the functionality available in an e-mail application, PST folders, and shared network drives to manage e-mail are coming to an end.

Using software designed to specifically manage electronic content (including e-mail) is becoming more prevalent. This includes e-mail archiving, document management (DM), and enterprise content management (ECM) applications. When coupled with records management capabilities, these types of systems provide the ability to properly manage e-mail.

E-mail archiving systems

E-mail archiving software has been available for many years. It's designed to extract e-mail messages and attachments, apply index values, and place the e-mail information in a *read-only* format in a separate database. The benefit of this approach is that it centralizes all e-mails, makes them accessible across the organization, and can assist in disaster recovery.

E-mail archiving doesn't promote effective records management. The primary reason for the development of e-mail archiving systems was to alleviate the storage load on e-mail servers. Archiving software allows e-mail information to be moved to another repository so that e-mail performance isn't negatively impacted, but e-mail archiving solutions are designed to keep all e-mail forever — by no means an effective approach. E-mail should be retained based on its content and deleted in accordance with an organization's records and information retention schedule. Archiving all e-mail indefinitely makes it harder to search and retrieve what you need, and can be a liability during lawsuits and governmental inquiries.

Optimizing with DM and ECM applications

A preferred option for managing your e-mails is to implement a document management (DM) or enterprise content management (ECM) system. These applications are designed to manage the life cycle of information. Using document and enterprise content management software provides the following benefits:

- ✔ **Integration:** Many DM and ECM applications integrate directly with e-mail systems such as Microsoft Outlook. This allows users to index and save e-mail to the software application while remaining in the e-mail system.

- ✔ **Metadata:** Software provides the ability to assign additional metadata (index values) to an e-mail file. This allows significantly better search and retrieval capabilities.

- ✔ **Sharing:** Enterprise content management systems are designed to make information available to the entire organization. This promotes knowledge sharing, better decision-making, and regulatory compliance.

- ✔ **Records management:** Document management and ECM systems equipped with records management functionality provide the ability to assign retention periods to e-mail based on content. This ensures that e-mail is only retained for a prescribed length of time and prevents the accumulation of unneeded information. DM and ECM applications can programmatically incorporate an organization's record and information retention rules so that retention can be automatically managed.

Note: The appendix, available online at `www.dummies.com/go/records managefd`, provides a listing of DM and ECM vendors and their contact information.

Part III
Capturing Records

The 5th Wave   By Rich Tennant

"Your database is beyond repair, but before I tell you our backup recommendation, let me ask you a question. How many index cards do you think will fit on the walls of your computer room?"

In this part . . .

The tale of the backup tape — here you'll find out how your information is backed up, the benefits of said backups, and how the benefits can turn into risks if tape backups aren't managed. Part III provides guidance on what to do with records and information that are part of a lawsuit, audit, or governmental inquiry. And last, but definitely not least, you'll dive in for a deep look at document imaging — the benefits, the equipment, and how to determine whether imaging is a good fit for your organization.

Chapter 7

Watch Out, I'm Backing Up

In This Chapter
▶ Identifying backup types
▶ Understanding backup tape risks
▶ Applying records management principles to backed-up data

*M*ost of us have experienced the frustration and panic of working on a spreadsheet or document when suddenly the computer freezes and the "blue screen of death" appears — you are immediately brought face to face with the realization that you are the victim of a *crash*. Or perhaps you've experienced disaster on an even larger scale, where you have been part of a department that was unable to log in to a critical business software application because the server crashed. It's times like these when *backups* can make the difference between recovering information in a short period of time and being able to resume normal business operations, or saying farewell to the information forever.

In this chapter, you look closer into what backups actually are, as well as analyze the different types of backups and their purpose. In addition, you find out how to best manage backups in an effort to ensure that they complement your records and information management program instead of becoming its nemesis.

Creating a Backup Plan

Every business, regardless of size, needs to routinely back up the information stored on its computers and servers. A backup is the process of transferring data from your computer systems to another storage device, with the objective of being able to restore the information in the event of data loss. Information in this case typically consists of structured (database) and unstructured (images, documents, and spreadsheets) data.

You have a number of different options for conducting backups, including what, when, and where to back up. The following sections cover each of these topics and provide the knowledge you need to ensure that your data is safe, accurate, and accessible.

Identifying different types of backups

It is critical to have a backup strategy, whether it's for the one computer you use for your small business or for the hundreds of servers your company has in a data center. Understanding the types of backups that can be conducted can help you determine what data you need to duplicate in the event of data loss. Listed as follows (and summarized in Table 7-1) are four types of backups that can be used by organizations of all sizes:

✔ **Full:** This type of backup makes a copy of all the data in all files and folders. Conducting frequent full backups allows a faster and simpler restore.

✔ **Differential:** A differential backup makes a copy of all data that has changed since the last full backup. Differential backups provide a fast restore. However, if differential backups are conducted too frequently, this can cause the size of the backup file to grow very large because it includes information from previous differential backups. In some cases, this can create a differential backup file that's larger than a full backup file.

✔ **Incremental:** This type of backup makes a copy of all data that has been modified since the last full or differential backup. An incremental backup takes the least amount of time to complete, but it can take longer to restore due to each individual incremental backup having to be processed.

✔ **Mirror:** A mirror backup is similar to a full backup with a few twists. The first time a mirror backup runs, it will back up all information. However, subsequent backups only make a copy of information that has changed or been modified. Mirror backups are not compressed or encrypted. Users are able to point to the backup location and quickly access the backed-up data.

Table 7-1	Different Backup Types			
Type	*Information Backed Up*	*Backup Time*	*Restore Time*	*Space Required*
Full	All information	Slow	Fast	High
Differential	All information since the last full backup	Medium	Fast	Medium
Incremental	Only new or modified files and folders	Fast	Medium	Low
Mirror	Only new or modified files and folders	Fast	Fast	High

Small businesses need to conduct full backups on a regular basis. This approach is feasible due to the limited amount of information that has to be backed up. Backing up your computer can be performed manually or on an automatic scheduled basis.

What works for small businesses, however, may not be manageable for medium to large organizations. Due to the extreme amount of data that these organizations possess, conducting full backups is more challenging. Companies have to dedicate staff, software, and other resources to developing, implementing, and maintaining a formal backup process.

The IT departments of large organizations typically conduct backups during nonpeak times (late at night and early morning) to ensure that all systems are operable and accessible during normal business hours. Most IT departments schedule different types of backups to be conducted throughout the week or month. As an example, this may include differential or incremental backups each night and a full backup at the end of each week.

Based on the significant volume of data that large organizations are required to back up and retain, the organizations are continuously evaluating new techniques, media, and applications to shorten backup times. Later in this chapter, you get a chance to see how you can apply records and information management principles to backups to help better manage the process.

Finding a place to back up

An important piece of the backup puzzle is determining a target location for your backed-up files. The amount of data your company possesses normally determines what medium you need to use for backups:

- **Magnetic tape:** Tapes are most commonly used by organizations that have a large amount of data to back up. Tapes are usually housed in cartridges or cassettes. Data is written to tapes and read by a tape drive. For years, this backup option has proven the most economical for backing up large amounts of information. A benefit of magnetic tapes is that they can be reused. Data centers create tape rotation schedules that allow tapes, after a prescribed period of time, to be overwritten with new data.

- **External hard drive:** For many years, it wasn't cost effective to back up large amounts of data to an external hard drive. However, the cost of drives has significantly decreased and is now comparable to magnetic tapes. Hard drives allow more flexibility than tapes, such as no winding or rewinding to locate information — meaning faster restore capability — and instant rewrite capability, because you don't have to deal with the erase cycle that comes with tapes.

✔ **Optical disc:** *Optical media* refers to recordable and rewriteable CDs and DVDs. Optical discs don't have the storage capacity of tapes or external hard drives and normally are only used to back up selected files rather than to perform full system backups. Still, optical discs are economical and simple to use. Most computers are now equipped with CD and DVD burners that allow you to drag and drop files to the Disc icon and record the data. This is a great backup option for small- and medium-sized businesses.

✔ **Flash drive:** Over the past several years, flash drive storage capacity has significantly increased. Today, most flash drives have several gigabytes (GB) of capacity and are rewriteable, making them a good option for backing up selected files. The flash drive shows as an additional drive on your computer. It is a very portable medium and can be used to move data between computers. Some flash drives can be password-protected and encrypted.

Even though flash drives can have significant storage capacity, and now contain encryption capability, most large organizations haven't adopted the use of flash drives for routine data backups. This is mainly due to the typical flash drive not having the storage capacity of disk drives or magnetic tapes, as well as being easy to lose based on their compact size. However, they are a good option for small- to medium-sized businesses.

✔ **Cloud:** The *cloud* refers to an Internet-based vendor-hosted or software as a service (SaaS) operating environment. As cloud computing has matured, the cost has decreased, and it is now becoming a viable option for small- and medium-sized businesses. Cloud backups are performed by transmitting data to a vendor's site via the Internet. However, if your organization is using the cloud for processing and other computer services, your information is most likely being backed up on a regular basis by the vendor. (For more on the potential of the cloud, check out Chapter 16.)

Distinguishing between backups and archives

As you read in the preceding sections, backups are performed to prevent data loss in the event that your computer crashes or your files become corrupt. Backups of this type are not meant for the long-term storage of organizational information that must be retained in accordance with the company's records and information retention schedules. This is the role and purpose of *digital archiving*.

Over the past decade, organizations have seen a dramatic increase in laws and regulations that impact corporate behavior, including the management of their information. Many of the laws and regulations that have been enacted require companies to retain their records (both paper and electronic) for specified time frames, to destroy the records after the time frame expires, and to ensure that the information is quickly accessible. Backing up to magnetic tapes — as most large organizations do — doesn't provide this capability because of the difficulty and operational inefficiencies related to deleting specific files from a tape after their retention period has expired.

While backup solutions provide data protection and recovery, *data archiving* provides efficient retrieval and retention, as well as the capability to meet the organization's regulatory, legal, and historical needs. Several media can be used for digital archiving, such as optical discs, hard drives, CDs, DVDs, and digital tapes. Although these preferred digital archiving storage options exist, the reality is that most organizations continue to store information required for regulatory, legal, and historical purposes on magnetic tape. Magnetic tape is not a good archiving medium for records whose retention must be managed. Magnetic tape is an "all-or-nothing" format. Magnetic tape doesn't provide the ability to delete specific files. If a magnetic tape contains various types of records with different retention periods, you must restore the tape to a disk and then delete the files whose retention period has expired. You then back up the remaining records to the tape again.

 If your organization is considering the creation of digital archives, it's important to plan ahead. Prior to creating an archive, you should first analyze and determine what data needs to be captured, how long it needs to be retained, and how frequently it will be accessed during its life cycle. After these details have been sorted out, the next step is to work with your IT department to determine the storage device that best meets your company's needs.

Archiving is a dynamic process. This means that new data will continuously be added to the archive. Therefore, because magnetic tape doesn't allow an organization to properly manage the retention of archived data, you should use a media format such as disk to archive your information. It's recommended that all information be evaluated prior to being archived. The evaluation process should be formalized and conducted by a knowledgeable business department representative, the records manager, and IT. For example, if the Workers' Compensation department is implementing a new administrative software application, certain data from the system probably needs to be retained for a specified length of time. The business unit, records manager, and IT should confer to determine what information needs to be archived and for how long. In the absence of an evaluation process, erroneous data could be archived or applicable data may be archived, but for an inappropriate time frame.

The tale of the mystery tape

Information accumulation breeds risk. Over time, organizational information accumulates in file cabinets, in desk drawers, on hard drives, and on network drives — and also on backup tapes! Although backing up company data is vital for resuming business operations and reducing risks, if not properly managed, it can be a source for a whole other set of risks. The following sections analyze the types of risks associated with data stored on backup tapes.

Yes, you may end up using different media to back up your data, but the vast majority of organizations still rely on magnetic tapes to handle their backup chores. Even if companies are using disks for backups, they probably still have legacy magnetic tapes in storage. It's not unusual for medium- to large-sized companies to have accumulated tens or hundreds of thousands of tapes over the years. The issue is that most organizations don't know what information is contained on the tapes.

Although magnetic tape cartridges are labeled, organizations rely upon employees to label the cartridges in a manner that allows a clear understanding of the contents of the tape. If the labeling is cryptic or fades over time, it can make it extremely difficult to decipher the contents.

For many years, organizations and their IT departments didn't have to worry much about accessing data stored on backup tapes. Aside from the occasional request to restore an employee's e-mail or other miscellaneous data, backup tapes sat idle in storage. Historically, retrieving specific information from magnetic tapes has not been easy. Digital storage mechanisms allow an employee to search and retrieve targeted information. However, magnetic tapes require users to scroll through the contents of the tape until they locate what they need. Although this approach isn't efficient, in years past, the volume and types of restore requests were manageable.

Organizations are now faced with increasing numbers of lawsuits and regulations that require access to and production of company information. A decade ago, most organizations weren't too concerned about having to produce information for a lawsuit or governmental inquiry from their backup tapes; they could invoke the *burden argument*. The burden argument is a claim that it's too cost prohibitive and burdensome to restore, search, and retrieve content from backup tapes. Times and technology have changed, however, poking holes in this argument. New technologies now make it affordable and viable for information from backup tapes to be produced.

The primary difficulty in producing information from backup tapes for a lawsuit involved organizations converting from one backup system application to another. To restore older tapes, a company needed access to the previous backup system application. If the application was no longer available, the company would have to send the tapes to a third party to be restored. However, new technologies allow tape data to be restored without having access to the previous backup operating environment.

Judges and lawyers are becoming more educated and savvy about *electronically stored information (ESI)* and related technologies. They understand what is feasible and what isn't. The result is that organizations are now faced with searching huge volumes of backed-up data to properly respond to discovery requests.

The cost to search and produce information from backup tapes can be significant. However, the primary risk of not managing backup tapes is the potential for judgments, fines, and penalties associated with information on backup tapes that proves to be a liability. Applying records and information management principles to tape backups can help reduce the risks.

Managing Backups

As digital information continues to grow at an astounding rate, IT departments are looking for guidance on how to manage the volume. Information Technology personnel are now frequently conferring with records managers in an attempt to apply life cycle principles to electronic data.

Applying records and information management principles can help control the accumulation of electronic data, make information easier to identify and retrieve, and ensure that it's appropriately deleted. In the following sections, you discover how to apply these principles so that you only back up what is needed, know how to determine the retention period of data backups, and have a strategy in place so that you can clean up what's accumulated over the years.

Determining what needs to be backed up

Prior to the events of September 11, 2001, most IT departments acted independently when determining what should be backed up and how frequently it should be backed up. After 9/11, organizations across the world quickly realized that their companies were not adequately prepared to resume business operations in the aftermath of a catastrophic event. This resulted in *business continuity planning (BCP)*. The purpose of BCP was to formulate a partnership between business departments and IT in an effort to identify and protect critical operating information that must be accessible within a specified time frame after a disaster to resume business operations. This process was the start of records managers and IT personnel working together to assist business areas in managing their information. If your organization hasn't yet forged the partnership between records management and IT, the organization should begin taking the steps to do so.

Determining what needs to be backed up is not solely based on preparing for a catastrophic event, but also on anticipated events such as computer crashes, file corruptions, and lawsuits. As a normal course of business, you need to regularly back up computer files that have been modified or conduct a complete backup. In the case of medium or large organizations, the IT department can ensure that files and applications are backed up. However, not all information should be (or is required to be) backed up or archived. When determining what additional data needs to be backed up or archived, you should consider the following factors:

- ✔ **Criticality:** How important or sensitive is the information? Critical information typically includes, but isn't limited to, data related to the organization's accounting, human resources, and customer applications.

- ✔ **Legal:** Could the information be important in the event of a lawsuit? Legal departments understand what types of information are considered high risk and should be backed up or archived for long-term storage.

- ✔ **Regulatory:** Is the information required to be backed up, retained, and accessible based on regulatory requirements? Organizations should ensure that they are familiar with regulations that govern their operating environment, and back up or archive associated information for the prescribed time frame.

- ✔ **Historical:** What information should be retained that has historical significance? Most companies have accumulated information over the years — press clippings and photos, for example — that serve as evidence of the organization's existence.

To help identify the types of information that should be backed up or archived, the Records Management department should work in conjunction with department representatives and IT to determine what information meets the criteria listed previously. In addition, the departments should work together to determine what software applications house the information, which servers they reside on, what retrieval frequency is most appropriate, and whether specific regulations govern how the information should be retained and for how long.

Applying retention to backups

After you know what to back up, you need to know how long to keep it. As detailed earlier in this chapter, most organizations conduct three types of backups:

✔ **Restore:** This type of backup ensures that information can be restored and accessed in the event of a system failure.

✔ **Disaster recovery:** Disaster recovery backups encompass predetermined information related to critical systems and files that are needed to resume operations after a disaster or catastrophic event.

✔ **Archives:** Archiving ensures that information that must be retained for legal, regulatory, or historical purposes are backed up.

Restore and disaster recovery backups are typically overwritten based on a tape rotation schedule. However, archive backups are used for retaining records that must be kept in accordance with operational, legal, and regulatory purposes and should be deleted when their retention period has expired. Archived records aren't routinely overwritten like disaster recovery backup tapes are. The focus of this section is how to apply appraisal and retention periods to archive backups.

Chapter 2 has more on how to evaluate information to develop an organizational retention schedule. The same approach should be applied when determining the retention period of archived information. Archived information has a life cycle just like information stored on a shared network drive, in a content management system, or in a file cabinet.

When determining how long to keep archived information, start with the retention schedule that you have already developed, even if the current schedule only addresses paper records. In many cases, you will find that you have already evaluated and assigned a retention period to physical information that is related to or is the same as its electronic counterpart. For example, you may have assigned a seven-year retention period to paper contracts, but you also have electronic contracts that are archived. The same retention period should be assigned to the electronic versions.

Creating a data retention schedule

Archived information consists of unstructured and structured data. Examples of unstructured data are documents, spreadsheets, images, PDFs, and e-mails. Structured data is information based on data fields, such as a database table in a software application.

Most companies are familiar with the concept of record retention schedules. Such schedules get used when managing the length of time you keep paper records such as invoices, employee files, and contracts. A smaller number of organizations utilize this same approach for unstructured electronic records and information. Then a small percentage of companies exist that have addressed the need to apply retention principles to structured data.

For most organizations, backing up and retaining structured information from software applications account for the majority of backed-up volume. Applying retention periods to structured data is a relatively new concept that is getting a lot of attention. Structured data poses some philosophical records management issues. To see what I mean, check out Table 7-2, which contains numerous fields of information with unique values. The question here is, does each individual value or *data element* — say, someone's first name — by itself constitute a record? Some say yes, and some say no.

Table 7-2			Dealing with Unique Values				
Employee ID	*fName*	*lName*	*Addr1*	*City*	*State*	*Zip*	*Phone*
111111	Ann	Doe	111 Main St	Anytown	AZ	88888	5555555555
222222	Bob	Doe	222 Main St	Anytown	AZ	88888	5555555555
333333	Charles	Doe	333 Main St	Anytown	AZ	88888	5555555555
444444	David	Doe	444 Main St	Anytown	AZ	88888	5555555555
555555	Arlene	Doe	555 Main St	Anytown	AZ	88888	5555555555

As the debate has progressed, more records managers have come to the conclusion that a data field in and of itself is not a record, but when it's combined with other related data fields through the software application, a record is born. For example, if you image a vendor invoice, it creates a digital replication of the document that can be viewed and understood. However, the individual data elements represented on the document, such as vendor name, number, and address, also exist in your organization's accounting system database in separate fields. If you view an individual data element in a field, it doesn't have much meaning, but when the software application brings all the associated elements together to form the invoice, it now has meaning.

To apply retention to structured information, you can use the same appraisal method used for unstructured and physical content. If you retain paper invoices for seven years, the structured information in the accounting system that relates to invoices should also be retained for seven years.

A word of caution is probably called for here. In a database environment such as an accounting software application, data elements in a table may be used for different purposes. For example, the Tax department may need to retain vendor information for seven years for reporting purposes, while the Accounts Payable department may need to retain vendor information for three years after the last transaction. Many of the data elements in the database used by each department are the same — vendor number, name, and tax identification number. Therefore, when appraising structured data information for retention purposes, these issues need to be evaluated.

Appraising structured information is a group effort. The appraisal allows you to understand the nature of a software application, see who uses it, determine where the application's information resides on the network as well as what data it produces, let you establish what information should be archived, and set up the required retention periods. Each department that uses an application should be involved in the appraisal along with the Records Management and IT departments.

Before new software applications are implemented, it's recommended that the system be appraised prior to placing the system into production. This approach ensures that only required data is archived and that appropriate retention periods are assigned.

Deleting backed-up and archived information

The thought of deleting records and information makes some people cringe, but don't fear. It's all part of the information life cycle and should take place on a regular and scheduled basis — as long as the necessary homework has been done, meaning that the information has been researched and the appropriate retention periods have been assigned.

As you discovered, magnetic tapes are still widely used for system and file restores, disaster recovery, and archive backups. Although tapes used for basic recovery and disaster recovery are erased and overwritten on a scheduled basis, archive tapes aren't; this poses a significant retention and deletion issue. Magnetic tapes don't allow you to delete or erase specific files — it's an all-or-nothing proposition when deleting content on backup tapes.

This is one more reason not to use magnetic tapes for archiving purposes. Instead, use optical discs or external hard drives that allow you to archive specific files and delete them when their retention period has expired.

Chapter 8

Know When to Hold 'em

In This Chapter

▶ Understanding the discovery process

▶ Issuing an information hold order

▶ Searching for relevant information

▶ Preserving information

▶ Maintaining an information hold order

▶ Lifting the hold

*I*nformation is a business asset that's used for a variety of purposes, such as processing work functions and decision-making. However, in this chapter, I focus specifically on how information supports an organization in the event of actions such as lawsuits, audits, and governmental inquiries.

In the event of a lawsuit, audit, or inquiry, relevant information must be identified and protected during the duration of the event and, in many cases, after the event has concluded. This chapter provides you with an understanding of how to ensure that these requirements are met.

Discovering Discovery

Discovery is a legal term that refers to the pretrial phase of a lawsuit where opposing sides request information from each other in an attempt to find facts that may be relevant to the case. Over the past decade, the term *discovery* has become commonly referred to as *eDiscovery*. The same definition applies, but eDiscovery refers specifically to electronically stored information (ESI, for short) and the process of producing it from electronic repositories and applications. For the purpose of this chapter, I use the term *discovery* unless specifically talking about electronic discovery.

Discovery is a process that includes several phases. Some of the phases involve records and information management, while others involve interaction solely between attorneys and the court. This chapter provides you with insight into the processes, but focuses primarily on what you need to know as it pertains to records and information management.

In terms of discovery, planning is the key to effective and compliant preservation. Organizations need to know ahead of time what steps must be taken to preserve relevant documentation, instead of attempting to figure it out after the event occurs. Due to the critical nature of preservation, every company should invest in the creation of a *preservation plan* and ensure that its employees are appropriately trained to follow it. When creating a preservation plan, remember that regardless of the nature of a lawsuit, audit, or governmental inquiry, standard procedures are applicable to each. The following steps should be detailed in the plan:

- **Communication:** The need to preserve relevant documentation should be communicated as soon as possible via the record hold. The record hold should clearly provide instructions to all appropriate recipients. Such instructions should include what documentation is considered to be relevant, as well as any date ranges that are applicable to the content.

- **Suspend the retention schedule:** When an order to preserve has been issued, the retention policies for the impacted relevant documentation should immediately cease and not resume until the legal hold has been lifted. Relevant documentation shouldn't be destroyed, deleted, or modified. The records manager should be involved in this process. If the organization uses a Records Management software application to programmatically manage record retention, the system will need to be updated to reflect holds on the impacted records. This helps ensure that the records are retained during the duration of the hold order.

- **Enlist the services of the IT department:** The organization should provide the IT department with a list of departments or employees (custodians) who are (or potentially are) the owners of relevant documentation. This allows the IT department to identify applications and repositories that the custodians use and ensure that electronically stored information is not deleted.

- **Preservation coordinator:** Organizations should determine whether a preservation coordinator should be assigned to oversee the protection of relevant documentation.

When an organization receives legal notice indicating that it is party to a lawsuit, or anticipates that it could happen, the wheels of discovery go into motion. Discovery happens prior to a trial and usually includes the following steps:

- ✔ **Disclosure:** This step involves each party to the lawsuit providing a comprehensive list of information that he or she feels is relevant to the matter. This may include a list of witnesses and documents.

- ✔ **Interrogatory:** An interrogatory is a formal set of written questions that a witness or party to the lawsuit is required to answer under oath.

- ✔ **Admissions of fact:** This step involves a written list of facts directed to the other party. The party receiving the list of facts is asked to admit to or deny each item.

- ✔ **Request for production:** This is a process where opposing sides request information that they believe may be relevant to the lawsuit.

- ✔ **Deposition:** A deposition is the process of gathering sworn testimony from witnesses or parties involved in the lawsuit.

Initiating a Legal Hold

When an organization receives a "request for production," the organization's Legal department issues a *legal hold*. A legal hold is a process a company uses to ensure that relevant or potentially relevant information is preserved and retained in the event of a lawsuit or in anticipation of a lawsuit. Some organizations use different terms to refer to a legal hold, such as *information hold order* and *record hold*.

The components of a legal hold

As mentioned previously, a legal hold is normally initiated and communicated by the organization's Legal department. Typically, it includes the following components:

- ✔ **Recipients:** This section lists all recipients who are to receive the hold notice. Each recipient has been identified as a custodian of relevant (or potentially relevant) information.

- ✔ **Date:** This is the official date of the legal hold order notification.

- ✔ **Matter:** This portion of the notice lists the formal name of the lawsuit or event that is causing the hold order.

- ✔ **Relevant documentation:** This section lists all records and information (paper and electronic) that are currently deemed relevant or potentially relevant to the matter. It includes, but isn't limited to, documents, spreadsheets, e-mails, notes, drafts, voice mails, and audio files. The legal hold may also provide specific time frames — all e-mails received or created between January 1, 2008, through December 31, 2010, for example.

✓ **Preservation instructions:** This section of the legal hold provides instructions to the recipients spelling out that they should cease, until further notice, all destruction or deletion of information listed in the Relevant Documentation section of the legal hold. The hold order instructs recipients not to alter or modify relevant information and to ensure that it's retained in its native format. Preserving information in its native format helps to ensure that all original metadata (data about data) is retained. In addition, the legal hold may also communicate to recipients the possible disciplinary action for failing to comply with the order.

✓ **Confirmation of receipt and hold:** Most legal hold notifications require recipients to acknowledge receipt of the order and indicate that they are preserving relevant information in their possession.

Although the hold notice applies specifically to a lawsuit, the same concept and approach can be used to communicate holds related to nonlawsuit matters such as a federal tax audit or a regulatory inquiry. In these cases, the Tax or Compliance department rather than the Legal department normally issues the hold order.

Organizations should educate and train their employees on the legal hold process. The effectiveness of a legal hold is dependent upon how well employees understand and comply with the order. In addition to understanding the hold process, employees need to understand that properly managing the organization's records and information creates the foundation for an efficient and compliant record hold. Applying records and information management principles ensures that content needed for a lawsuit can be quickly identified, retrieved, and protected.

A legal hold supersedes the organization's retention schedule. This means that when the information related to the hold has been identified and communicated to the recipients, it's critical that the information not be destroyed. Even if the retention period for some of or all the information has expired, the information still must be retained. Failure to do so can lead to significant fines and penalties.

When relevant documentation has been identified and located, it is made accessible to the Legal department for review and analysis. In some cases, the information is quarantined or segregated so that it cannot be destroyed or altered. This ensures that the information is appropriately preserved in case it has to be produced for the lawsuit.

In many cases, the information that an organization must hold, preserve, and produce for a lawsuit is comprised of a significant volume of records and non-record content that wasn't destroyed in accordance with the organization's records and information retention schedule. An effective records and information management program helps ensure that you appropriately retain information and destroy it on a scheduled basis in the normal course of business.

Organizing the search party

During the discovery and legal hold process, Legal departments and attorneys typically work closely with the records manager or with departmental employees who have responsibility for managing records. Records managers and their staff are knowledgeable of the organization's records. They know which departments are the custodians of the records, where the records are located, and whether the records still exist or have been destroyed. When a legal hold is received, the records manager and all departmental employees who have been identified as potentially being in possession of relevant information should review the nature of the hold and begin the process of searching for the information.

Before starting your record hold information search, remember these things:

- ✔ **Format:** Relevant documentation may include information in paper or electronic formats, or both. In addition, electronic information can encompass structured and unstructured data.

- ✔ **Category:** The relevant documentation section of a legal hold may list specific company records that are listed in the organization's record retention schedule. However, in some cases, the communication may include broader categories such as "All information related to employee training." In this case, relevant documentation may be comprised of official records and nonrecord information. As a reminder, nonrecord information consists of content that is not considered an official company record or listed on the organization's record retention schedule, but may have business value, such as a spreadsheet or a report.

- ✔ **Location:** In the event of a legal hold, all relevant information needs to be located, placed on hold, and preserved. This includes information stored within the organization's facility as well as any information stored at offsite storage and cloud vendors. (For more on the new wrinkle that is cloud computing, check out Chapter 16.)

- ✔ **Repositories:** The records manager should become familiar with the different information repositories used by the organization. This may include file cabinets, document and content management systems, e-mail servers, and shared network drives. For small- to medium-sized businesses, this may be a task the records manager can commit to memory. However, in large organizations, it's recommended that a *data map* be created. (Data mapping gets its own coverage in Chapter 16. For now, just know that the purpose of a data map is to list all the repositories of data used by an organization, including application and server names, nature of the data, business purpose, and who owns the application. A data map can be very helpful in locating information during discovery.)

- ✔ **New information:** A legal hold will list historical information needed for a lawsuit. However, sometimes it will require that all new content that is generated or received that meets the criteria of the legal hold also be preserved.

If the legal hold requires that specific company records be placed on hold and preserved, the records manager should use the company's retention schedule to help assist in locating the records. A departmental retention schedule lists all records by department, which can expedite the search process.

Searching in the dark

This section isn't meant to depress you, but rather to detail common issues that most organizations encounter when conducting discovery searches. Searching for relevant documentation is the most problematic phase of discovery — especially eDiscovery. While the legal hold may clearly communicate the type of information that needs to be located, placed on hold, and preserved, in many cases, the information is difficult to find. If your organization doesn't use a Records or Content Management software system to manage its information, the search process may be very time consuming and result in not finding content that's needed.

It's important for the Compliance, Legal, Records Management, and Risk Management departments to understand what searching challenges the company faces. For example, paper records are routinely removed from file cabinets, placed into boxes, and sent to storage, where they accumulate over time. Some boxes may be labeled in a manner that allows you to quickly and accurately determine the contents, while many boxes may be poorly labeled and must be opened and physically reviewed for relevance. Some departments may maintain a spreadsheet of boxes that they have sent to storage, which can be valuable when attempting to find information; other departments may not keep any storage documentation. (Chapter 11 provides an example of a spreadsheet that can be used in lieu of Records and Content Management software for tracking records sent to storage, as well as insight into how to utilize a storage vendor's website for this purpose.)

The following approaches can be used for locating paper records:

- ✔ **Record retention schedule:** If your organization uses a departmental retention schedule, each department's records are listed individually. This allows you to quickly identify which departments may have relevant documentation. (Functional and Big Bucket retention schedules don't provide the same level of detail, but they can provide a starting point for your search.)

- ✔ **Record storage spreadsheets:** Departments may keep a spreadsheet or other documentation that lists the boxes of records and their contents that they have sent to storage. The listing can be reviewed to determine whether any information relevant to the lawsuit is in storage.

✔ **Record storage vendor website:** Many record storage vendors provide their customers with a website that the customers can use to monitor their inventory. The website allows customers to view box storage details such as bar-code number, contents, department, record-classification code, and content date ranges. However, the adage "garbage in, garbage out" applies in this case. If the department didn't provide box detail information (or provided inadequate information) to the vendor, the website may not be of much use.

Searching for electronic information poses the greatest organizational challenge. This is based on the large amount of electronic content that organizations retain, the numerous repositories used, the lack of filing structure, and the absence of standard file-naming conventions. These issues significantly increase the chances that information required for a lawsuit will never be located. The challenges of searching for electronic information are so great that companies have been created whose sole purpose is to assist organizations with eDiscovery. Such eDiscovery companies use a variety of logic and algorithms to search through repositories of information looking for certain words, phrases, dates, and probabilities.

E-mail — the smoking gun

While searching for electronic content on hard drives and shared network drives is a challenge, in many organizations, it pales in comparison to the challenges of searching and producing e-mails. For some companies, e-mail is the single largest source of information. Employees tend to archive e-mails rather than delete them. When employees reach their e-mail space quota, they save e-mails to a variety of storage devices, such as local and network drives and removable media. In addition, the e-mail application servers are regularly backed up and archived to tape by the IT department. In most organizations, backup and archive tapes contain mountains of e-mails that may have to be reviewed during the discovery process. Organizations spend millions of dollars annually reviewing e-mails for lawsuits.

To compound the discovery issue, e-mail has become the number-one electronic information focus of attorneys. E-mail is considered a "smoking gun." It has proved to be detrimental in many lawsuits. E-mail is used by many employees, at all levels of an organization, as an informal communication tool. There have been numerous instances of employees communicating a personal opinion or corporate position on a matter, never thinking that the communication may be retrieved and entered into evidence in a lawsuit. Attorneys have become very knowledgeable and savvy of how companies use e-mail and how to use it against them.

Keying in on keywords

Now that you're schooled on the nature of the search challenges you'll be facing, it's time to talk about what you can do to find the information you need. In the absence of eDiscovery and Records, Document, and Content Management software to assist you, your options are limited. However, you do have some tools at your disposal.

To assist you in locating electronic information, it's recommended that you perform *keyword searches.* A keyword search allows you to look for a specific word in a folder or filename, as well as in the text of a document or spreadsheet. Keyword searches can be used to find information on hard drives, shared network drives, and removable media. Keyword searching is a function of your computer operating system; no additional software is needed.

A record hold notice contains many potential keywords that can be used when searching for electronic information:

✔ Parties named in the lawsuit

✔ Dates

✔ Subject matter

Following is an example of how you conduct a keyword search on a computer hard drive for the term *asbestos* in Windows:

1. **Click the Start button, located in the lower-left corner of the Windows screen.**

    The Start menu opens, as shown in Figure 8-1.

2. **Type the keyword *(asbestos)* in the Search Programs and Files field.**

    This searches the computer's local hard drive for any files or documents containing the word *asbestos.*

3. **Press Enter.**

    Your search results are displayed. See Figure 8-2.

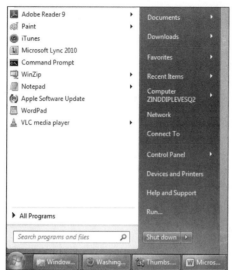

Figure 8-1:
Initiating the
search.

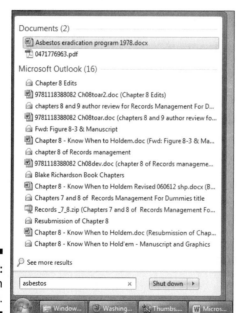

Figure 8-2:
Search
results.

Searching made simple

If your company uses a Records, Document, or Content Management software system, congratulations — searching may be a lot easier. These types of software applications provide many benefits that are covered in detail in Chapter 10, but two major benefits are worth mentioning now, just because such benefits are especially suited for helping assist organizations during discovery:

- ✔ **Single repository:** Applications such as Content Management systems can provide a single repository where all (or the majority) of an organization's information can reside. This significantly reduces the number of repositories that have to be searched during discovery.

- ✔ **Metadata:** Records, Document, and Content Management systems allow users to assign metadata (information about information) to your information. For example, if you are saving an employee file to the system, you can apply metadata such as employee ID, name, hire date, division, department, and title. Subsequently, you can conduct searches on each attribute or a combination of the metadata attributes. This can significantly reduce the time spent looking for the information you need.

Preserving what you find

The game isn't over yet — after you find what you're looking for, it needs to be preserved. Preservation is a critical step in the discovery process. Preservation means keeping the relevant documentation valid and intact. After relevant documentation has been identified and located, it must not be destroyed, deleted, or altered. Preserved information should remain in its native format, such as paper, word processing document, and spreadsheet. The failure to preserve information relevant to an active or pending lawsuit can result in significant fines and penalties.

Maintaining the legal hold

After the legal hold is initially communicated, the issuing department should send all recipients periodic reminders letting them know that the hold is still in place. This approach allows the initiating department to communicate any changes in the scope of the legal hold, including documentation that is no longer considered relevant or additional documentation that must now be preserved.

Periodic legal hold reminders can be distributed by reissuing the original hold notice or through e-mail or an e-mail attachment, a posting on the company's intranet, pop-up messages, or voice mail. The initiating department should document all periodic reminders to provide proof that the organization executed the proper due diligence to ensure that employees continued to preserve relevant documentation.

We have liftoff

A legal hold is usually lifted after the lawsuit has concluded or when a lawsuit is no longer anticipated. The steps in lifting a legal hold are similar to initiating one. The Legal department will distribute a legal hold *rescission notice*. This is a formal communication alerting all recipients that the hold is no longer in effect. Legal, audit, and regulatory compliance holds can be in effect for months or years, resulting in the mandatory retention of records and information that may have otherwise have been eligible for destruction. After the hold is lifted, it's time to take a look at the information that was impacted.

After a hold is lifted, it's recommended that you take some time to review the information that has been on hold to determine its status. To determine the status of the information, follow these steps:

1. **System update:** If your organization uses a Records Management software application or vendor website to manage your content, you should ensure that the hold is removed in the system so that programmatic retention monitoring of the records can resume.

2. **Evaluation:** All content impacted by the hold should be evaluated to determine whether it should be destroyed or deleted. Departmental record custodians, IT, and the Records Management department should conduct the evaluation.

3. **Destruction:** Based on the evaluation, you should ensure that all impacted content that is eligible to be destroyed is disposed of appropriately.

Content can be placed on multiple holds. This means that multiple lawsuits, audits, or governmental inquiries can impact the same record. In large organizations, it's common for attorneys to handle specific types of legal matters. For example, one group of attorneys may be responsible for human resources matters, while another group of attorneys may handle issues related to regulatory compliance. The potential exists for each group to be unaware that records they placed on hold may be on a hold for an additional lawsuit, audit, or governmental inquiry. Therefore, when evaluating whether information can be destroyed after a hold is lifted, it's critical to verify that no other holds apply to the content.

Chapter 9

Imaging Documents

. . . .

In This Chapter

▶ Understanding how document imaging works

▶ Reviewing the benefits

▶ Conducting a needs assessment

▶ Studying the approaches

▶ Determining what you need

▶ Determining the return on investment (ROI)

▶ Evaluating hardware and software

. . . .

*A*lthough the paperless office hasn't yet come to fruition, document imaging can allow organizations to rely less on paper processing. *Document imaging* (commonly referred to as *scanning* or *imaging*) uses technology to convert paper documents to electronic format. Document imaging provides many benefits, such as reductions in physical storage space, productivity increases, and better customer service.

Sounds great, right? Not so fast. Although document imaging *can* provide many benefits, it first requires a thorough understanding of your business processes to determine whether imaging is a good fit for your organization. This chapter provides the knowledge you need to make an informed decision. In this chapter, you find out how to assess your document-imaging needs, review implementation options, and discover how to evaluate imaging hardware and software.

From Paper to Paperless

Paper isn't going away. Although it's certainly true that, in today's corporate environment, most organizations have more digital volume than paper, many employees nevertheless continue to send electronic information to their printers so that they have a hard copy for filing and reference purposes. Therefore, it can be argued that the explosion of personal computing and electronic information has actually *prevented* the paperless office from becoming a reality, instead of speeding it on its way. Some companies still require all e-mails to be printed and filed. Worse yet, in some cases, the printed documents are later imaged, thus creating a digital copy!

Implementing a document-imaging program is a significant *business culture* change. In many cases, it changes (for the better) the way that departments currently process their business functions. Even though document imaging can improve a process, it's a change. It requires employees to reshape years of a paper-based mind-set. Companies should anticipate initial resistance from some employees, but after a short period of time, you will find employees singing the praises of document imaging.

Understanding the basics of document imaging

Document imaging is simply converting paper to an electronic format through the use of imaging software and hardware. The hardware and software take a digital picture of the paper document, which allows you to store and retrieve the image by using your computer.

The two main components of a document-imaging system are hardware and software. Depending on a company's imaging needs, the investment in hardware and software can be minimal to hundreds of thousands of dollars. The extent of an organization's investment depends upon the following factors:

- ✔ **Volume:** The volume of documents to be scanned determines the type of scanning device and software that need to be used. Low-volume imaging can be performed on an inexpensive desktop scanner or *multifunctional device (MFD)*. (An MFD is a device that allows you to print, scan, and fax from the same machine.) For organizations that need to scan a large volume of information, it may be necessary to invest in high-volume production scanners and software.

- ✔ **Frequency:** Frequency refers to how often you need to image documents. Volume alone doesn't always provide an accurate picture of your imaging needs. For example, you may have a significant amount of documents that need to be imaged for a one-time project. In this case, you don't want to invest a lot of money in scanners and software. However, if you have documents that need to be scanned on a regular basis, you may want to make the investment.

- ✔ **Location:** Organizations that are geographically dispersed may have a need for each location to image its own documents, which can result in purchasing more scanning equipment than would be needed if the organization used a centralized imaging approach.

Later in this chapter, I tackle each of these issues in greater detail so that you have the info you need to determine your specific document-imaging needs.

Benefiting from an image makeover

Every organization struggles with managing paper-filing systems. Some common issues associated with paper-based file management include lost or misfiled information, decreased productivity, poor customer service, space constraints, and limited access to information. Document imaging can help you resolve each of these issues. The following list explains how:

- **Productivity increases:** Employee productivity is increased by eliminating the time it takes to walk to a file cabinet, search for a file, and then refile the information. Document imaging allows users to quickly search and retrieve information without ever leaving their computer. Document imaging also significantly reduces the occurrence of lost and misfiled documents, which is a definite productivity boost.

- **Expense reductions:** Imaging documents can reduce or eliminate the costs associated with maintaining paper-based filing systems. This includes the purchase of filing equipment, costs of archival storage, and labor costs related to manually retrieving physical information.

- **Customer service enhancements:** Document imaging enhances customer services by providing quick access to customer and vendor information. It eliminates the need to place a customer "on hold" while you walk to a file cabinet and search for his information, or worse, telling the customer you have to call him back because you have to order his file from a centralized filing area.

- **Storage reductions:** Transitioning to document imaging can significantly reduce the number of file cabinets and the amount of expensive office space needed for paper-based filing. Document imaging eliminates the need to make copies of documents and physically distribute them; a document is imaged once and becomes available to multiple users.

- **Improved access to information:** Document imaging makes information readily available to employees, whether they are located in the same department or in another country. This approach allows organizations to effectively collaborate on projects and assists in rapid and informed decision-making.

- **Disaster recovery and vital records protection:** Document imaging allows vital information to be backed up electronically and protected. In the event of a disaster, imaged documents can assist in the business resumption.

To Image, or Not to Image

Document imaging can provide organizations with many benefits. However, not all paper documents should be imaged. Before investing in scanning hardware and software or outsourcing the process, it's recommended that you take time to assess your imaging needs. The lack of proper planning can be expensive in the end. Many companies have learned this the hard way by scanning years of documents that are no longer referenced and in some cases should've been destroyed.

In the following sections, I walk you through the process of evaluating your imaging needs, determining what documents make good imaging candidates, anticipating the cost and effort, and calculating your return on investment.

Conducting an imaging needs assessment

Large volumes of paper don't always translate into a need for document imaging. Some organizations feel that they need to explore document imaging because they are at a point where they need to purchase additional file cabinets or they have grown tired of paying a vendor to store their documents.

In many cases, overflowing file cabinets may seem like a good reason to scan documents, but usually they're a symptom of not managing the information life cycle. Full file cabinets may mean that you need to send inactive information that's not yet eligible for destruction to offsite storage for the remainder of its retention period. The cost to store a box of records with a vendor for a few years is usually less expensive than imaging the documents.

Before you invest in document imaging, you should be asking yourself one question — Why do I want to image my documents? It's essential to know your document-imaging objective. For example, what issues or problems are you attempting to resolve? To help you answer the question, it's recommended that you conduct an *imaging needs assessment.* The assessment is a tool every organization should use if it has file cabinets and file rooms full of paper and is interested in the benefits of document imaging. The assessment lists a series of questions that allow you to determine what documents are good candidates to be imaged — kind of like what you see in Figure 9-1. (Feel free to use it — think of it as my gift to you.)

The imaging needs assessment should be conducted with someone knowledgeable of the document-imaging process. This may include an employee with prior imaging experience, a qualified consultant, or a document-imaging vendor. This approach allows you to receive clarification regarding the assessment questions and ask additional questions if needed.

	Question	Response
1.	Why does your department need imaging services.	
2.	What are the main functions of the department.	
3.	List the documents related to the functions.	
4.	Is this a request for an imaging project or continuing production.	
5.	What is the estimated daily volume of documents.	
6.	What is the number of pages per document.	
7.	Are the documents single or multi-sided.	
8.	Are there any initiatives to begin receiving the documents electronically.	
9.	If the answer to question 8 is yes, when do you anticipate receiving the documents electronically.	
10.	How frequently are the documents accessed after initial processing or receipt.	
11.	How long are the documents stored in the department before they are transitioned to archive storage.	
12.	How many filing cabinets are today to house the documents.	
13.	Does your department currently need additional filing space.	
14.	Is the retention of the documents governed by legislation or regulations.	
15.	Are the documents accessed by other departments, operation or external parties.	

Figure 9-1:
Imaging
needs
assessment
form.

The assessment questions are designed to ensure that the answers provide a comprehensive picture of an operation's imaging needs. Upon completion, most companies will find that they have a valid imaging need if the documents that are being assessed fall into one or more of the following categories:

✔ **Heavy volume and frequent retrieval:** A major benefit of document imaging is eliminating the time it takes to walk to a file cabinet, file a document, retrieve a document, and then refile the information. If an organization has a large volume of different document types that are frequently retrieved, imaging is a good fit.

✔ **Workflow process:** In this scenario, the volume of paper documents may or may not be significant. However, the manual processing of the documents requires multiple handling and authorizations. In this case, implementing automated workflow in conjunction with document imaging can provide productivity gains, reducing labor costs and improving customer service.

✔ **Protection:** This scenario refers to the need to digitally protect information that is organizationally and operationally vital to the organization. This can include documents such as articles of incorporation, bylaws, board of directors meeting minutes, pension records, accounts receivable records, and employee-related information. In this scenario, the amount of paper may be insignificant and the information rarely accessed. However, the risks associated with losing the information outweigh the expense of imaging.

Small businesses are sometimes an exception to these scenarios. Small businesses may have significant space constraints that don't allow many file cabinets or box storage of paper documents. In this case, an inexpensive desktop scanner or multifunctional device can be used to scan documents and store them on a computer, helping to reduce the amount of needed storage space.

Stepping through the imaging process

Now that you have a good understanding of the basics of document imaging and what documents make good imaging candidates, it's time to look at the steps in the document-imaging process. The imaging process consists of four primary phases:

- ✔ Prepping
- ✔ Scanning
- ✔ Indexing
- ✔ Quality control

Note: Depending on the complexity of an imaging operation and the software technology being used, you may have additional processing phases such as recognition and release. Each of these processes is reviewed later in this chapter.

Prep school

Document preparation (commonly referred to as *document prep*) means ensuring that your documents are in the proper condition to proceed through the scanning process. Preparing your documents to be imaged is a very important step. Properly prepping your documents helps to make sure that you receive accurate scanning results. Improperly prepped documents slow the scanning process, result in invalid output, and may damage the scanning equipment.

Depending on an organization's document-imaging approach, prepping may be performed by the department that owns the information or by a centralized scanning department. Departments usually prep documents when the company uses a *back-end,* or *postprocessing,* imaging approach. This means that documents are imaged after they have been used to process a function. Back-end imaging allows the documents to be electronically stored and retrieved for future reference. A centralized scanning department typically preps the documents when an organization uses a *front-end* imaging approach. Front-end imaging involves scanning departmental documents when the company receives them. For example, when paper invoices enter the mailroom, they are forwarded to the scanning department. The scanning department will prep and scan the documents, allowing the Accounts Payable department to process them electronically. ***Note:*** Later in this chapter, you see how a process such as invoice payments can be automated by using document imaging and *workflow*.

Prepping usually involves inserting a *separator sheet* (also referred to as a *cover sheet*) between each document. This allows the scanning software and, in some cases, the scanning hardware to determine where one document ends and another begins. Separator sheets use a patch code to trigger separation by using a pattern of alternating black bars and spaces, as shown in Figure 9-2.

Figure 9-2:
Document-
imaging
separator
sheet.

Patch codes don't contain embedded data like a traditional bar code. However, some scanning operations use bar codes rather than patch codes to automate the indexing of documents. (See Figure 9-3.) For example, a Human Resources department that scans employee files can place bar-code sheets between each document to trigger separation and also provide indexing values such as department name, document type, employee ID, and employee name. (I cover index automating and bar-code sheets in more detail later in this chapter.)

Figure 9-3:
Document-
imaging
separator
sheet with
bar codes.

In addition to inserting separator sheets, you need to remember some basic prepping "dos and don'ts" for your documents to flow smoothly through the imaging process and to ensure that you receive an accurate electronic replication of your paper documents:

- ✔ **Highlighting:** Don't highlight text on a document that is to be imaged. In some cases, it can "black-out" the text.

- ✔ **Staples:** Staples should be removed from all documents before they are imaged. Staples slow the imaging process and can scratch the scanner's glass. Using a staple remover helps to ensure that the corners of the paper do not tear. Torn paper corners can result in *jams* during the scanning process and *double feeds* (two pages feeding through the scanner at one time).

- ✔ **Tape:** Sometimes it is necessary to tape a document such as a receipt to another document or a blank piece of paper. When taping a document, you need to ensure that it's taped at least ½ inch from the top and side edges of the paper. Items taped too close to the edges can result in the paper not feeding properly through the scanner. Some scanners are equipped with a *double-feed* detection device. If the tape is too close to the edges, the detection device may interpret the thickness of the tape as two pages going through the scanner at the same time. In addition, avoid taping over text on the document. Tape is reflective and can cause information to be blacked out.

- ✔ **Corners:** It is important to ensure that the corners of a document are smooth and unfolded prior to being imaged. Folded corners can cause jams and misfeeds. In some cases, folded corners can cover up information on a document.

Scanning documents

Scanning documents can be a simple process or involve several steps, depending on the size and complexity of an imaging operation. For a small business using a desktop scanner or multifunctional device, it may involve placing a document in a feeder tray and clicking an icon on your desktop. However, the process for large departmental and centralized production scanning operations is more complex.

Larger scanning operations typically use high-speed scanners in conjunction with *capture* software. Document capture software is used to profile different document types. Document profiling occurs by creating a *batch class* in the software. The batch class indicates the type of document, whether all documents are single page or multipage, and the different software-processing queues the documents will pass through.

Prior to scanning a document, the operator will invoke the software and choose the proper batch class. For example, if the operator is preparing to scan invoices, she will select the invoice batch class, which triggers the software to automatically know that the documents about to be imaged are all one-page, double-sided documents. This results in the software creating a separation between each one-page invoice, creating separate documents, and scanning both sides of the invoice. The capture software also knows to send the documents through the appropriate queues after they are imaged. (I say more about processing queues in the upcoming sections.)

Recognizing a good thing when you see it

Document capture software provides functionality that can read information on a document and assign the information as metadata to the image; this is referred to as *recognition.* Although recognition is not listed as one of the four primary steps in the document-imaging process, it plays a very important role in subsequently finding information and making the process more efficient.

In a production-oriented imaging operation, the scan operator will send the imaged documents to the recognition processing queue after the documents have been scanned. This allows the recognition module to read and apply metadata to the image. The batch class determines where on the document the software needs to look for data to read and what type of data format to expect. Capture software with recognition capability can typically read and extract the following types of information:

✔ **Bar code:** This includes a variety of commonly used bar-code formats such as 3-9, 128, and 2-D. (See Figure 9-4.)

✔ **Optical Character Recognition (OCR):** OCR refers to computer or machine print.

✔ **Intelligent Character Recognition (ICR):** ICR refers to handwriting.

✔ **Optical mark reader:** Check boxes and radio buttons are examples of optical marks. (See Figure 9-5.) Optical marks are commonly used on surveys, as well as on various other applications. (Remember the SAT?)

Figure 9-4:
Bar codes.

The recognition process significantly reduces the amount of manual data entry, referred to as indexing. (More on indexing in the next section.)

Applying indexes

In some cases, automated recognition may not be able to be used due to poor-quality print or handwriting, or due to the inconsistency of the location of information on a document. When this occurs, the documents need to be manually *indexed*. Indexing involves data entry by a scan operator. For example, if an organization receives a high volume of invoices from multiple vendors, information such as account number, purchase order number, vendor name, and invoice amount may be located in different places on each vendor's invoice. In this case, it's difficult to program the capture software recognition module to know where to find the information. This usually results in a scan operator visually inspecting the scanned invoice and keying the index values into the appropriate fields in the capture software screen.

It is recommended that you minimize the amount of manual indexing that has to be performed. For many scanning operations, manual indexing is the most labor-intensive part of the document-imaging process. One tool that can be used to reduce the amount of indexing is *autopopulation*. Autopopulation allows you to key in one index value and, based on the value you enter, the other index fields automatically populate.

1 Ⓐ ● Ⓒ Ⓓ Ⓔ	31 Ⓐ Ⓑ Ⓒ Ⓓ ●	61 Ⓐ ● Ⓒ Ⓓ Ⓔ	91 Ⓐ Ⓑ Ⓒ
2 Ⓐ Ⓑ Ⓒ Ⓓ ●	32 Ⓐ Ⓑ Ⓒ ● Ⓔ	62 Ⓐ Ⓑ Ⓒ ● Ⓔ	92 Ⓐ ● Ⓒ
3 Ⓐ Ⓑ Ⓒ ● Ⓔ	33 Ⓐ Ⓑ Ⓒ Ⓓ ●	63 ● Ⓑ Ⓒ Ⓓ Ⓔ	93 Ⓐ Ⓑ Ⓒ
4 Ⓐ Ⓑ Ⓒ Ⓓ ●	34 Ⓐ Ⓑ ● Ⓓ Ⓔ	64 Ⓐ Ⓑ Ⓒ Ⓓ ●	94 Ⓐ Ⓑ Ⓒ
5 Ⓐ Ⓑ Ⓒ Ⓓ ●	35 Ⓐ Ⓑ Ⓒ ● Ⓔ	65 Ⓐ Ⓑ ● Ⓓ Ⓔ	95 Ⓐ Ⓑ Ⓒ
6 ● Ⓑ Ⓒ Ⓓ Ⓔ	36 ● Ⓑ Ⓒ Ⓓ Ⓔ	66 ● Ⓑ Ⓒ Ⓓ Ⓔ	96 Ⓐ Ⓑ ●
7 Ⓐ Ⓑ ● Ⓓ Ⓔ	37 Ⓐ ● Ⓒ Ⓓ Ⓔ	67 Ⓐ Ⓑ Ⓒ Ⓓ ●	97 ● Ⓑ Ⓒ
8 Ⓐ Ⓑ ● Ⓓ Ⓔ	38 ● Ⓑ Ⓒ Ⓓ Ⓔ	68 Ⓐ Ⓑ ● Ⓓ Ⓔ	98 Ⓐ Ⓑ Ⓒ
9 Ⓐ Ⓑ Ⓒ ● Ⓔ	39 Ⓐ Ⓑ Ⓒ ● Ⓔ	69 Ⓐ Ⓑ Ⓒ Ⓓ ●	99 Ⓐ Ⓑ Ⓒ
10 ● Ⓑ Ⓒ Ⓓ Ⓔ	40 ● Ⓑ Ⓒ Ⓓ Ⓔ	70 Ⓐ Ⓑ ● Ⓓ Ⓔ	100 Ⓐ Ⓑ Ⓒ
11 Ⓐ ● Ⓒ Ⓓ Ⓔ	41 Ⓐ Ⓑ Ⓒ Ⓓ ●	71 Ⓐ Ⓑ Ⓒ ● Ⓔ	101 Ⓐ Ⓑ ●
12 ● Ⓑ Ⓒ Ⓓ Ⓔ	42 Ⓐ Ⓑ Ⓒ Ⓓ ●	72 Ⓐ Ⓑ ● Ⓓ Ⓔ	102 Ⓐ Ⓑ ●
13 Ⓐ ● Ⓒ Ⓓ Ⓔ	43 Ⓐ ● Ⓒ Ⓓ Ⓔ	73 Ⓐ Ⓑ Ⓒ ● Ⓔ	103 Ⓐ Ⓑ Ⓒ
14 Ⓐ Ⓑ Ⓒ Ⓓ ●	44 Ⓐ Ⓑ ● Ⓓ Ⓔ	74 Ⓐ ● Ⓒ Ⓓ Ⓔ	104 Ⓐ Ⓑ ●
15 Ⓐ Ⓑ Ⓒ ● Ⓔ	45 Ⓐ Ⓑ Ⓒ ● Ⓔ	75 Ⓐ ● Ⓒ Ⓓ Ⓔ	105 Ⓐ Ⓑ Ⓒ
16 Ⓐ Ⓑ Ⓒ ● Ⓔ	46 Ⓐ Ⓑ Ⓒ Ⓓ ●	76 Ⓐ Ⓑ Ⓒ ● Ⓔ	106 Ⓐ Ⓑ Ⓒ
17 Ⓐ ● Ⓒ Ⓓ Ⓔ	47 Ⓐ Ⓑ Ⓒ ● Ⓔ	77 Ⓐ Ⓑ Ⓒ Ⓓ ●	107 ● Ⓑ Ⓒ
18 Ⓐ Ⓑ Ⓒ ● Ⓔ	48 Ⓐ Ⓑ ● Ⓓ Ⓔ	78 ● Ⓑ Ⓒ Ⓓ Ⓔ	108 Ⓐ Ⓑ Ⓒ
19 Ⓐ Ⓑ ● Ⓓ Ⓔ	49 ● Ⓑ Ⓒ Ⓓ Ⓔ	79 ● Ⓑ Ⓒ Ⓓ Ⓔ	109 Ⓐ Ⓑ ●
20 Ⓐ ● Ⓒ Ⓓ Ⓔ	50 Ⓐ ● Ⓒ Ⓓ Ⓔ	80 Ⓐ Ⓑ Ⓒ Ⓓ ●	110 Ⓐ Ⓑ ●
21 Ⓐ Ⓑ ● Ⓓ Ⓔ	51 Ⓐ Ⓑ Ⓒ ● Ⓔ	81 Ⓐ ● Ⓒ Ⓓ Ⓔ	111 Ⓐ ● Ⓒ
22 Ⓐ Ⓑ ● Ⓓ Ⓔ	52 Ⓐ ● Ⓒ Ⓓ Ⓔ	82 Ⓐ Ⓑ Ⓒ ● Ⓔ	112 Ⓐ Ⓑ ●
23 Ⓐ ● Ⓒ Ⓓ Ⓔ	53 Ⓐ Ⓑ Ⓒ ● Ⓔ	83 Ⓐ Ⓑ Ⓒ Ⓓ ●	113 Ⓐ Ⓑ Ⓒ
24 ● Ⓑ Ⓒ Ⓓ Ⓔ	54 Ⓐ Ⓑ ● Ⓓ Ⓔ	84 Ⓐ ● Ⓒ Ⓓ Ⓔ	114 Ⓐ Ⓑ ●
25 Ⓐ ● Ⓒ Ⓓ Ⓔ	55 Ⓐ Ⓑ Ⓒ Ⓓ ●	85 Ⓐ Ⓑ ● Ⓓ Ⓔ	115 Ⓐ Ⓑ ●
26 Ⓐ Ⓑ ● Ⓓ Ⓔ	56 Ⓐ Ⓑ Ⓒ ● Ⓔ	86 Ⓐ ● Ⓒ Ⓓ Ⓔ	116 Ⓐ Ⓑ Ⓒ
27 Ⓐ ● Ⓒ Ⓓ Ⓔ	57 ● Ⓑ Ⓒ Ⓓ Ⓔ	87 Ⓐ Ⓑ Ⓒ ● Ⓔ	117 Ⓐ Ⓑ Ⓒ
28 Ⓐ Ⓑ Ⓒ Ⓓ ●	58 Ⓐ Ⓑ Ⓒ Ⓓ ●	88 Ⓐ Ⓑ Ⓒ Ⓓ ●	118 Ⓐ Ⓑ ●
29 Ⓐ Ⓑ Ⓒ ● Ⓔ	59 Ⓐ Ⓑ ● Ⓓ Ⓔ	89 Ⓐ Ⓑ ● Ⓓ Ⓔ	119 Ⓐ Ⓑ Ⓒ
30 Ⓐ Ⓑ ● Ⓓ Ⓔ	60 Ⓐ ● Ⓒ Ⓓ Ⓔ	90 ● Ⓑ Ⓒ Ⓓ Ⓔ	120 Ⓐ Ⓑ ●

Figure 9-5: Optical marks.

No, it's not magic. It happens by programmatically connecting your document capture software to another organizational system such as a human resources or financial application. For example, if you are indexing an employee file, you can type in **John Doe** in the Employee Name field. Then the capture software looks up the employee ID, division, and hire date in the human resources application and populates the other respective index fields.

Organizations that use automated recognition and manual indexing typically *release* documents to either a document or content management system after the imaging process is completed. This is in contrast to smaller companies, which may scan a document and then save the electronic image to a computer. Most small-volume desktop scanners or multifunctional devices apply cryptic names to imaged files such as SCAN014B12. Therefore, after the document is scanned and saved, it must be renamed.

Applying index attributes to imaged files and releasing them to a document or content management system greatly improve your ability to quickly find the information you are looking for. You can search by one of or all the index attributes that were assigned to the image. However, when you image a document and save it to your computer, you have to rely on the effectiveness of the filename and where it was saved to find the information.

Document owners (departments) usually predetermine index fields. When determining what index fields should be assigned to a document type, you need to focus on how you will need to retrieve the information in the future. I show you how to determine your index attributes in the "Gathering Requirements" section, later in this chapter.

Controlling the quality

The last major step in the scanning process is *quality control (QC)*. Quality control involves examining imaged documents upon completion of the scanning and indexing process to ensure that the imaged document is an accurate replication of the paper document and that the appropriate indexes were assigned to the image. Quality control is a very important step in the document-imaging process. Most companies destroy the *source document* (paper document that's imaged) after a predetermined period of time and rely solely on the imaged version for processing, inquiries, legal, and tax matters. Therefore, it is essential to ensure that you receive accurate scanning and indexing results.

Sampling is typically the basis for determining which imaged documents are selected for QC. An organization may determine that a 10 percent sampling is adequate for determining the accuracy of the document-imaging process. However, organizations operating in highly regulated industries such as nuclear energy and pharmaceuticals may require that QC be performed on all imaged documents.

The QC process should encompass a review of the following items:

- ✔ **Image quality:** During the scanning process, a document may be skewed (turned) as it feeds through the scanner. In addition, speckling can occur during the scanning process if a page has excessive dust on it or if dust has collected in the scanner. Most production capture software is equipped with deskewing and despeckling functionality. In some cases, it may be necessary to rescan the document to improve the image quality.

- ✔ **Readability:** Image quality can negatively impact the automated recognition process, as well as the ability of a human to read the contents of the imaged document. Therefore, during the QC process, it's important to ensure that the document is readable and that the context or intent of the information has not been jeopardized.

✔ **Indexing:** This step involves verifying that the appropriate index values were assigned to the document. This may include checking the accuracy of both automated recognition and manual indexing.

✔ **Page count:** This process ensures that the page count of the imaged document equals the page count of the paper document. During the scanning process, it's possible for two pages of the document to be fed through the scanner at the same time, resulting in only one of the two pages being imaged. Additionally, scanners occasionally jam. After clearing the jam, it's important to verify the last page that was successfully imaged so that you know what page to image next.

Determining Your Imaging Approach

If you determine that imaging can provide benefits to your organization, it's time to think about the approach. Depending on an organization's size, imaging can be an expensive proposition. Therefore, it's critical to understand your options and iron out a plan *before* imaging any documents.

You have two basic options for imaging documents — create an in-house document-imaging operation or outsource your needs to a qualified vendor. However, both options have their own subset of options. The following sections can help you sort out the approaches and determine what best meets your organization's needs.

What happens in-house stays in-house

One option you have for imaging your documents is establishing an in-house scanning operation. The primary advantage of this approach is that it allows an organization to maintain control of its documents. Normally, when you outsource your imaging, your documents will need to be forwarded to the vendor's location for scanning, and in some cases, the vendor will subcontract the indexing process to a third party, sometimes offshore. Some organizations may not be comfortable with relinquishing control of their documents, so for such a company, in-house imaging may be more attractive.

Before establishing an in-house document-imaging operation, you should consider the cost and effort of the investment. The investment will vary depending on the volume of information to be scanned and how quickly employees need the imaged documents. For small businesses, the expense is minimal. However, the investment is significant for large organizations wanting to create a production-level imaging operation. The following sections examine the different components needed for in-house imaging and the investment you can plan to make.

Equipping your imaging operation

Document-imaging equipment typically includes scanners, computers, and monitors. Document scanners come in many shapes and sizes. Low-volume, quality desktop scanners can be purchased for $200–$300. However, high-volume, production-level scanners capable of imaging over 120 pages per minute can cost in excess of $30,000. Depending on your organization's imaging needs, several scanners may need to be purchased.

Before purchasing scanning equipment, it's essential to perform a document-imaging needs assessment (reviewed earlier in this chapter) for each department interested in scanning its documents. The results of the assessment can provide you with the information you need to determine the best approach to scanning within the organization, forecast potential volume, and also see how quickly the documents need to be imaged.

After you have an understanding of the document volume and service-level requirements, it's time to understand which approach to scanning best meets the organization's needs. Most companies that decide to image their documents in-house use one or a combination of the following approaches:

- Departmental (decentralized)
- Remote
- Centralized

Read on to see the pluses and minuses of each approach.

Taking a departmental approach

Departmental imaging, commonly referred to as *distributed capture,* is a decentralized approach that provides individual departments with the ability to scan their own documents. Department imaging can be beneficial when documents need to be quickly imaged. For example, a healthcare operation may have a need to scan documents as a patient completes them instead of sending the documents to a centralized imaging department to be scanned later.

Using a departmental imaging approach allows departments to maintain control of sensitive information. Some departments such as Legal and Human

Resources may decide, due to the confidential nature of their information, to image their own documents rather than to send them to a centralized imaging operation, where other employees could view the information.

The need for departmental imaging needs to be carefully evaluated. If this approach is not carefully researched, it may lead to the following issues:

✔ **Inconsistency:** When multiple departments are responsible for imaging their own documents, it can lead to inconsistencies in the management of the document-imaging process. Such inconsistencies could include the types of scanning equipment that's purchased, the manner in which documents are prepped, how quality control is performed, and how scanning equipment is maintained.

✔ **Unneeded expense:** Departmental imaging requires scanning equipment to be purchased and maintained for each individual department. In some cases, this may lead to departments buying their own scanners from different manufacturers or purchasing different model types. This approach may reduce an organization's overall buying leverage and require support from different vendors.

   If your organization decides to implement departmental imaging, it's very important that consistent procedures be developed and implemented across the company to ensure that expenses are minimized and the quality of the imaged document output is acceptable.

   If an organization decides to use departmental imaging, a centralized group or committee should control the purchase process to ensure that the scanning equipment and software meet each department's needs and that it maximizes its buying power.

   Some organizations decide to forgo departmental imaging due to labor costs. Typically, it's more expensive to have higher-paid departmental employees such as accountants, human resource specialists, or paralegals scan and index their documents rather than entry-level employees who may staff a centralized document-imaging department.

✔ **Underutilization:** Locating a scanner (or scanners) in each department can lead to underutilization of the equipment. If a department has a valid need to image its own documents, it's important to ensure that the right equipment is purchased based on the department's volume and service-level requirements.

   Purchasing a scanner that is capable of imaging 100 pages per minute when the department's volume warrants less throughput will result in underutilization. The document-imaging needs assessment should be used to determine a department's volume, which will allow you to select the appropriate equipment.

In a land far, far away

Remote imaging is a decentralized approach geared toward organizations that have operations in different geographical locations. Remote imaging allows the location to both scan and index documents and then transmit the information via the Internet or company's network, where it can be deposited in a document or content management application. Or, the documents can be scanned and then transmitted to a centralized processing department, where they are indexed.

In the absence of remote imaging, locations may have to ship their information via the postal service or express courier to a centralized imaging operation. This can result in significant expense, delays in documents being imaged, and lost documents.

Like departmental imaging, you should ensure that the appropriate equipment and software are purchased to prevent unnecessary expense and underutilization. In many cases, a satellite office's volume may not require the purchase of a dedicated scanner — multifunctional devices are sometimes perfectly adequate.

Bringing it all together

Centralized imaging operations are mainly utilized by large organizations that have significant volumes of paper documents that need to be imaged. Centralized imaging may provide departments with less flexibility in the imaging of their documents, but it provides the organization with several important benefits.

A centralized document-scanning operation is comprised of a dedicated staff that's trained and knowledgeable in all facets of imaging. This increases the overall efficiency, consistency, and accuracy of the process. Whereas a departmental imaging approach requires that numerous scanners be placed throughout the organization, centralized imaging uses fewer scanners, but those they do have are of a higher quality and are considerably faster.

Although centralized document imaging may use fewer scanners, they *are* more expensive. You may be able to purchase ten or more departmental scanners for the price of one production-level scanner. Therefore, it's a good idea to thoroughly assess your imaging needs before purchasing scanning equipment. However, regardless of the in-house scanning approach you use, you need to account for equipment failure and repair time. It's recommended that you purchase enough scanners to allow you to meet your service requirements in the event that a scanner is inoperable for a limited period of time.

Out with it!

Many organizations decide to outsource their document imaging. This is usually based on two factors — core functions and investment. *Core functions* refers to allowing employees to focus on their main tasks rather than spending time on ancillary administrative tasks such as prepping, scanning, and indexing documents.

The *investment* in document imaging can be significant. Instead of investing in additional staff, scanning equipment, and software, some companies decide to pay a vendor that already has the imaging infrastructure to scan their documents. However, if you decide to use a document-imaging vendor, you need to ensure that it meets your operational and regulatory requirements. You should consider the following factors when evaluating a vendor:

- ✔ **Use:** How do you plan to use the imaged documents? Do you need them to process a function, or do you need an image of the documents for retrieval purposes after they have been processed? Defining your imaging needs is essential in determining your vendor requirements.

- ✔ **Indexing:** You should determine what indexing you need the vendor to perform. This starts by determining how you plan to retrieve the documents. The more indexing you require the vendor to perform, the more the vendor will charge. One option is to have the vendor scan your documents and then have them transmitted back to you for indexing. In the section "Applying indexes," earlier in this chapter, I show you how you can use autopopulation to programmatically apply indexing values by integrating the capture software with different organizational applications. By transmitting a daily snapshot of application databases to the vendor, it can also use autopopulation.

  Some vendors contract with offshore companies to perform indexing. If this is the case, you should ensure that the information is encrypted during the transmission process. You should require the vendor to encrypt all information that it transmits to a subcontracted organization. The subcontract vendor should encrypt the data when sending it back. It's recommended that you consult with your IT department to ensure that the vendor and its subcontractors are using the most updated encryption methods. In addition, the vendor should provide you with information on the offshore company regarding its reputation, security controls, and accountability.

- ✔ **Service-level agreement:** You should establish a *Service Level Agreement (SLA)* with the vendor. An SLA defines your processing timeline and quality requirements and remedies you have if the vendor doesn't meet your requirements. For example, the SLA may include how and when you will provide documents to the vendor, how the documents are to be prepped and indexed, and when and how the information should be provided back to you. If the vendor fails to meet any aspect of the agreement, the SLA should provide a reduction in the costs normally charged by the vendor. The amount of reduced fees should be specifically communicated in the SLA.

Some organizations take a hybrid approach to outsourcing document imaging. This approach involves the vendor using its personnel, equipment, and software within the organization's facility. This option is typically used by companies that want to maintain control of their documents through the process, but don't want to make the investment in additional employees, equipment, and software.

Gathering Requirements

Whether an organization decides to perform document imaging in-house or to outsource the process, it's vital that you understand — and document — your imaging requirements. Defining your requirements typically occurs after the initial document-imaging needs assessment has been reviewed and approved. Departmental imaging requirements form the basis for determining how documents need to be processed and what it will cost.

The imaging needs assessment provides a high-level overview of the types of documents to be imaged, the volume, and the retrieval rate. The assessment provides a good starting point for understanding the basics of a department's imaging needs, but it doesn't provide enough detail to begin imaging the department's documents. The requirements definition phase of the initiative starts the process of collecting the details needed to move the initiative into production. It's recommended that the requirements be gathered by someone knowledgeable of the document-imaging process, including hardware and software functionality.

Conducting a document analysis

A document analysis involves obtaining a proficient understanding of a department's documents. This can help to ensure that the imaging process is configured to be efficient and to produce accurate results. When conducting the document analysis, you need to evaluate several distinct factors:

✔ **Size:** Documents of a very large or small nature need to be accounted for during the analysis. Most scanning equipment can process standard-size paper dimensions such as letter, legal, and executive. However, larger-dimension paper may have to be imaged by using a large-format scanner. Smaller documents such as receipts sometimes don't feed well through a scanner and may have to be taped to a blank letter-size piece of paper.

✔ **Paper characteristics:** During the analysis, you need to identify any documents with unusual thickness issues. Paper thickness can impact scanning equipment. Most document capture software and scanners (not multifunctional devices) have document-thickness control settings. This allows you to program the software to accommodate variations in document thickness to prevent the triggering of the scanner's double-feed detection sensors.

✔ **Print characteristics:** Faint print may not be captured by the imaging software. In some cases, you may be required to produce a darkened copy of the document, which is scanned in lieu of the original document. In addition, the capture software may drop out certain color ink. The software will have to be configured to prevent the dropout of ink.

✔ **Raised seals:** Some documents may contain raised seals or watermarks. After being imaged, a document will reflect the seal and its verbiage, but will not be raised. The department needs to determine, based on the type of document and how it's used, whether *not* having a raised seal will create an operational or legal issue.

✔ **Automated recognition:** Documents should be evaluated to determine whether the document text and format will be conducive to automated recognition such as OCR, bar codes, and Optical Mark Recognition (OMR), or whether automated recognition will not be possible. Documents with a small font, minimal spacing between fields, or certain colors such as red or blue may prevent effective recognition. During the analysis, you need to document the font size and other characteristics to select the best automated recognition settings in the capture software.

End of the beginning

The next step in gathering requirements is deciding on what values to use to index a document. This means looking into the future to determine how the information needs to be retrieved rather than how it needs to be filed in a document or content management system. It's common for a department to want to assign numerous index values to a document to allow every conceivable retrieval scenario. However, this approach should be discouraged. Assigning too many index values results in a significant amount of time spent by the department or the centralized imaging operation applying indexes that may not be used. Departments should be encouraged to assign a minimal number of values (one to three) needed to retrieve their documents. If a valid need exists for more index values, you should determine whether autopopulating the additional attributes from an enterprise resource system, such as a human resource or financial system, is possible.

Calculating the Return on Investment (ROI)

Whether you decide to image your documents in-house or to outsource the process, it's recommended that you develop a method for calculating your *return on investment (ROI)*. Most organizational initiatives require an investment of either money, effort, or both — document imaging is no exception.

Determining the ROI can help you decide whether you need to perform imaging in-house or send your documents to a vendor for processing. In addition, it can assist in determining whether a department is a good candidate for document imaging. The following sections provide tips and tools you will need to make your decisions.

Investing in the benefits

Calculating the imaging ROI involves two basic components:

- ✔ **Investment:** The investment in document imaging depends on whether you image in-house or outsource the process. An in-house operation usually includes the hiring of additional staff, purchasing equipment, and buying software and maintenance, while outsourcing the process involves paying a vendor an agreed-upon amount of money for its services.

- ✔ **Benefits:** Document imaging can provide many benefits, such as reductions in physical storage space (file cabinets, paper archiving), process efficiencies, and improvements in customer service. To calculate the imaging ROI, you should apply a monetary value to the benefits.

The primary index used to determine the expense related to a document-imaging operation is *price per image*. Price per image refers to the cost of imaging each individual sheet of paper. Price per image is calculated by accounting for all or certain costs related to an imaging operation. Figure 9-6 shows what might go into such a calculation.

Item	Cost
Annual volume (pages)	6,500,000
Annual labor costs (including benefits)	324,000
Annual management costs (including benefits)	81,000
Scanner depreciation	16,800
Software depreciation	20,000
Computer depreciation	4,800
Equipment maintenance	16,000
Supplies	5,000
Cost per square foot	150
Total square footage	1,500
Total square footage expense	225,000
Total operational expense	692,600
Price per image	$0.11

Figure 9-6:
Calculating price per image.

Note: To determine the price per image, divide the total operational cost by the annual number of imaged pages.

Many outsource vendors can provide you with a price-per-image quote. You should use your internally generated price-per-image estimate as a comparison to determine whether it's more economical to do it yourself. *Note:* It's important to ensure that you are making an apples-to-apples comparison. You need to determine from the vendor how it derived and itemized its price-per-image costs and see whether you included the same expense factors.

Knowing your customer

If you take another look at Figure 9-6, you see that it shows a macro-view of the overall cost of an imaging operation and the resulting price per image. However, some organizations create a micro-view for determining the imaging expense and price per image related to providing imaging services for individual departments.

Whether your organization uses a departmental or centralized approach to scanning, the expense related to imaging will vary based on a department's needs. One department's documents may require more prepping, while another department's documents may require less prepping, but need more indexing. Figure 9-7 provides a micro-view of the expense and resulting price per image for scanning an individual department's documents.

Figure 9-7:
Price per
image
(micro-
view).

Daily volume - pages		2,000				
Daily volume - documents		500				
Hourly labor rate (Imaging Department)		$19.00				
Functions	Number	Minutes Required	Hours Required	Daily Labor Costs	Annual Labor Costs	Price per Image
Prepping (documents/minute)	30	17	0.28	$5	$1,372	
Scanning (pages/minute)	70	29	0.48	$9	$2,352	
Indexing (documents/minute)	4	125	2.08	$40	$10,292	
Quality control (documents/minute)	15	33	0.56	$11	$2,744	
Total		204	3.39	$64	$16,761	$0.03

Developing a departmental price per image requires an understanding of a department's imaging requirements. Based on the requirements, the Imaging department can estimate how many documents can be prepped and indexed per minute. Figure 9-7 indicates the amount of minutes and hours required to process the department's documents. This information can be used to determine the impact on available labor hours in the imaging department. The information allows management to decide whether additional staff needs to be hired. In addition, Figure 9-7 can be modified to include other document-imaging department overhead, such as square-footage cost, depreciation, and maintenance.

Valuating the benefits

Determining your total annual imaging costs and price per image is one-half of the ROI equation. Next, you should determine the value of the benefits that document imaging can provide the organization. The value of the benefits may come in the form of soft-dollar and hard-dollar cost savings. Soft-dollar savings may include items such as reductions in floor space needed for file cabinets and archive storage. Although the elimination of these items increases the square footage available for other uses, it's not a direct cost savings to the organization. However, hard-dollar savings result in the elimination of direct expenses such as labor, processing time, and offsite storage costs.

When evaluating an organization's or department's need for document imaging, you should determine the cost savings that it will realize from the process. This typically includes the following items:

✔ **Filing:** Document imaging eliminates the need to manually file, retrieve, and refile documents. Time studies should be performed to estimate how much time is spent on a daily or weekly basis related to these activities. After you determine how much time employees spend filing, multiply the time by the average labor rate to arrive at total annual filing cost. This results in an annual labor savings.

✔ **Efficiencies:** Imaging documents in conjunction with automated work-flow can significantly increase an organization's efficiencies by reducing processing time. Steps should be taken to document and valuate the reduction in processing time. The efficiencies gained result in a direct labor expense savings related to document imaging.

✔ **Storage:** Document imaging may eliminate the need to send paper documents to a vendor for storage. Most organizations retain source documents (paper documents) for a period of time after they are imaged in the event that a document needs to be rescanned. However, companies typically retain imaged source documents for a lesser period of time than they would if the information was not imaged. This may allow a company to retain the source documents onsite instead of sending them to a vendor for storage, resulting in a cost savings.

After you have calculated the savings related to document imaging, the savings should be compared to the cost of scanning to determine an anticipated return on investment. The organization may have a valid need to image documents that doesn't result in a monetary benefit. This includes imaging organizationally and operationally vital information so that it's protected in the event of a catastrophic event.

Evaluating Imaging Hardware and Software

Selecting the right hardware and software is critical in the success of your document-imaging operation. You find numerous manufacturers, software vendors, and resellers that sell their products and services. Before buying scanning equipment and software, you need to define your current needs and imaging objectives as well as forecast future needs.

Purchasing equipment and software that doesn't meet your needs may counter the document-imaging benefits you hope to attain. Therefore, it's important to understand your options. The following sections help you evaluate different types of scanners and imaging software to help you determine what best fits your needs.

Examining document scanners

Scanner manufacturers have evolved their products to accommodate many types of document imaging; from small to large formats, color, and throughput.

Although you have many models of scanners to choose from, you'll come across three primary scanners in use by most organizations:

- ✔ **Desktop (workgroup):** Desktop scanners are used for low-volume imaging — usually less than a 1,000 pages per day, depending on the model. Desktop scanners are typically used to support just a few employees' imaging needs. Most employees use desktop scanners to scan a few documents at a time. In some cases, multifunctional devices are used in lieu of desktop scanners. A quality desktop scanner can be purchased for approximately $400 to $600.

- ✔ **Departmental:** Departmental scanners are designed to support the imaging needs of a single department. Departmental scanners come in several models able to scan approximately 4,000 to 10,000 pages per day. Departmental scanners typically cost between $2,000 and $8,000.

- ✔ **Production:** Production scanners are mainly used in centralized imaging operations. They are able to scan tens of thousands of pages per day. One production scanner is normally able to support the imaging needs of multiple departments and operations. Depending on the model, production scanners usually cost between $18,000 and $30,000.

The rated speed of a document scanner is normally derived by imaging under optimal conditions. This means scanning one-sided (simplex), letter-size (8 ½" x 11"), portrait-oriented documents scanned at a lower resolution such as 200 dpi (dots per inch). If your organization has a need to scan documents that fall outside these parameters, you can expect to see a reduction in the number of rated pages that a scanner can process per minute.

While speed and cost are important factors in selecting a scanner, other equally important features should be taken into account:

- ✔ **Ease of use:** A document scanner should require minimal employee training. If the equipment is too complicated to use, it will reduce the efficiency of the document-imaging process and potentially increase scanning errors. Many vendors now offer one-touch buttons that are very convenient for desktop and departmental scanning. They allow users to easily select scanning functions such as OCR or scan to PDF, Microsoft Word, or Outlook, as well as to direct the imaged document to be sent to a specific file folder. One-touch functionality can significantly increase productivity.

- ✔ **Mechanics:** You should choose a document scanner that is equipped with features that prevent or minimize mechanical errors such as double feeds and jams. Without these capabilities, employees may spend a significant amount of time correcting problems and ensuring that all pages of a document were scanned. Most scanners are now equipped with multiple sensors that detect multifeeds and prevent jams.

✔ **Feeder trays:** Feeder trays are used for stacking documents that will be fed into the scanner. If you have a medium or high volume of documents that need to be imaged, you need to ensure that the feeder tray can hold hundreds of pages and can be adjusted for different document dimensions. If a feeder tray's capacity is too low, employees will spend more time placing documents in the tray, thus reducing their productivity. Front-loading feed trays are recommended in most cases because they are easier to load than side trays.

✔ **Maintenance:** Just like any mechanical device, scanners have to be maintained on a regular basis to ensure that you continue to produce high-quality images. Depending on the daily volume of paper you image, scanners need to be cleaned frequently due to the accumulation of paper dust. Paper dust can cause *noise,* or spots on your images. In addition to regular cleaning, *preventive maintenance (PM)* should be performed on high-volume scanners at least two to three times per year. A technician certified by the equipment manufacturer should perform preventive maintenance. Between PMs, you will need to replace the scanner *consumables* based on the manufacturer's recommendation. Consumables consist of parts such as tires and rollers. These are parts of the scanner that grab the pieces of paper and feed them through the scanner. The parts wear down over time and can cause double feeds and jams if they're not regularly replaced.

Consumables are expensive. Therefore, you should ensure that you select a scanner that uses quality consumables so that they don't have to be replaced as often.

The role of document-imaging software

Document scanners come bundled with software. Therefore, during the evaluation process, it's essential to assess both the scanner's capability as well as the software's capability. Document-imaging software is the brains behind the scanner and can provide functionality that makes the imaging process more accurate and efficient. When evaluating document-imaging software, you should look for the following features:

✔ **Recognition:** Scanning software should have automated recognition capabilities that can read bar codes and perform OCR on your documents.

✔ **Back-page detection:** You may have the need to scan duplex pages. This means pages that have print on both sides. Rather than having to scan these pages separately from one-sided pages or manually choosing a duplex setting on the scanner, the software should automatically detect the presence of print on the back side of a page.

✔ **Page order:** Sometimes it's necessary to reorder the pages in a document. The software should allow you to rearrange the page order after the document is scanned.

✔ **Deskew/despeckle:** *Deskew* software functionality allows you to straighten the orientation of an image that may be slightly skewed or crooked. *Despeckling* allows you to remove noise or spots from an image. These features provide better readability.

✔ **One-touch buttons:** Although this feature was reviewed in the preceding section, it's important to note that while a one-touch button may be on the scanner, it's the software the scanner uses that enables the functions.

Although all document scanners come bundled with software, in many cases, production imaging departments purchase software with advanced capabilities that allow profiles (*batch classes*) to be created for different document types or imaging jobs. Prior to imaging a batch of documents, the scan specialist will select the corresponding batch class that instructs the software on how to process the information. This may include performing OCR, autopopulation, and scanning of the back side of the documents.

Equipment manufacturers and their resellers understand that purchasing scanning equipment and software can be a significant investment. In many cases, they will allow you to test their products in your environment. This will allow you to thoroughly evaluate the equipment and software and compare different models before making a purchase.

Chapter 10

Software Applications

In This Chapter
▶ Examining software
▶ Seeing what you actually need
▶ Checking out potential vendors
▶ Implementing guidelines

*T*he sheer volume of information that companies have to deal with, in combination with legal requirements and regulatory compliance, has made the task of records and information management a daunting challenge. In today's business environment, attempting to manage information without the help of technology makes the task even more difficult.

This chapter provides a comprehensive approach to assessing your need for software, as well as clues you in on how to evaluate vendors and their applications. (For good measure, I throw in some tips for a successful implementation.) Using software to manage your records and information will create efficiencies and help ensure that you are in compliance with laws and regulations by automating policies and many existing manual processes.

Examining Software Options

In the following sections, I first examine the fundamentals of Records and Information Management software so that you understand the differences between the applications and the functionality they provide. Later in this chapter, I analyze the process for documenting your software requirements. Although technology shouldn't dictate your requirements, it's a good idea to understand what the software applications are capable of doing.

During the past 15 years, companies have experienced the impact of significant growth in information as well as laws and regulations. The growth in these areas and the resulting organizational needs that such growth has created haven't gone unnoticed by software vendors. It only takes a single Internet search to see how many vendors are in the business of providing Records and Information Management software.

Numerous software applications are designed to meet specific records and information management needs. It's important to be able to differentiate between the different systems and their capabilities. Some software provides comprehensive records and information management functionality, while other applications only address certain areas.

Laying the software foundation

As you work your way toward understanding how software can help manage your records and information, it's important to understand two primary classifications of software functionality:

- ✔ **Document management:** Sometimes the term *Document Management software* is used synonymously with *Records Management software.* Although they complement each other, a distinct difference exists. Document Management software provides functionality that helps manage document storage, retrieval, processing, and collaboration, but does not provide any records management functionality.

- ✔ **Records management:** Records Management software provides functionality that's focused on compliance-related issues, such as information holds, retention monitoring, and disposition (the "managing" part of records management, as it were).

For many years, Document Management and Records Management applications were provided as two separate software packages. However, over the past decade, they have joined forces. Vendors and clients realized that the functionality offered by each type of system could significantly enhance the other. Admittedly, a limited number of reputable vendors still provide separate Document and Records Management software applications, but most organizations are making the choice to purchase and implement comprehensive solutions.

Many vendors now offer companies options for acquiring and using software. The more readily available options can be summarized as follows:

- ✔ **Premises-based:** This option refers to the client purchasing the software and using its data center (its *premises*) and equipment to run the application.

- ✔ **Hosted:** In a hosted environment, the client purchases the software, but the vendor operates the software in its (the vendor's) data center.

- ✔ **Subscription and hosted:** Some software vendors allow companies to subscribe or "rent" their software. The software is then operated in the vendor's data center.

Types of software

Several types of software are used to manage records and information. The following list of software categories are used in many medium- and large-sized organizations:

- ✔ **Records management (paper and electronic):** This type of software focuses on the classification, storage, retrieval, and disposition (permanent archiving, destruction, and deletion) of organizational records.

- ✔ **Document management:** Document Management software is designed to manage the classification, storage, and retrieval of company information. This includes records and nonrecord content. Document Management software by itself doesn't provide records management functionality.

- ✔ **eDiscovery:** This type of software has comprehensive search tools and the ability to isolate information relevant or potentially relevant to a lawsuit.

- ✔ **Enterprise content management (ECM):** Enterprise Content Management applications provide comprehensive records and information management functionality designed to support certain organizational operations or the entire company.

Small businesses may not have a need for (or are unable to afford) these types of commercial applications, but would still like to have a way to use software to help manage their records and information. In this case, software such as Microsoft Excel (for spreadsheets) and Microsoft Access (for databases) can provide functionality that allows businesses to manage small volumes of records and information.

Records Management software used to be segregated and provided as two distinct applications — physical and electronic. For many years, managing paper records was the most pressing issue that organizations faced. With the rapid growth of electronic information came the need to purchase and implement an electronic records management system. Based on these needs, vendors began creating one software tool that allows companies to manage both physical and electronic records.

Records Management software

Records Management software functionality focuses primarily on compliance-related matters such as information holds, retention monitoring, and disposition, rather than on features found in Document Management applications. The following list highlights the functionality common to most Records Management software:

- ✔ **Classification:** Records Management software applications provide users with the ability to apply classifications to records. This involves assigning a categorization or code to different record types.

- ✔ **Security:** To ensure that records are protected from unauthorized use, the software provides security settings at an individual user or departmental level. This allows only authorized employees to search and request boxes of records or files.

- ✔ **Box storage (physical):** The software provides users who have onsite storage areas or facilities used for boxed record storage to configure their shelving units (including bar-coded locations) in the system. The software accounts for your boxed record inventory, allowing you to track its location and movement throughout the organization. Tracking functionality can be used for records stored on-site as well as with an offsite storage vendor.

- ✔ **File management:** Records Management software applications provide the ability to account for records at the file level, including files located in cabinets, boxes, or (electronically) in the application repository. Typically, the systems will create a parent-child (hierarchical) relationship between boxed records and the files they contain. This allows you to search the system and request a specific file located in a box.

- ✔ **Search/request (physical):** The software creates an inventory of all boxes of records and files accounted for in the system. This allows users to search their inventory based on their security and privilege settings and submit retrieval requests.

- ✔ **Check-out/check-in (physical):** Records Management software applications provide the ability to check boxes and files out to requestors and check them back in to a storage location after the requestor is finished reviewing or processing the information. The system uses bar-code technology and optional hand-held bar-code readers to scan the boxes and files when they are delivered to the requestor and when they are sent back to storage. In each case, the scanned information is uploaded into the software application so that the location of boxes or files can always be determined.

✔ **Record holds:** The software enables Information Hold orders to be placed on records and files. This prevents the items from appearing on Destruction Eligibility reports produced automatically by the application. In addition, most systems have the ability to assign specific Hold Order titles to related groups of records that are placed on hold for the same lawsuit or investigation.

✔ **Audit controls:** This feature lets organizations track and report on data and setting changes, including information about who made changes and when they occurred. For example, if a classification is assigned a new retention period, the system will record what the previous retention was, what it was changed to, who made the change, and when it was changed.

✔ **Retention management:** When a classification is created in the system, it's assigned a corresponding retention period. For example, you create a classification of "Invoice" and assign it a seven-year retention period. When a box of invoice records or an invoice file or document is entered into the application, the Invoice classification is applied and the date ranges of the information are entered. After this occurs, the software will begin the process of automatically monitoring the retention of the records and will generate a notification when the information is eligible to be destroyed or deleted.

Document Management software

The lines between Records Management and Document Management software systems are often blurred. Each type of application possesses some of the same capabilities as the other, but also has some distinct differences. The objective of a Document Management application is to make it easier to find electronic information, while the objective of a Records Management system is to apply records management principles to the content.

Both systems allow you to store, classify, search, and retrieve documents. However, a Document Management system provides additional features that enhance the overall management process:

✔ **Annotations:** This feature allows you to attach electronic notes and watermarks to documents. The annotation is an overlay of metadata that becomes connected to a document, but doesn't alter the document. Annotations can be helpful in providing additional information about a document.

✔ **Redactions:** A redaction involves the blacking-out of sensitive information on a document. The redaction is an overlay that doesn't alter the underlying document in any fundamental way.

✔ **Keywords:** This feature provides the ability to assign multiple key-words (indexes) to a document type for efficient retrieval. For example, if you are attempting to locate an employee file, you don't want to look through every active and inactive file. By using keywords, you can assign the employee ID, name, and date of hire to the document. Subsequently, if you need to locate the document, you can enter the key-word information, which will retrieve the specific file you need.

✔ **Full-text searching:** Full-text searching provides additional search capa-bility beyond the use of keywords. This feature allows you to search for specific words and phrases in the body of a document. Full-text searching is commonly used in Legal departments for contract reviews and disputes.

✔ **Workflow:** Workflow software allows an organization to programmati-cally automate existing manual processes. Workflow is a feature that can significantly enhance organizational efficiency. Through the use of business rules and preconfigured software functions, workflow allows you to automate processes that are currently performed manually. For example, in most organizations, invoice routing and processing may involve several manual steps. By implementing workflow, the invoice can be imaged and then automatically attached to the purchase order that was previously imaged along with the packing slip. The scanned packet of information is then sent through the workflow to an invoice processor. If the invoice is over a certain dollar limit, it can route to a second approver and then be automatically sent for payment.

✔ **Software integration:** This feature gives companies the ability to integrate Document Management software with other organizational applications. For example, if you are in your Financial or Accounting system and you're reviewing a vendor payment dispute, you can access an image of the invoice, which resides in the Document Management system, without leaving the financial application.

✔ **Version control:** Document Management systems allow you to create and track document revisions. This feature allows a document to be checked out by an employee, revised, and then checked back in. During the time the document is checked out, other employees can view it, but it can't be modified until it is checked in. The software tracks the revisions made to a document so that employees know whether they're viewing the most updated version.

✔ **Access:** Vendors provide two primary methods for accessing their appli-cation: thick client and thin client. A thick client approach requires that each computer used to access the system must have files loaded on it. The process of distributing the files to each computer can take a signifi-cant amount of time and IT effort unless an organization has the ability to programmatically distribute the files.

Most companies prefer thin clients. A thin client allows you to access an application through the organization's intranet, eliminating the need to load files on each computer. In addition to thick and thin clients, more vendors are now offering cloud-based solutions. Cloud applications are hosted on the vendor's network and allow organizations to access applications via the Internet. This eliminates the need for companies to purchase and maintain servers needed to support the vendor applications.

Some Document Management systems are designed for small businesses and departmental use, while other applications are developed for use throughout an organization. You find more on these types of applications in the section "Enterprise Content Management software," later in this chapter.

Discovering eDiscovery software

Traditionally, medium- to large-sized organizations have outsourced eDiscovery to vendors or outside law firms that specialize in the process. However, in recent years, companies have made a push to bring eDiscovery back in-house. In the United States, the move is primarily due to the 2006 changes in the Federal Rules of Civil Procedures (FRCP).

The changes to the FRCP focused on electronically stored information (ESI) and how it is to be handled during eDiscovery. Whereas for years organizations viewed eDiscovery as a one-off or individual event based on the nature of a lawsuit, the changes to FRCP brought structure to the process. Organizations now treat eDiscovery as a routine event that has repeatable procedures. This has led to companies bringing eDiscovery back in-house and purchasing software to manage the process and control costs.

eDiscovery software is a niche application. It doesn't provide standard Document Management or Records Management functionality, but it is equipped with features that provide significant eDiscovery benefits, including the ability to search comprehensively, isolate potentially relevant information so that it's not modified or deleted, and *cull* unneeded content such as duplicates and information outside certain date ranges.

Enterprise Content Management software

Enterprise Content Management (ECM) software supports the overall ECM concept of bringing people, processes, and technologies together to capture, manage, store, preserve, and deliver information throughout a company. Enterprise Content Management software can provide organizations with extensive web, collaborative, records management, and document management functionality.

Enterprise Content Management systems use two approaches for managing unstructured content residing in multiple repositories, such as Microsoft SharePoint, e-mail servers, and Records and Document Management systems:

- **In-place:** Managing content *in-place* means that information can be managed by the ECM application while residing in other software repositories or locations. For example, a document that currently resides in Microsoft SharePoint can be declared a record in the ECM system through software integration. The document can continue to reside in SharePoint while the ECM system monitors its retention.

- **Centralized:** In a centralized environment, content that's declared a record or content that needs to be managed by the ECM system must be moved to the ECM software repository. After the information is transferred from the source repository, the ECM system creates a *pointer* to the information for use by the source application. A pointer gives employees the ability to continue to access the content from the source repository although the content is in the ECM system.

Most ECM applications are module based. Modules are *add-ons* or *plug-ins* that provide additional functionality. In some cases, the software comes *out of the box* with basic capabilities such as content storage and retrieval. The module-based approach can be beneficial for companies that want to pay for only what they currently need with the option to add additional functionality in the future.

Traditionally, ECM systems have required a significant amount of IT support. This includes software deployment, administration, and modification. For many organizations, it's difficult to allocate the IT resources needed to implement (and provide ongoing support for) an ECM system. Some vendors recognize this issue and have begun to introduce software that decreases an organization's reliance upon IT to administer and support ECM applications. These ECM systems use a *point-and-click* configuration approach.

Point-and-click configuration allows non-IT employees, knowledgeable in the system's operation, to administer the majority of the application's functions. Traditional ECM systems require a significant amount of IT programming to configure an application for initial and ongoing use. Point-and-click configuration systems have the necessary programming already embedded in the application, which significantly reduces the need for IT programming.

Most organizations don't have a problem creating content; they have a problem subsequently finding information and sharing it. A key feature of ECM software is enterprise search. Internet search engines such as Bing, Google, and Yahoo! locate content from millions of websites based on your search criteria. Enterprise search works in a similar fashion. Enterprise Content

Management systems have the ability to search for relevant content that resides in multiple organizational repositories as well as on external websites. Content Management systems perform enterprise searches by integrating with other organizational applications.

An additional benefit of system integration is the ability to *deduplicate* data. Deduplication is the process of identifying duplicate or *near-duplicate* content located in the same repository or multiple repositories. Deduplication is performed by using a *crawler* — a program that runs through the company's unstructured repositories, identifying duplicate and potentially duplicate information. The program uses algorithms that analyze content metadata. For example, if you send an e-mail with an attachment to ten employees within the organization, the deduplication crawler will identify the duplicate copies and only store one instance of the e-mail message and attachment. This process reduces the amount of information that must be stored, backed up, and collected during eDiscovery.

Enterprise Content Management systems can provide needed organization and structure to unstructured data such as Microsoft Excel spreadsheets, Word documents, PDF files, and scanned images. In most organizations, this content resides in folders on hard drives or shared network drives. The folders and files are often unorganized and named in a manner that doesn't support searching and retrieving. In addition, you're unable to apply retention rules to content stored on drives. These issues can significantly increase organizational risks and reduce operational efficiency.

Enterprise Content Management systems can be used in lieu of hard drives and shared network drives for storing files. This approach allows you to establish and assign keywords (index values) and retention periods to spreadsheets, documents, and other unstructured content.

Assessing Your Needs

Records, Document, and Enterprise Content Management systems can provide many benefits to companies. Numerous software vendors and options are available. The costs range from several thousand to millions of dollars. The issue is determining what software package is right for your organization.

Without the proper planning, you run the risk of selecting an application that doesn't meet your records and information management needs or long-term objectives. The following sections focus on how to identify and document your current and forecasted needs and requirements in an effort to ultimately select a software system that will make your organization more compliant and efficient.

Calculating the return on investment (ROI)

The requirements analysis can help you determine your *return on investment (ROI)*. Due to the significant investment of money and time related to the implementation of a Records, Document, or Enterprise Content Management system, senior management may require you to calculate and document the initiative's ROI.

Calculating the ROI for these types of software applications has historically been difficult. For example, Records Management software systems typically don't reduce costs or improve the efficiencies of routine operational processes, but focus on improving compliance to laws and regulations. Attempting to calculate cost savings related to compliance is at best an educated guess. However, Document and Enterprise Content Management applications can help organizations realize significant monetary savings. Some areas where a company's bottom line could be improved include the following:

- ✔ **Process automation:** Using imaging and workflow to automate manual processes can produce significant savings through the reduction in labor costs.

- ✔ **Reduction in copying and faxing:** Document Management and ECM applications improve an organization's access to information, reducing labor and paper costs involved with printing and physically distributing documents to recipients. The ability to electronically route information can eliminate the need to fax documents, which can reduce equipment needs and costs.

- ✔ **Improved search and retrieval:** Through the use of Document Management and ECM applications, you reduce the instances of lost or misfiled information, reducing the labor costs involved with searching for content.

A number of so-called "soft-dollar" benefits are derived from these types of applications, but they are more difficult to quantify. They may include enhanced decision-making, customer service, and compliance. Even if you are unable to determine their value, they should be mentioned in the ROI document.

Many vendors recognize the issues faced by organizations that are attempting to calculate the ROI related to the purchase of Records, Document, and Enterprise Content Management systems. Some vendors offer ROI calculators to assist in the process. Before relying on a vendor ROI calculator, ensure that you understand the formulas, calculations, and assumptions that it is using.

You should avoid using a calculator whose output can't be substantiated or isn't an accurate reflection of your organization's operations.

Identifying your "pain points"

In most cases, when an organization reaches a position where it is considering the purchase of software to manage its records and information, it's because the company is attempting to address *pain points*. Pain points in this case are specific records and information management issues. Common issues organizations face include

- ✔ Too much paper
- ✔ Lost documents
- ✔ Compliance concerns
- ✔ Multiplying document versions
- ✔ Inefficient processes

Before purchasing software to help manage your records and information, it's critical that you identify your organization's specific pain points. The process of identifying and documenting your current and anticipated issues is vital in helping you evaluate a vendor's software features.

Conducting a requirements analysis

The *requirements analysis* lays the foundation for documenting your records and information needs. The analysis is comprised of two parts — *operational* and *technical*. The operational analysis addresses specific business issues such as compliance and processes, while the technical analysis addresses attributes that software must possess to be supported in the company's IT infrastructure.

Records, Document, and Enterprise Content Management systems can impact an entire organization. Therefore, the planning and requirements gathering process shouldn't be conducted in a vacuum. Producing an accurate and comprehensive requirements analysis will take a group effort. The analysis process should include input from operational areas as well as the Legal, Compliance, Records Management, and IT departments, with a focus on the end-user experience.

The requirements analysis involves several sequential steps. Following this process helps to ensure that you address all areas relevant to the success of the initiative.

1. **Justification:** This step involves documenting the business case for software. During this phase, you should calculate a preliminary return on investment, or ROI. (Keep in mind that the ROI can be modified as additional information is gathered in subsequent steps.)

2. **Committee:** To ensure that the requirements you document are accurate and comprehensive, it's recommended that a committee or group representing relevant stakeholders be established.

3. **Requirements gathering:** This step involves meeting with different operational areas to determine their current and anticipated pain points as well as the nature of their content and how it's used.

4. **Business-use cases:** After operational requirements have been gathered, you should develop business-use cases in conjunction with the committee. Business-use cases are operational scenarios that are used to test vendor applications. In addition, the committee should develop a testing document that is to be used to indicate the results of testing each vendor's system against the business-use cases. *Note:* More information is provided on business-use cases later in this chapter.

5. **Initial research:** After the business-use cases and testing document have been developed, you should begin conducting vendor research to develop a list of prospective vendors. You can research vendors and their applications by using the Internet, colleague recommendations, and research reports from firms such as Forrester and Gartner. It's recommended that you limit your list to three or four prospective vendors.

6. **RFI/RFP:** After you have compiled a list of prospective vendors, you should submit a request for information (RFI) or request for proposal (RFP) to each vendor. The RFI instructs a vendor to provide information about his company and applications. The RFP provides the vendor with your requirements and asks the vendor to submit a proposal indicating specifically how his applications will meet your requirements and resolve your pain points. *Note:* You should enter into a nondisclosure agreement (NDA) with each vendor whom you supply with your requirements and information. The NDA helps to ensure that the vendor doesn't inappropriately divulge any of your organization's confidential information during or after the evaluation process.

7. **Vendor review and selection:** Upon return of the RFI or RFP from the vendor, it's time to begin the evaluation process, with the objective of selecting a vendor that best meets your organization's records and information management needs. The process usually involves narrowing the list of prospective vendors to one or two. The evaluation process may

include a request to the vendor to configure a test system within your organization. This approach is referred to as a proof of concept (POC). It allows the committee and end users to test the system within your own IT environment. In addition, a POC can be established for a cloud-based approach.

Evaluating Vendors

How you conduct the vendor evaluation process will have a significant impact on the success of the initiative. The organizational future of a Records and Information Management department hinges on how thorough applications are evaluated. The evaluation process can take several months to complete and require a significant investment of time.

Approaching the vendor evaluation with the appropriate tools and knowledge of business content and processes can help ensure that the correct application is selected. To provide you with what you need to know to make the evaluation process a success, I provide you with examples of business-use cases and a comprehensive test plan in the following sections.

Determining your evaluation approach

You can take two approaches when evaluating vendor applications:

- ✔ **Demos:** This approach involves reviewing and evaluating an application through demonstrations conducted by the vendor. This isn't an optimal approach because it doesn't allow you to evaluate the application at your own pace. It also doesn't let you use your own data or determine how the system will perform within your IT infrastructure.

- ✔ **Sandbox:** The term *sandbox* refers to having the vendor set up its application within your facility, running on your network. This approach is preferred. It provides all employees involved in the evaluation process with access to the application. A sandbox allows you to determine how the system will perform on your network and enables you to import your own data for testing. If your organization is interested in a cloud-based solution, you can have the vendor provide the evaluation team with access to the application. This approach gives the team the ability to evaluate the application's functionality, as well as to determine the performance of the vendor's cloud system.

Using business-use cases

Business-use cases are essential for evaluating vendor applications. They provide the testing road map that you need to assess system functionalities and capabilities (see Figure 10-1). Business-use cases are developed by determining current and anticipated organizational pain points and requirements. The best business-use cases cover a comprehensive range of items and issues.

Business Use Case Name	Audit Trails
Business Use Case ID	DM-1234
Desired Outcome	Reporting and online access to audit trail information. This includes, but is not limited to, system changes, change type, reason for change, initiator and date of change.
Summary	Audit trail functionality allows the organization to verify system and data modifications, who made them, when they were made and why. This information is important to show evidence of normal course of business transactions or potential issues.
Actors	Records management, compliance and information security departments.
Assumptions	No assumptions made in this business use case.
Functionality	**Access:** The system must provide audit trail information regarding who has accessed information, when the information was accessed, if the information was printed or distributed internally or externally via email, including recipients names and email addresses.
	Versioning: The system must be capable creating and retaining document version history. This includes who checked-out a document, when it was checked-out, creating a version control number and when the document was checked back in.
	Location: For physical records, the application must provide an audit trail of file and box-level record activity through the use of barcodes and scanners. The audit trail must provide details on who requested the information, when the request was made, when the requestor received the information, when the information was sent back and its current location.
	Security: The application must provide an audit trail of changes made to individual or group security profiles including the previous security settings, new security settings, who requested the change, who approved the change, who facilitated the change, when and why.
	Retention: The system must create and maintain a detailed audit trail of record and information retention period changes. This includes who requested the change, who approved the change, who facilitated the change, the reason for the change, previous retention period and when the change was made.

Figure 10-1:
Business-use case.

Detailing the results

The business-use cases should be used in conjunction with a detailed test plan. As illustrated in Figure 10-2, the test plan is used to document the results of your business-use case testing. The results of the test plan should be used to communicate your testing results to the vendor. One of the primary objectives of the test plan is to expose functionality gaps in the vendor's application.

Business Use Case ID	DM-1234
Business Use Case Name	Audit Trails
Expected Results	Provide comprehensive audit trails for access, security, data and retention modifications.
Tester 1 Name	John Doe
Pass/Fail/Partial	Pass
Actual Results	Application meets all business use case requirements for audit trails.
Comments	Application isn't intuitive. It's difficult to determine how to access audit trail information.
Tester 2 Name	Jane Doe
Pass/Fail/Partial	Partial
Actual Results	Application meets all business use case requirements except retention period modifications. The application doesn't retain information regarding the prior retention period assigned to record types.
Comments	Application isn't intuitive. It's difficult to determine how to access audit trail information.

Figure 10-2:
Test plan.

Functionality gaps may involve the complete inability of the application to meet a specific requirement, or it may be that the application partially meets a specific requirement. In either situation, the evaluation team should communicate the results to the vendor to allow the vendor to address what steps can be taken to resolve the gaps.

When testing an application's functionality, it's recommended that you use a primary and a secondary tester (two different employees). This helps ensure the thoroughness of the evaluation. For example, in Figure 10-2, the first tester passed the application's audit trail functionality, while tester 2 indicated that the system partially met the requirements of the business-use case.

It's not all about functionality

An application's functionality and features are important, but some equally important nonsoftware issues should be evaluated as well:

✔ **Vendor/reseller:** Prior to investing in a Records, Document, or Enterprise Content Management system, you should get to know the vendor. This includes understanding its stability. Over the past decade, numerous software vendor acquisitions have occurred. Although it's difficult to predict whether a vendor will be acquired, you can use business-reporting agencies such as Dun & Bradstreet to obtain information regarding a vendor's financial stability and strength.

It's important to know how long the vendor has been in operation and how many installations of its application are in use. You should obtain references for organizations currently using the application. When contacting references, ensure that you inquire about the vendor's performance as well as the application's performance.

In many cases, vendors use resellers to market, sell, and support their products. You should take the same approach to evaluating a reseller as you would if you were evaluating the vendor.

✔ **Support:** In addition to evaluating the functionality of an application, you should assess the vendor's ability to support the system after implementation. This includes the number, type, and experience of employees the vendor uses to support its application. You should obtain an understanding of its service response times and the support staff's ability to assist you with your additional programming needs. When you decide upon an application, it's recommended that you include Service Level Agreement (SLA) language in the contract that clearly states your expected response and resolution times to issues.

✔ **Cost:** In many cases, the cost of the software is just the tip of the proverbial iceberg. Depending on the size of your organization, licensing costs can significantly exceed the cost of the application. Therefore, it's essential to understand the vendor's licensing requirements and cost structure. Most software vendors offer two primary license types — named and concurrent. *Named* licenses are assigned to a specific user such as a system administrator, while *concurrent* licenses aren't assigned to specific employees but to any user with access to the system. For example, if you purchase 20 concurrent licenses, this allows 20 employees who are not specifically assigned to a license to access and use the system. In addition, some vendors require that you purchase additional license types for functionality such as workflow and software integration.

Maintenance is an additional cost you will incur with the acquisition of a Records, Document, or Enterprise Content Management system. This is an annual cost charged by the vendor or reseller. In most cases, it ranges from 15 to 20 percent of your total software and license costs. For example, if you purchase $150,000 in software and licenses, you can expect to pay approximately $27,000 in annual maintenance fees. It's recommended that you negotiate the annual maintenance percentage. It is common for vendors to offer discounts on their software. If this is the case, ask for your maintenance fees to be based on the discounted software price.

Professional services refers to the services offered by the vendor or reseller. This includes services for customizing its software, consulting, programming, and training. Professional services costs are high. They typically range from $1,000 to $2,000 per day. Therefore, it's important to understand the vendor or reseller's cost structure. You should negotiate and include the agreed-upon rate in your contract.

✔ **Scalability:** As your organization grows, it's important to select an application that can keep pace with your records and information management needs. *Scalability* refers to the software's ability to handle an increased workload without diminished performance. Over time, it's common for most organizations to increase the number of users of an application and add significant amounts of data that need to be managed. You should ensure that the application can appropriately handle the increase. *Load testing* or *stress testing* can be used to rate an application's performance under increased transactional and volume conditions. Some companies provide software specifically designed to load-test applications. It's recommended that you consult with your IT department to determine how to appropriately load-test an application.

Comparing the results

After you have evaluated each vendor's features and functionality, it's time to compare the results. Figure 10-3 provides a comparison grid that you can use to summarize the results and to serve as justification for your software selection.

Features	Weight (1-3)	Vendor 1 Rating (1-3)	Vendor 1 Score	Vendor 2 Rating (1-3)	Vendor 2 Score
Administration	3	1	3	2	6
Annotations	2	2	4	2	4
Audit trails	2	1	2	3	6
Cost	3	3	9	2	6
Deduplication	1	3	3	2	2
Deletion	3	1	3	1	3
Encryption	1	2	2	2	2
Federated searching	1	2	2	3	3
Information hold orders	3	3	9	3	9
Intuitiveness	2	1	2	2	4
Level of IT support required	3	2	6	3	9
Redaction	2	2	4	1	2
Reports	2	3	6	1	2
Retention	3	2	6	3	9
Scalability	3	2	6	3	9
Security	2	2	4	3	6
Software integration	2	2	4	2	4
Support	3	2	6	2	6
Versioning	3	1	3	3	9
Warehouse configuration	2	3	6	1	2
Watermarks	1	1	1	3	3
Vendor	3	2	6	2	6
Score			97		112

Figure 10-3: Vendor application comparison grid.

Guiding You through Implementation

Implementing a Records, Document, or Enterprise Content Management software system is challenging; the approach you take can determine the initiative's success or failure. The reality is that implementations of a smaller scope or of a localized nature statistically are more likely to be successful than larger implementations. For example, Records and Departmental Document Management applications have a higher success rate than that of

Enterprise Content Management systems because fewer employees or departments are involved and the scope is more focused.

Researching, planning, and managing expectations are the keys to a successful implementation. The following sections address each of these topics and provide you with tips for ensuring that your implementation succeeds.

Why implementations fail

I'll get the negative stuff out of the way first. Whether you're planning to implement a Records, Document, or Enterprise Content Management application, it's good to know why implementations of any of these applications typically fail:

- ✔ **Lagging adoption:** One of the most important factors that determines the success or failure of an implementation is user adoption. If the application doesn't provide a convenient end-user experience, employees won't use the system. Convenience is a relative term. Any new system will require employees to perform some aspects of their job differently; employees understand this. However, if employees perceive that the changes outweigh the benefits, they will be reluctant to adopt the system.

- ✔ **Big bang:** An additional factor at the root of implementation failure is the *big bang*. The big bang refers to a large-scale initial implementation. Implementing an application across multiple departments at one time can create significant operational problems if an unforeseen problem with the application occurs.

- ✔ **Overcustomization:** Overcustomization of an application can significantly delay implementation as well as future upgrades of the system.

- ✔ **Faulty evaluation and testing:** If the wrong business scenarios are evaluated and tested, this will result in the application not meeting the company's needs.

- ✔ **Lack of strategic thinking:** It's essential to ensure that the application be aligned with and be able to support the organization's strategies. For Records and Departmental Document Management system implementations, most organizations have a relatively clear understanding of how the systems will be used to support the business. However, most companies don't have a comprehensive vision or strategy for enterprise content management or how ECM software can support their objectives.

- ✔ **Budget shortfalls:** In this context, budget includes money and labor resources. Implementations that run over budget or require additional employee time and effort may cause senior management to rethink whether to proceed with the project.

How to ensure that your implementation is a success!

The following items are proven steps and guidelines that you should evaluate and incorporate to ensure that your implementation is a success:

- ✔ **Plan well.** Implementing applications of this type requires extensive planning and involves many different employees. It's essential to appoint a project manager and establish a project plan. This approach helps to ensure that the proper resources are allocated to the project and that the initiative stays on track.

- ✔ **Focus on adoption.** During the evaluation of an application, it's critical to consider the end-user experience. Employees should be involved in the evaluation and testing process to receive their feedback on how the system meets their needs and to incorporate modification or configuration changes to the software. However, if possible, you should avoid or minimize actual system customization.

- ✔ **Try a pilot program first.** A pilot involves implementing the system in one or two departments and evaluating its performance over a period of time. This approach allows you to quickly respond to any issues that occur and take immediate corrective action if needed.

- ✔ **Avoid customization.** You should avoid or minimize customization to the software. This approach can help expedite the implementation and make future software upgrades easier.

- ✔ **Do the right evaluation and testing.** It's important that appropriate business-use cases be used to evaluate and test an application. The evaluation team, as well as end users, should develop them to ensure that they are comprehensive and that they accurately reflect the proper business scenarios. In addition, end users should be involved in the evaluation and testing process. This provides two benefits: Employees understand their business functions, and they want a system that can meet their needs. In addition, this can improve the end-user adoption rate.

- ✔ **Strategize.** As part of the project process, the evaluation team should partner with senior management and other key stakeholders to understand and document the organization's near- and long-term initiatives and strategies to ensure how they impact the management of records and information. This can enable the evaluation team to select an application that best supports the company's efforts.

- ✔ **Budget correctly.** Properly evaluating and testing an application's functionality before implementation increase your ability to accurately forecast the implementation time frame and employee involvement. The evaluation team should work closely with senior management on the project and frequently communicate status updates.

✔ **Provide awareness and training.** During the evaluation and testing phases of the project, the evaluation team should begin the process of bringing awareness of the initiative to employees who will ultimately be using the application. This helps to gradually prepare employees for the upcoming change. As the implementation phase grows closer, the evaluation team should develop a training curriculum and schedule employee training sessions.

Part IV
Parking Spaces

The 5th Wave   By Rich Tennant

"We take security of records very seriously here."

In this part . . .

Out with the old and in with the new. It's time to get the old stuff out of the file cabinets and into storage. Part IV helps you with the process of sending records to storage — onsite or offsite — and looks at how you can develop storage requirements and evaluate offsite storage vendors. You also examine proper ways for destroying your records and information.

Chapter 11

Storage Locations

. . . .

In This Chapter

▶ Storing records onsite

▶ Understanding vendor services

▶ Establishing vendor offsite storage requirements

▶ Examining vendor contracts

. . . .

*O*ver time, organizations produce and receive a significant amount of paper documents. Most documents are subject to two phases — active and inactive. Active documents normally reside in file cabinets or in shelving units, allowing employees to readily access them. Active documents are needed for processing and inquiries related to recent transactions.

Inactive documents are not frequently accessed, but still may need to be retained based on the company's record retention schedule requirements. Inactive documents that still need to be retained are usually placed in boxes and sent to either on-site or offsite storage. This chapter addresses how to ensure that your records are protected and remain accessible during their inactive phase and provides tools to evaluate offsite storage vendors.

Storing Inactive Records Onsite

Some organizations with adequate space may make the decision to store their inactive records onsite. Prior to making this decision (or if your company already stores inactive records onsite), you should evaluate several factors to ensure that your records are being stored and accessed in an appropriate manner.

Just because records are stored within your own facility doesn't mean that they're properly stored. In the following sections, you find out what requirements and processes should be established for onsite records storage.

Protecting your inactive records

This section addresses how to create the proper environment for the long-term storage of inactive paper records — primarily records stored in record storage boxes. Organizations typically don't allocate prime office space for the storage of inactive boxed records. In many cases, records are stored wherever a company has available space, such as in utility rooms, basements, rental trailers, and other areas that may not provide a suitable record storage environment.

Improperly stored physical records are susceptible to damage from a variety of elements such as water, humidity, temperature, fire, and infestation. To minimize these risks, it's important for organizations to put measures in place to ensure the records' protection. The following requirements should be established for areas housing boxed records:

- **Smoke/fire (heat) detection:** The storage area should be equipped with the appropriate number (and type) of smoke- and heat-detection equipment. Your facility manager or engineer can serve as a resource for information on smoke- and heat-detection equipment and maintenance.

- **Fire suppression:** A *wet* sprinkler system should be installed in all areas housing records unless the temperature in a storage area could (potentially) not be high enough to prevent freezing (below 40 degrees Fahrenheit). If freezing temperatures inside the storage location are a possibility, a *dry* sprinkler system (where the pipes are filled with air rather than water to prevent the pipes from freezing) should be used. It's very important to ensure that nothing is stored in close proximity to a sprinkler head. If the sprinkler head is struck by an object it can become dislodged and cause water damage to the records.

- **Ventilation:** The storage area should be well ventilated to prevent the buildup of heat, which can negatively impact paper records. Excessive heat can decrease the stability of the chemicals in most paper, leading to fading of the print and deterioration of the paper. It is recommended that areas used for the long-term storage of paper not exceed 65 degrees Fahrenheit.

- **Adequate pest control:** Areas used for records storage should be regularly treated for pests and vermin. Pest such as termites and silverfish can quickly destroy boxes of records. Rat droppings can cause damage to records and create unsanitary conditions for employees.

- **Cleanliness:** Areas designated for record storage should be kept free of accumulations of dust and dirt. Employees should be prevented from eating or drinking in storage areas.

✔ **Proper shelving:** Records should be stored at least 3 inches off the floor. This helps to protect the records in the event of flooding. Preferably, sturdy shelving should be used to store boxes of records. Stacked boxes may become crushed and unstable over time, increasing the potential for employee injury and damaged records.

✔ **Adequate moisture control:** Excessive humidity may cause mold. It's recommended that the relative humidity in areas used for the long-term storage of paper records remain below 55 percent. If you store records in a basement, it's important to ensure that the area is not prone to excessive dampness or standing water. In addition, you should avoid storing records in areas with overhead plumbing. This increases the potential for water damage due to leaking pipes.

✔ **Proper boxes:** When storing inactive records in boxes, it's important to use boxes specifically designed for records storage. The boxes should be *low-lignin* and *acid free*. Over time, lignin and acid can degrade paper. (Lignin is a chemical compound derived from wood. When it breaks down, it turns paper brown.) Many vendors offer record storage boxes. The boxes should have a crush weight of at least 200 pounds. The appropriate crush weight can prevent or reduce box damage (especially at corners) from occurring. The preferred box size is 1.2 cubic feet. This allows better handling of the box and can reduce employee injuries related to lifting large box sizes.

Storing your inactive records in the proper environment helps to ensure the safety of employees who must access them. Storage areas should be equipped with adequate lighting, ladders, and stools to assist in record retrieval. In addition, you should ensure that aisles between shelving units are at least 30 inches wide to allow adequate employee movement, and ensure that boxes are not stacked more than three high and two deep to reduce employee injuries and ensure efficient retrieval.

Implementing access control procedures

In addition to ensuring that physical records are protected from environmental elements, it's important to establish proper access controls. In many cases, organizations store inactive records from multiple departments together based on available space. As an example, it's not uncommon for a business to store Facility Maintenance records alongside Human Resources or Customer Account records. While Facility Maintenance records may not contain any sensitive or confidential information, the latter record types do contain information of this nature.

Often organizations use a *self-service* approach for retrieving inactive records in storage areas. This means that numerous employees have access to a storage area and can retrieve, refile, or reshelve information as needed. This method increases the potential that unauthorized employees may access sensitive, confidential, and competitive information.

To eliminate or minimize the unauthorized access of inactive records, companies should implement security and access controls. The following is a list of topics to consider when securing inactive storage locations:

- ✔ **Access:** Access to inactive storage areas should be secured through a lock and key or security card access. Warehouse operations will often store inactive records on shelving in open areas. If this is the case, the area should be fenced in or walled off.

- ✔ **Employees:** Access to inactive storage areas should be granted to the minimum number of employees needed to retrieve, deliver, and refile or reshelve the records. Typically in this scenario, the employees may be assigned to a shared-services area such as Mail Services or the Records department.

- ✔ **Training:** Employees responsible for the security and operation of a storage area may have to handle sensitive information governed by legislation such as HIPAA (personal health information) and Gramm-Leach-Bliley (privacy). In this case, it's important for employees to be trained on the proper handling of this type of information.

- ✔ **Segregation:** If a company is unable to assign dedicated custodians to a record storage area, and needs to have departmental employees retrieve their records, sensitive information should be segregated and secured. This can occur by fencing off and locking a portion of the area.

- ✔ **Chain of custody:** *Chain of custody* refers to having a paper or electronic audit trail of who has had (or currently has) possession of specific records, files, or boxes of records. The audit trail allows you to keep track of your information. When inactive records are removed from storage, you should have a method for establishing chain of custody. Most Records or Enterprise Content Management systems provide this functionality. However, if you don't have access to this type of system, you can document the movement of records usingby using a simple Microsoft Access database form. (See Figure 11-1.) (The next section addresses the importance of using bar codes and shelving locations in an inactive records storage area.)

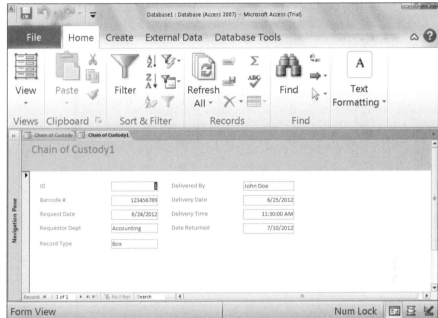

Figure 11-1: Chain-of-custody form.

Optimizing your inactive storage

Although inactive records shouldn't need to be frequently accessed, it's important that you can easily find them when they're needed. To assist in the retrieval and refiling or reshelving of inactive records, it's recommended that you use tools such as shelf and bar-code labels. Most Records and Enterprise Content Management software applications that have even bare-bones physical records functionality allow you to configure your storage area in the system. This means that you are able to create *locations* in the software that correspond to actual locations in your storage area. Before entering this information in the system, you should label each storage location in the area. For example, if your storage area is equipped with shelving, you should label each row of each shelving unit with a unique identifier, including a corresponding bar-code label if you plan to use a hand-held scanner to automate the process. (See Figure 11-2.)

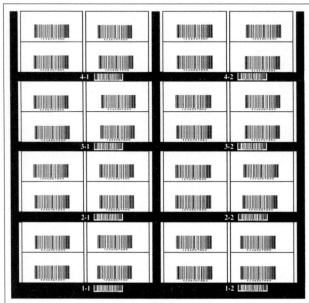

Figure 11-2:
Shelf
labeling.

If your organization doesn't have a Records Management application, you can still track where a box is located by labeling each row of each shelving unit along with placing (writing) a unique identifier, such as a department identifier, plus a number on each box. (See Figure 11-3.) This approach allows you to use a spreadsheet to identify and keep track of where a box is located on a shelving unit.

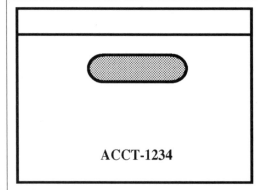

Figure 11-3:
Box
identifier.

ACCT-1234

Getting to Know the Record Storage Vendor

If you have more boxes of inactive records than space to store them, or if it will take too much money and effort to create the proper onsite storage environment, you should explore enlisting the help of a record storage vendor. Record storage vendors offer a variety of storage, transportation, and document management services. However, not all record storage vendors are created equally. It's important to get to know the vendor and its operation before allowing it to store your records.

In the following sections, you find out how to evaluate vendor fee structures, how to develop a requirements checklist, and how to negotiate a storage contract. Developing a proficient understanding of each of these areas provides the foundation for an effective partnership with a storage vendor.

Understanding the fee structure

A good starting point for determining whether to use a storage vendor is to understand what the storage is going to cost. Although I'm unable to tell you specifically what you'll be charged, I can provide you insight into how vendors structure their fees and what can impact your costs.

Record storage vendors provide numerous services, resulting in numerous fees. Often, organizations are not aware of all the cost components involved with storing their records with a vendor. The following is a list of services that most organizations will need (and will need to pay for) when they store their records with a vendor:

✔ **Receiving and entry:** This involves the vendor entering new boxes of records into its computer system. Most vendor fees are based on the cubic foot of a box — meaning that the price it quotes has to be multiplied by the cubic feet of the box. For example, most storage boxes are 1.2 cubic feet in volume.

Therefore, if the vendor quotes a receiving and entry price of $1.50 for a 1-cubic-foot box, the actual cost will be $1.80 (1.2 x $1.50). Additionally, the vendor will charge more if you want files in the box to be entered into its system (file indexing). Indexing files in a box creates a parent-child (hierarchical) relationship. This allows you to request either the entire box to be delivered back to you or just a file (or set of files) from the box.

✔ **Storage:** Vendors charge a monthly fee for the cubic feet of each box that you have in storage.

✔ **Retrieval:** This is a fee charged by the vendor when you request a box or file from storage. It relates to the vendor's labor cost for locating and retrieving a box or file from a shelving unit. (Most vendors charge a higher rate for retrieving a file from a box due to the increased time it takes to look for the file inside the box.)

✔ **Refile:** Like a retrieval fee, this is the cost you are assessed when you return a box or file to the vendor. It involves the labor cost for placing a box back onto a shelving unit. (Vendors typically charge more for refiling a file into a box.)

✔ **Handling:** When a vendor delivers boxes to your location, you are charged for each box the vendor unloads from its vehicle. In turn, when a vendor picks up boxes from your location, you are charged a handling fee for each box it places in its vehicle.

✔ **Transportation:** Vendors usually have a three-tiered price structure for delivering your records — next day, half-day, and rush. Next-day delivery is the most common and economical delivery method. Vendors may charge significantly more for half-day and rush delivery. In addition, a vendor may levy a fuel surcharge depending on the cost of fuel. This fee normally isn't based on the volume of a box.

✔ **Destruction:** Most record storage vendors offer secure destruction services (shredding). The vendor will charge you for each box of records you have it destroy (based on the volume of the box). The charge includes a fee for destruction plus a fee for retrieving the box from its shelving units.

✔ **Permanent withdrawal:** Commonly referred to by clients as *hostage fees,* permanent withdrawal refers to permanently withdrawing your boxes from the vendor prior to the expiration of the contract. Vendors claim that permanent withdrawal fees are necessary to cover the cost of removing client information from their systems, while clients feel, due to the high cost of the fee, that permanent withdrawal is used as a deterrent from moving their business to another vendor — thus earning the nickname hostage fees.

The price range for these services normally depends upon how many boxes of records you plan to store with the vendor. The majority of the costs an organization incurs are related to transactional services rather than monthly storage fees. For example, if you store 1,000 boxes of records with a vendor and your monthly storage fee is $0.30 per box, your monthly storage cost will be $360 (1,000 x 1.2 cubic feet x $0.30). However, if you request 50 boxes be delivered to you during the month and send back 20 of them during the same invoice period, your *estimated* costs will be closer to what you see in Figure 11-4.

Transactional Services	Volume	Estimated Cost per Cubic Ft.	Total
Retrieval	50	$2.50	$150.00
Handling	50	$1.50	$90.00
Transportation	-	$15.00	$15.00
Transportation	-	$15.00	$15.00
Handling	50	$1.50	$90.00
Refile	20	$2.50	$60.00
Total	90	°□	$420.00

Figure 11-4:
Transactional costs (estimated).

The moral to this story is to ensure that you only send *truly inactive* records to offsite storage in an effort to minimize the transactional costs.

Making sure that your requirements are met

Inactive records may consist of a significant amount of personal and confidential information, some of which potentially needs to be managed and retained in accordance with laws and regulations. Therefore, it's important that you select a storage vendor that can meet these requirements.

Before selecting a storage vendor, it's recommended that you tour its facility. Conducting an onsite review of the vendor's facility provides you with the opportunity to inspect the physical structure where your records will be stored, as well as to evaluate the vendor's security procedures. To assist you in completing a comprehensive review of the vendor's operations, you should develop an *off-site records storage requirements checklist*. A sample checklist is shown in Figure 11-5. The checklist should encompass the following areas:

✔ **Company information:** It's important that you familiarize yourself with a prospective vendor. You should determine its financial stability, how long it has been in business, and its expertise in records storage. In addition, you should request that the vendor provide references.

✔ **Location:** The vendor's location should be carefully evaluated. For example, records shouldn't be stored in areas prone to flooding. If possible, you should also avoid areas susceptible to other natural disasters such as tornadoes and earthquakes. Other factors to consider include whether the vendor's facility is in a known high-crime zone or near an airport. Many companies avoid locating critical operations near airports due to the potential for air disasters that could damage surrounding facilities.

✔ **Facility:** Storage facilities should be constructed in accordance with local zoning laws and fire ordinances. In addition, if the facility is located near a known earthquake zone, it's important to determine what additional structural precautions have been implemented. The facility should be equipped with an adequate smoke- and fire-detection and sprinkler system. The system should be tested on a regular basis. Some vendors are now incorporating shelving units that have a flue space that, in the case of a fire, would channel the flames away from the boxes.

- ✔ **Security:** You should ensure that the vendor has 24-hour monitored surveillance cameras in key areas of its facility. The property should be fenced in, and visitors should be identified before they are able to enter the property or facility. The vendor should have documented security procedures that are internally and externally audited at least twice per year.

- ✔ **Disaster preparedness:** The vendor should have documented disaster preparedness procedures that are tested at least semiannually. Determine whether the vendor has backup power such as a diesel generator.

- ✔ **Customer service:** It's important to ensure that the vendor can allow you 24/7 access to your records in the event of an emergency. The vendor should incorporate bar-code and tracking technologies. Many record storage invoices can be difficult to decipher. Therefore, you should ask to see a sample copy of its format.

- ✔ **Vehicles:** The vendor's vehicles should be well maintained and equipped with alarms, GPS systems, a fire extinguisher, and communication devices. Some vendors' vehicles will sound an alarm if the vehicle is left unsecured.

- ✔ **Policies:** The vendor should conduct extensive background checks and drug testing on each employee at least once every three years. Employees should also sign confidentiality agreements.

In addition to these requirements, you should assess the overall cleanliness and organization of the vendor's facility and property. These factors can be good indicators of how your records will be handled while in the vendor's possession.

Contracting with the vendor

After you have found a vendor that meets your off-site record storage requirements, it's time to think about the contract. Contracts impact many aspects of your offsite records storage experience. The first thing to remember is that *everything* is negotiable. However, your negotiating leverage will be based on the volume of records you plan to store with the vendor. The more volume you send the vendor's way, the more negotiating power you have.

		Poor	Fair	Average	Good	Excellent	N/A
Company							
1	Financial stability						
2	References						
3	Years in business						
Facility							
4	Is the area prone to flooding or other natural disasters.						
5	Does facility meet local construction standards including earthquake codes.						
6	Stand-alone or multi-tenant facility.						
7	Smoke/fire detection and suppression.						
Security							
8	24-hour monitored surveillance.						
9	Access control.						
10	Secure loading and unloading.						
11	Property is fenced.						
12	Security checks (multiple per day)						
Vehicles							
13	Well maintained.						
14	Security alarms.						
15	Communication device.						
16	GPS device.						
17	Fire extinguisher.						
18	Alarm activates if door left open.						
19	Climate controlled.						
Policies							
20	Employee background checks.						
21	Employee drug testing.						
22	Employees are HIPAA trained						
23	Employees sign confidentiality agreements.						

Figure 11-5:
Storage vendor requirements checklist (excerpt).

A vendor's price structure is based on volume and a tiered level of discounts. A small business that needs to store 50 boxes of records may pay $0.40 per box per month for storage, while a large company with 50,000 boxes may pay $0.25 per box per month (both are estimated costs). Transactional fees for services such as retrievals and refiles are also based on the same volume scale.

Although your attorney may review the legalese of the contract, you should ensure that you fully understand the operational aspects of the agreement and how it can impact you going forward. You should carefully review the following areas included in most vendor contracts:

✔ **Term:** The term refers to the contract period. Most record storage vendors would like you to sign a long-term contract such as five years. Many times, the vendor will provide discounted rates for a longer-term contract. However, if this is your first experience with a vendor, you should be wary of locking yourself into a contract for longer than three years. Although most contracts have an *exit clause* that allows you to terminate the relationship with written notice (usually 30 or 60 days), if operational issues are unable to be rectified, the vendor may levy charges such as permanent withdrawal fees against your account if you terminate the contract before the stated expiration date.

✔ **Pricing:** Although the contract provides rates for services (the so-called Schedule A — see the next bullet item), vendors typically include language in their contracts that allows them to increase your costs after the first year. If you agree to this approach, it's important for your attorney to add verbiage in the contract that specifies an increase ceiling such as "not to exceed 3 percent." In addition, you can require that the vendor base the increase on a specific price index.

✔ **Pricing schedule:** The pricing schedule, commonly referred to as *Schedule A,* provides the pricing for all the services that the vendor proposes to offer. It's important to ensure that the rates you previously agreed upon are reflected in the schedule. You should negotiate the removal of any permanent withdrawal fees or use a diminishing schedule approach. For example, if you enter into a three-year contract and terminate the contract in the first year, you agree to pay 100 percent of the stated permanent withdrawal fees. If the contract is terminated in year two or later, you agree to pay a lesser percentage.

✔ **Liability:** Most vendors will only compensate you a small amount ($1–$2 per box) if your records are destroyed while in their possession. In some cases, this is listed in the contract as *value of deposit* or *limitation of liability.* Usually, the vendor is not going to budge on such compensation fees — or, in budging, insists on a significantly higher rate for storage and transactional services. If this is the case, you may have to acquire third-party insurance to insure items of high value.

An additional item you may consider adding as an addendum to the contract is a Service Level Agreement (SLA). Although most record storage vendors will provide you with a document outlining their customer service commitment, it's not contractual. A Schedule A may reflect a set charge for next-day delivery, but it doesn't provide the customer any remedy if the vendor fails to deliver the records to you as stated. The SLA addendum can provide a remedy such as, for example, you will not be charged for any service failures on the part of the vendor.

Chapter 12

Compliant Destruction

· ·

· ·

*R*ecords and information should be retained in accordance with the organization's retention schedule and hold orders. However, when a record's (and information) retention period has expired, and it's no longer subject to any holds, it should be scheduled for destruction.

It's important to understand how to appropriately destroy information. Consumer and privacy laws now make the proper destruction of some information mandatory. In this chapter, I walk you through the various destruction methods for different types of information, help you determine whether you need to outsource your destruction, and show you how to develop an effective information destruction policy. Although I focus heavily in this chapter on the destruction of physical (paper) information, I also review the issues involving the deletion of electronic information.

Determining the Appropriate Destruction Method

Organizational information is diverse. It may consist of a lunch appointment reminder on a Post-it note stuck to your computer monitor to a terminated employee file relegated to inactive storage. The point is that most companies have a variety of record and information types, some of which is inconsequential, while others contain personal, confidential, and competitive information.

Understanding the different types of information you have is a starting point for determining the appropriate destruction method. In Chapter 1, I talk about three types of organizational information — records, business value, and nonvalue. Records serve as evidence of business transactions and legal obligations and status. Items of business value don't meet the criteria of a record, but contain useful operational or referential information, while nonvalue content is of a personal, nonbusiness nature. For destruction purposes, it's important to understand each category of information.

When eligible for destruction, records and information of business value should always be shredded and never placed in a trash can or recycle bin. The potential exists for this type of content to contain personal, confidential, and competitive information. Nonvalue information should be discarded in a recycle bin.

To ensure that information of a personal, confidential, and competitive nature doesn't fall into the wrong hands, some organizations have implemented a *shred-all* policy. This approach involves the shredding of all company information, regardless of category, when it's eligible for destruction. This takes the employee guesswork of whether items should be shredded or placed in a recycle bin out of the equation.

Deciding on Your Shredding Approach

Organizations use two approaches for shredding documents — in-house or outsource. Before deciding on a shredding method, you should carefully evaluate your options. Typically, the decision is based on the size of the organization and the volume of documents to be shredded. The following sections analyze each option to help you determine which approach best fits your needs.

Shredding your own documents

In-house shredding is most often performed by small businesses that have lower document volumes. However, some medium- to large-sized organizations have made the decision to shred in-house due to the nature of their information. This may include organizations that have highly sensitive information and don't want the information to be transported to a vendor for shredding or to have a third party involved in the destruction process.

If you decide to shred in-house, you need to evaluate several operational and logistics factors:

✔ **Equipment:** Depending on the amount of documents and the frequency of shredding, the investment in shredding equipment can be minimal or substantial. Most small businesses can get by with a few personal shredders at a minimal cost. However, medium to large businesses may have to purchase an industrial shredder (see Figure 12-1) that is more expensive, but capable of shredding significantly more volume.

✔ **Costs:** In addition to the cost of equipment, in-house shredding in medium to large organizations will result in additional labor and supply costs. In-house shredding usually requires dedicated employees to gather information to be shredded and perform the shred process, as well as additional equipment and supplies, such as personal or departmental shred bins that serve as collection points for documents that need to be shredded. Also, organizations that decide to use an industrial shredder for all their shredding needs should dedicate a secure area for the process. This can result in additional costs. If you require the use of an industrial shredder, it's important to know that they require regular maintenance, in many cases by a certified technician. You should factor in the maintenance costs of your shredding equipment.

✔ **Process:** Organizations should develop procedures for their in-house shred program and train each employee on the process. This helps to ensure that the program is appropriately followed. The organization should appoint a management employee to administer and monitor the program. In addition, a process should be developed that provides proof of destruction. Proof of destruction, commonly referred to as a *certificate of destruction,* allows an organization to prove that it is no longer in possession of specific information in the event of a lawsuit, audit, or regulatory investigation.

✔ **Information sensitivity:** In most medium to large organizations, in-house shredding requires employees not affiliated with the departments they're servicing to collect and shred documents. This approach means that the employees will have access to a broad range of information, some of which may be of a sensitive nature. Some organizations may determine this approach isn't acceptable or require the employees to sign *internal nondisclosure agreements.*

Figure 12-1:
Industrial
shredder.

Getting to know the shredders themselves

If you decide to shred your documents in-house, you should understand the different types of shredders and their capabilities. You want to ensure that the shredder you select shreds your documents in a manner that prevents them from being reconstructed. You find four primary types of shred cuts:

- ✔ **Strip-cut:** A *strip-cut* shredder slices your documents into strips. The problem is that it's feasible to reconstruct the strips into their original document format. Although strip-cut shredders normally shred documents faster with lower maintenance than other types of shredders, I nevertheless recommend that you avoid using a strip-cut shredder to destroy your documents for precisely that reason.

- ✔ **Cross-cut:** *Cross-cut* shredders (sometimes referred to as confetti shredders) provide more security by shredding documents vertically and horizontally. Cross-cut shredders are more expensive than strip-cut shredders.

- ✔ **Diamond-cut:** *Diamond-cut* shredders cut documents vertically and diagonally. After it is shredded, the paper is in small diamond-shaped pieces that are extremely difficult to reconstruct. Diamond-cut shredders are typically more expensive than strip- or cross-cut shredders.

- ✔ **Tear and crush:** Many industrial shredders have transitioned from cross-cut shredding to *tear and crush.* This approach punctures and tears the paper instead of cutting it. This leaves the paper fibers intact, making it easier to recycle. After the paper is torn, it's then crushed to compact it. This method provides a high level of security

For many years, personal, low-volume shredders only offered strip-cut shredding. Now they're available in cross- and diamond-cut. Industrial shredders mainly use cross-cut and tear and crush.

Shredder prices range from less than $100 for low-volume (100 sheets per day) to over $100,000 for high-volume shredding (hundreds of sheets at a time). Heavy-duty industrial shredders can be fitted with conveyor belts to feed the paper into the shredders and have balers so that the paper can be recycled.

When implementing an in-house shredding program, it's recommended that you shred your documents at a minimum on a weekly basis. Documents that need to be destroyed shouldn't be allowed to accumulate excessively. The longer you wait to shred your documents, the greater the potential is for them to be compromised. Therefore, prior to purchasing shred equipment, it's important to understand the volume of documents that need to be shredded and the frequency of your shredding needs. Personal shredders are available from most office supply retailers. The Internet is a good source of information for customer reviews of personal shredders. In most cases, if you plan to purchase an industrial shredder, you need to contact the manufacturer directly.

Outsourcing your shredding

Outsourcing your shredding is a recommended option for most medium and large organizations. Companies that decide to outsource shredding usually make their decision based on document volume and the hassles of having to create an internal process, as well as concerns about initial investment and ongoing costs. Many companies would rather leave the job of document destruction to vendors specifically trained and certified in the process.

Different approaches are available for outsourcing your document shredding. Some vendors provide on-site shredding in mobile shred vehicles, some pick up your documents and transport them to their facility for shredding, and others provide both services.

Vendor onsite shredding is a good option for organizations that want to retain some control over the destruction process. This approach allows a company to witness its documents being shredded rather than having its documents transported to the vendor's facility, where they are later shredded. Although this option does have benefits, it typically costs more than offsite shredding.

If you choose offsite shredding, the vendor will transport your documents in secured containers to its facility. Vendors normally ensure that your documents are shredded with 24 hours after they arrive at their location. This approach is more economical than onsite vendor shredding, but it does come with an increased risk associated with transporting your intact documents. In the following section, I show you how to evaluate shred vendors in an effort to minimize risks associated with the process.

Some vendors offer a hybrid approach. They have on-site mobile shred vehicles as well as the ability to shred your documents at their facility. This approach is beneficial if you have separate operations with sensitive information that you don't want to have transported, but don't want to pay the increased costs for onsite shredding at all your locations.

Selecting the Right Shred Vendor

Over the past decade, many laws have been passed and regulations created to protect consumer privacy. This has resulted in more vendors offering document-shredding services. Before selecting a shred vendor, you should do your homework to ensure that you select a reputable organization.

A resource you should use in searching for a shred vendor is the National Association for Information Destruction (NAID). NAID is an international trade association for companies providing information destruction services. Its mission is to promote the information destruction industry and the standards and ethics of its member companies (courtesy of the NAID website, `www.naidonline.org`).

NAID's website provides information on member vendors that provide document-shredding services. NAID offers a certification program to its member companies. The certification program involves NAID audits of the vendors' mobile and plant-based shredding operations. The goal of the certification is to set standards for a secure information destruction process. This includes operational security, employee hiring and screening, the destruction process, responsible disposal, and insurance. It's important to remember that a difference exists between a vendor that's a NAID *member* and one that's NAID *certified.* It's recommended that you select a certified provider.

How to ensure that electronic information is unrecoverable

Most organizations understand the need and proper process for destroying physical information. Items of a personal, confidential, and competitive nature should be shredded in a manner that reduces the potential for reconstruction. However, organizations are less knowledgeable about the proper destruction of electronic information. Deleting a file isn't adequate. With the proper technology and knowledge, deleted files can easily be recovered. Special methods must be used to ensure that electronic information is unrecoverable.

Some vendors now offer electronic information destruction services. The vendor will shred your hard drives and peripheral devices such as CDs, DVDs, and flash drives. This method ensures that the information is unable to be electronically recovered.

Another effective method for rendering electronic information unrecoverable is degaussing. Degaussing disrupts or demagnetizes magnetic storage found on hard drives, CDs, DVDs, and flash drives. This prevents the information from being recoverable. However, the effectiveness of degaussing depends on the type of media and degaussing equipment. For example, some hard drives have a higher magnetic field than others. Therefore, the degausser should possess enough strength to ensure that it thoroughly demagnetizes the media. Some electronic media types such as hard drives may not be able to be reused after degaussing has occurred.

Establishing your shredding requirements

Before selecting a shred vendor, it's important to define your business requirements. It isn't difficult to find a vendor to shred your documents. The challenge is finding a vendor that can meet all your operational and security needs. Following are important factors that you should evaluate during the requirements gathering process:

✔ **Locations:** If your organization has multiple operations in different geographical areas, you need to determine which locations will need to be serviced. After you identify the locations, you must determine whether the vendor can service the area. In some cases, vendors will subcontract shredding services if they are unable to serve a specific market. If the vendor informs you that it must subcontract services in certain areas, ask the vendor to provide you information about the subcontracted vendor so that you can determine whether it meets your operational and security requirements.

✔ **Frequency:** It's important to determine how frequently you will need to have your documents shredded. If your organization has multiple locations that need to be serviced, you should also determine their shredding frequencies. If your business or any of your operations are located in a rural or remote area, the vendor may only be able to service you every few weeks or when it has enough volume from several customers to offset its travel and labor expenses.

✔ **Costs:** You should estimate how much it's going to cost to have a vendor shred your documents. Vendors typically charge by the pound of paper they shred or by the number of bins they service, regardless of whether they shred on-site or at their facility. You should avoid pricing that is based on time. Some vendors will charge based on the time it takes to collect your documents and shred them. This approach contains too many subjective variables.

Costs per pound can vary depending on your volume — the higher the anticipated volume, the lower the rate per pound. A typical charge per pound may range from $0.05 for higher-volume customers to over $0.50 per pound for lower-volume and onsite shredding. If the vendor is basing its costs on the number of bins it services rather than weight, you can expect a minimum charge to service your location. For example, the vendor may assess a minimum charge of $30 to service your facility or charge $10.00 per bin. If you only use two shred bins, you are paying $15 per bin ($30/2 bins = $15 per bin). However, if you use five shred bins, you will automatically meet the minimum charge, resulting in a cost of $50 or $10 per shred bin ($50/5 shred bins = $10 per bin). You should ask the vendor for its shredding fee structure.

✔ **Security:** You should ensure that the shredding vendor meets the security needs of your organization. This includes how quickly the vendor shreds your documents after it picks them up from your facility. You should select a vendor that can shred documents within 24 hours of receipt. It's recommended that you select a NAID-certified vendor for your document destruction needs. The NAID certification involves audits of several security-related issues, such as facility security, employee background checks, and security procedures.

✔ **Shred bins:** Most shred vendors provide their clients with secure document destruction bins. The bins are equipped with locks that allow them to remain secure at your facility. They come in several sizes and models (see Figures 12-2 and 12-3). Figure 12-2 is a security console bin that is frequently used in an office environment, while Figure 12-3 shows a larger bin that can be used in an office or warehouse environment. It's important to determine what types and quantity of bins you'll need to adequately service your organization. For large organizations, it's recommended that you work with department representatives to develop a floor plan that indicates where each shred bin will be located. This is an important step. It helps to ensure that the appropriate number of bins are placed in strategic locations, making them convenient for employees to use.

✔ **Electronic media:** It's important to determine whether your organization will need electronic media destruction. Vendors can provide separate secure bins for plastics and electronic content. Electronic media such as DVDs, CDs, and flash drives shouldn't be placed in bins containing paper documents.

✔ **Certificate of destruction:** The vendor you select needs to be able to provide you with a *certificate of destruction.* Certificates of destruction provide evidence that the vendor destroyed the information. The certificate usually provides information such as the weight and date of destruction. It normally doesn't provide specific information about the documents' contents, but it can be helpful during a legal matter or regulatory inquiry to demonstrate that the organization destroys records and information on a regular schedule and in the normal course of business.

Figure 12-2:
Security
console
shred bin.

Figure 12-3:
Document
shred bin.

After you have determined and documented your shredding requirements, you should include them in a request for proposal (RFP) to each prospective vendor candidate. The vendor should specifically communicate how it will meet each of your requirements, including a price schedule. It's recommended that you tour the vendor's facility to observe its security practices and witness the shredding process.

Developing an Information Destruction Policy

A destruction policy is an essential part of a Records and Information Management program. It provides specific information on what must occur before content can be destroyed, and how it should be destroyed. The policy helps to establish that an organization destroys information in the *normal course of business* on a regularly schedule basis. This is important in the event that the courts or regulatory entities question your destruction practices.

In addition to legal benefits, a destruction policy also provides compliance benefits. It provides the guidance and framework for employees to understand how information should be destroyed and how sensitive information can be kept from being compromised. The following sections analyze what to include (and what not to include) in your policy.

If you can't do it, don't include it

Company policies are perceived as corporate gospel. What you state in a policy is often viewed by outside parties such as attorneys and regulatory bodies as fact, and adherence to the policy is assumed. Therefore, avoid including anything in a policy that can't be followed by employees. Moreover, operationally, including policy direction with no hope of adherence confuses and frustrates employees.

As you begin the process of considering what to include in your destruction policy, determine your organization's capabilities. Know what technologies you have and what is lacking. It's important to remember that company policies should be enforced and audited. You can't enforce what you can't do. Therefore, it's critical that the elements of your policy be supported by the organization's capabilities.

Elements of an effective destruction policy

An effective destruction policy should include elements that address what should take place prior, during, and after information has been destroyed. The policy should encompass the following items:

- ✔ **Purpose:** The purpose states the reason for (or the objective of) the policy. For example, "The purpose of this policy is to ensure that organizational information eligible to be destroyed is done so in the normal course of business on a regularly scheduled basis and in a manner that renders it unrecoverable."

- ✔ **Scope:** The scope refers to what the policy applies to. In this case, the scope covers the destruction of physical and electronic content that is eligible to be destroyed or deleted based on the organization's record retention schedules. In addition, the scope includes all parties responsible for adhering to the policy.

- ✔ **Approvals:** The policy should address who should approve the destruction of information. For example, the destruction of nonrecord information may only require departmental management approval, while the destruction of official company records may require several levels of approval, such as the department head, the records manager, and the designated representatives from the Legal and Tax departments.

- ✔ **Information hold orders:** It's important to include policy verbiage that addresses the requirement to retain content that is currently (or anticipated to be) part of a hold order, even if the retention period of the information has expired.

- ✔ **Destruction methods:** This section of the policy should address acceptable destruction methods for physical and electronic information.

- ✔ **Vendors:** The policy should instruct employees to only use information destruction vendors approved by the organization.

- ✔ **Destruction log:** Most organizations maintain documentation or a log of destroyed information. The log normally includes items such as the department, information type or box bar-code number, date of destruction, and who approved the destruction. The policy should state that a destruction log will be maintained and retained for a specified time frame.

- ✔ **Certificate of destruction.** The policy should address the requirement that a certificate of destruction be provided by vendors that destroy the organization's information.

Instead of creating a separate policy to address information destruction, some organizations include it as part of their overall records and information management policy. This approach reduces the number of individual policies that need to be distributed or made available to employees.

Part V
Creating a Plan

The 5th Wave   By Rich Tennant

"The new technology has really helped me keep my records organized. I keep my project reports under the PC, budgets under my laptop, and memos under my smart phone."

In this part . . .

Part V puts some structure around your Records and Information Management program in the form of policies, auditing, and training. This part provides insight into what should (and shouldn't) be included in your Records and Information Management policy, as well as profiling effective methods for training employees and for auditing the policy for compliance.

Chapter 13

Codifying the Policies

- -

- -

*A*n effective Records and Information Management policy is essential to the success of your program. Policies provide the operational framework that employees need to make proper decisions. Therefore, it's important to develop a Records and Information Management policy that not only encompasses key aspects of the program but also provides employees with the guidance they need to manage the life cycle of organizational content. In this chapter, you find out what a policy can do for you, what makes it effective, and how to increase policy compliance.

Developing a Records and Information Management Policy

If you've been tasked to help develop your company's policy — congratulations, you have a great opportunity to shape how your organization will manage its records and information. As you prepare for the process, it's a good idea to understand what makes a policy effective; the better the policy, the better the compliance. The following sections guide you through the objective of a policy, the basics needed for a good policy, and what not to include in your policy.

Understanding what a policy is (and isn't)

A good starting point in developing a Records and Information Management policy is to understand what a policy is — and isn't. A policy isn't a procedure. A policy instructs employees what to do; a procedure provides steps on how to do it. It's important as you draft a policy to provide direction, but not the steps to get there. However, as you draft your policy, it's recommended that you make notes of subject matter included in the policy that will require an associated procedure.

Some organizations refer to their retention schedule as their Retention policy or Records Management policy. It's important to understand that a retention schedule isn't a Records and Information Management policy; it's a tool, like your policy, that supports your overall Record and Information Management program.

The basic characteristics of a good policy

Policies are meant to be communicated and followed. A concise, clear policy has a better chance of being accurately followed than one that's open to employee interpretation. To create an effective policy, some basic guidelines should be followed:

- ✓ **Simple:** Employees need to be able to understand what you're trying to communicate. Avoid using overly formal wording, acronyms, and long sentences.

- ✓ **Concise:** A policy doesn't have to be long to be effective. Employees have core functions that they're responsible for performing each day. Many employees will not take the time to review a policy unless it's mandatory and the company has the ability to monitor participation. To improve your chances that employees will actually review the policy, keep it as brief as possible.

- ✓ **Relevant/specific:** The policy should address relevant issues and provide specific direction that will guide the employee's decision-making. Policies that aren't specific inevitably lead to inconsistent employee behavior. Inconsistency leads to reduced policy compliance and an increase in organizational risks.

- ✓ **Enforceable:** It's assumed that what's contained in a policy can and will be followed. Therefore, the policy shouldn't include any elements or directions that are impossible for employees to follow due to issues such as lack of technology, resources, or training.

Talking records and information

After you have an understanding of basic policy characteristics, it's time to determine what Records and Information Management topics to include in the policy. You should cover several important areas. The following is a list of specific areas that should be included in your Records and Information Management policy:

- ✔ **Purpose:** The purpose states the reason for (or the objective of) the policy. For example, "The purpose of this policy is to ensure the complete life cycle management of organizational information."

- ✔ **Scope:** The scope communicates what and who the policy applies to. For example, "This policy applies to all company employees and governs the management of physical and electronic information."

- ✔ **Glossary:** A policy often includes terminology that's unfamiliar to employees. It's recommended that the policy contain an appendix with definitions, or if you plan to post the policy on the company's intranet, you can create *hyperlinks* between the terms and their definitions. This eliminates the need for the employee to scroll to the glossary page to look for a definition.

- ✔ **Audits:** The policy should inform employees that all topics and matters contained within the policy should be complied with and are subject to internal and external audits.

- ✔ **Vital records:** It's recommended that the policy contain a section on the identification and protection of the organization's vital records. The policy may indicate that it's the responsibility of each department head to identify his or her vital records and work with the appropriate parties to ensure that the information is appropriately protected.

- ✔ **Retention schedule:** The policy should contain a section that specifically addresses the purpose of the retention schedule and the requirement that the schedule be followed. Additional information can be provided that informs employees that all modifications to the existing retention schedule must be authorized and specifies who to contact if they need to request a modification.

- ✔ **Information hold orders:** All employees should fully understand their responsibility regarding information hold orders. The policy should clearly state that any information on hold as part of an active or anticipated lawsuit, audit, or regulatory investigation should be retained, even if its retention period — according to the organization's records and information retention schedules — has expired.

- ✔ **Record storage:** The policy needs to state that organizational records should be stored with approved vendors only. In addition, the policy should inform employees that requirements exist for the onsite storage of records, and that said requirements can be accessed via a link or as a policy appendix.

✔ **Hard/shared network drives:** The policy should provide guidance on the use and maintenance of hard drives and shared network drives. One such rule could be as follows: "Hard drives (C: drives) are not to be used for the storage of company records or information of business value. These content types must be stored in a repository accessible by employees with appropriate authorization." The policy should instruct employees to regularly maintain files located on hard drives as well as on shared network drives.

✔ **E-mail:** How an organization manages e-mail is largely dependent upon available technology. When developing this section of the policy, you should determine what technological resources are available to employees. Some items often addressed in this section include prohibiting employees from forwarding company e-mail to their personal e-mail accounts and/or minimizing the distribution of attachments and retention of e-mails. Often the management of e-mail is addressed in two separate policies. The Records and Information Management policy addresses e-mail from a content management perspective, while Human Resources may issue an *e-mail usage policy* that instructs employees on the proper use of e-mail — the injunction not to send offensive or harassing messages, for example.

✔ **Information destruction:** The policy should include a section on information destruction. Topics here could include proper methods for the destruction of physical and electronic information, a stipulation that only those vendors preapproved by the organization be used, or an insistence that certificates of destruction be both received and maintained.

The items listed here are general Records Management topics that should be addressed in your policy. However, depending on your organization and the industry in which it operates, you may need to add additional items.

To develop an accurate and comprehensive policy, it's recommended that you consult with key departments that have a stake in the policy outcome such as the IT, Legal, Tax, and Compliance departments. Discussing the proposed subject matter with these areas can provide you with additional perspectives and ideas on how to make the policy more effective and ensure that you don't include items that are unenforceable. After creating your initial policy draft, you should distribute the policy to the stakeholder departments for their review, feedback, and approval.

Making the Policy Available

After your Records and Information Management policy has been documented and approved, it's time to put it into action. Depending on the size of your organization, it may be a challenge to ensure that employees are aware of its existence. However, creating awareness of the policy is only part of the equation; employees also need to read, understand, and follow it.

The following sections examine options for distributing the policy throughout your organization. Some options may be a better fit for your company than others, but one of them will likely meet your needs.

Distributing the hard copy

Distributing a paper copy of the Records and Information Management policy to each employee is the least recommended option. Like most organizational documents such as procedures and organizational charts, policies are periodically modified. When you distribute a hard copy of the policy, employees may place it in a file or a binder and refer to it as needed. When a modification is made and distributed to employees, they may not update their file or binder, which results in employees following an outdated policy.

However, this approach may be the only option for small businesses. Due to having fewer employees, smaller organizations are normally more effective at controlling the distribution of hard-copy documentation. If you must distribute the Records and Information Management policy in hard-copy format, you should attempt to collect the old policy from employees as you are handing out the updated version.

Attaching a soft copy

A soft copy is an electronic version of a document. So, if distributing a hard copy of the policy is not recommended, distributing a soft copy should be okay, right? Unfortunately, this approach is also not recommended. When you distribute the policy as a soft copy, such as an e-mail attachment, you face the same issues related to hard-copy distribution. Employees may save the policy and periodically refer to it. When changes are made to the policy, employees may still continue to use the old version. Compared to hard copies, it can be more difficult to ensure that previous soft-copy versions of the policy are not used due to the various repositories in which they can be stored.

Although distributing the policy as a soft copy or hard copy has drawbacks, soft-copy distribution offers some advantages over hard-copy distribution. The policy can be distributed efficiently as an e-mail attachment. This approach can help ensure that all employees receive a copy of the policy while reducing paper and printing costs. In addition, distributing the policy via e-mail allows you to provide additional comments regarding the policy and the need to review it. You can also require employees to respond to you via e-mail by a certain date, acknowledging their review of the policy. This allows you to save the responses as evidence of policy distribution and review.

The missing link

REMEMBER

The best approach for distributing the Records and Information Management policy is to have employees come to the policy instead of sending the policy to employees. You can accomplish this by using the company intranet. For example, you can send an e-mail to all employees notifying them that the policy has been posted to the intranet. The e-mail should contain a hyperlink that, when clicked, takes the employee to the policy posted on the intranet. An example is shown in Figure 13-1.

Additionally, you can create a Records and Information Management Department page on the intranet that allows you to post other related documents, such as the retention schedule, storage requirements, and request forms. This approach allows you to maintain the most current version of documents on the intranet, eliminating the need to manually distribute updates.

TIP

It's important to remember that employees may still be able to print documents such as the policy from the intranet. To help reduce printing of forms that are periodically updated, you can insert verbiage on the form instructing employees not to print them. In addition, you can include a sentence at the end of the policy that states, "Only current as of date printed."

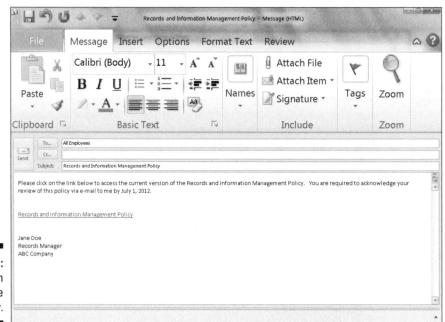

Figure 13-1:
E-mail with a link to the policy.

Auditing the Policy

Unaudited policies lack credibility. Organizational policies are frequently called into question by the courts and regulatory entities. Companies should be able to provide evidence of establishing relevant policies, training employees to follow them, and auditing their policies for compliance.

Audits are conducted to measure levels of organizational risk. Risks are categorized as compliance, financial, operational, and external. The categories associated with records and information typically involve compliance and operational risks.

Traditionally, audits are intended to determine whether employees are following the organization's policies and procedures. However, audits can also provide insight into whether a policy or procedure is effective or whether such policies and procedures need to be modified. Organizations should take steps to periodically audit their Records and Information Management program to ensure that the company is in compliance with laws, regulations, and operational mandates — and to determine whether the policy needs to be revised. The policy is the foundation for determining what should be audited, as well as for developing an audit plan.

Developing an audit plan

An audit plan involves developing a strategy or course of action for conducting an audit. Prior to conducting an audit, the auditor will develop an audit plan consisting of the following elements:

- **Audit areas:** A key process in developing an audit plan is determining what needs to be audited. The primary objective of an audit is to identify areas of risk. Therefore, a Records and Information Management audit will typically include policy areas that, if not complied with, create the greatest potential for risks.

- **Testing:** After the elements of the policy that need to be audited have been identified, a process must be established that allows the auditor to accurately test for compliance.

- **Communication:** A communication plan should be created and distributed to company departments and operations that are subject to the audit. The communication provides management with insight into when the audit will occur, what will be audited, and how to prepare for the audit.

- **Audit findings report:** After the audit is completed, the auditors will consolidate their findings into a report that will be distributed to management for review.

In medium to large organizations, an employee from the Internal Audit department normally develops the audit plan in conjunction with the Records manager or company employee assigned responsibility for overseeing the management of records. Companies that don't have an Internal Audit department may use an external audit firm to conduct the audit or assign the audit task to the Records manager.

Determining what to audit

An effective and comprehensive Records and Information Management policy provides a road map for determining what key areas to audit (*audit points*). The Records and Information Policy areas that should be regularly audited are listed as follows, along with testing recommendations for each item:

- ✔ **Policy acknowledgment:** Policy acknowledgment refers to a process for verifying and documenting employee review of the policy. Proof of acknowledgment can exist in the form of e-mails from employees, communicating that they've reviewed the policy and when the review took place. In addition, some organizations require employees to review the policy via the company intranet and use the employee's network ID to track whether the employee reviewed the policy.

- ✔ **Vital records:** During the audit, the auditor may ask the department head to identify which record types have been classified as vital and request information on how the records are being appropriately protected. This may include the creation of digital copies, nightly disaster recovery backups, and hard copies sent to off-site storage.

- ✔ **Retention schedule:** To test retention schedule compliance, the auditor can review records in storage and compare them to the schedule to determine whether any content is being retained longer than prescribed by the schedule. A list of information hold orders should be provided to the auditor. This allows the auditor to determine whether records being held beyond their retention period are part of a hold. In addition, the auditor should examine the destruction log to determine whether any information was destroyed or deleted prior to the expiration of its retention period.

- ✔ **Inactive records:** An audit of inactive records may include determining whether departments are routinely transitioning inactive records from active storage such as file cabinets to inactive or archive storage to reduce the number of file cabinets that need to be purchased.

- ✔ **Information hold orders:** The auditor should review all information hold order notifications and ensure that the appropriate records and information have been placed on hold. Depending on the size of an organization, the auditor may perform a *sampling*. A sampling is a test population that represents a percentage of the total applicable volume. The auditor should also review the destruction log to determine whether any records associated with a current hold have been destroyed.

✔ **Record storage:** This portion of the audit involves inspecting all onsite areas used for the long-term storage of company records. The auditor should reference the organization's on-site storage requirements checklist to ensure that the area meets the necessary standards. The auditor should determine whether any operations are sending their records to an offsite storage vendor. If they are, the auditor should verify that the vendor has been approved by the organization. In addition, the auditor can review invoices to see whether any payments are being made to unauthorized storage vendors.

✔ **Hard/shared network drives:** The objective of this portion of the audit is to determine whether employees are saving company records and business-value information on their hard drives and whether employees are regularly maintaining information saved to shared network drives. To test compliance, the auditor should visibly inspect all pertinent drives.

✔ **E-mail:** Typically an e-mail audit doesn't involve Records Management–related issues, but is focused on areas such as security and proper use. However, for Records and Information Management purposes, an auditor can test to determine whether employees are forwarding work messages to personal e-mail accounts, sending attachments rather than links, and retaining messages for the appropriate time frame. The auditor may have to work in conjunction with IT to view employee e-mail activity. If the organization is using an ECM or e-mail archiving system, the auditor may be able to view audit trail and history reports to collect the needed information.

✔ **Destruction:** When auditing an organization's compliance with destruction policies, the auditor should determine whether employees are using approved destruction methods such as shredding for records and content of business value. The auditor can test for compliance by inspecting recycle bins and waste receptacles to determine whether they contain items of a personal, confidential, or competitive nature. The auditor should also inspect shred bins to ensure that they are locked. The company's destruction log should be reviewed for accuracy and completeness, including the appropriate destruction approvals. If the organization uses a Records Management software application, the log should be compared to the system to determine whether items reflected as destroyed or deleted in the system match the log. Certificates of destruction should be maintained for each vendor that provides destruction services and retained in accordance with the records and information retention schedule.

Communicating the audit

Before conducting an audit, it's recommended that you notify the management of each department or operation that is subject to the audit. A communication plan should be developed that informs the management team that an audit will be conducted, the proposed dates of the audit, what will be audited, and how to prepare for the event. The communication should also provide auditor contact information in case management has any questions prior to the audit.

Prior notification allows management to ensure that information needed for the audit is collected and made available to the auditor upon his or her arrival. It also allows management to plan for any operational or personnel changes that may be needed to accommodate the auditor during the process.

Documenting the audit findings

The Audit Findings report is a comprehensive document that provides information on the results of the audit. This includes areas of compliance and noncompliance. The auditor will classify the severity and causes of the risks posed by noncompliance and provide recommendations to resolve the issues. When management is notified of noncompliance areas, an action plan should be put into place that provides resolution of the issue by a certain date, at which time the issue may be reaudited for compliance.

Chapter 14

Train the Troops

In This Chapter

▶ Generating program awareness

▶ Coming up with a training plan

▶ Seeing your training plan through

*E*quipping yourself with the tools to implement an effective and compliant Records and Information Management program is only half the battle — you also have to figure out how you get the word out to everybody else. Like any new company program, you will need to generate awareness and train employees how to use and follow it. The level of understanding that employees have of the program will determine its success. Generating awareness is especially important for new Records and Information Management programs, but also applies to existing programs that need a boost.

This chapter provides you with the guidance you need to generate awareness through developing marketing campaigns and effective training methods designed for small and large groups of employees, plus tips on conducting refresher training.

I'm Aware of That!

Employees appreciate being given advance notice of new company programs, especially if the program has the potential to impact the way they perform their functions. The organization's Records and Information Management program is no exception. You should take advantage of the opportunity to make employees aware of the program through establishing an awareness campaign.

From the top

The success of the organization's Records and Information Management program relies heavily upon employee cooperation and buy-in. The most effective way to ensure employee compliance to the program is to secure senior management support. As part of your marketing and awareness plan, you should request that senior management distribute a communication to employees introducing the program, its benefits, and their expectation that all employees will comply with the program. It's important to note that it's common in these situations that senior management will ask you to draft the communication, which they will then distribute on their letterhead.

What's in it for me?

It's important to generate awareness prior to rolling out the Records and Information Management program. Generating awareness of the program prior to implementation gives employees time to familiarize themselves with the important points and benefits of the program.

Good marketing programs have one key concept in common — they generate a perception of need. The same should be true for your Records and Information Management Program Awareness campaign. Your campaign should focus on how the program will benefit employees and why they need it. Therefore, it's essential for you to understand how the program will positively impact an employee's daily work life. Following are some examples of benefits that employees will realize:

- ✔ **Greater ease in finding information:** A huge source of employee frustration is not being able to locate needed information. An effective Records and Information Management program can significantly increase an employee's ability to find what he needs, when he needs it.

- ✔ **Eliminating guesswork:** In the absence of a Records and Information Management program, employees, out of necessity, are forced to make decisions on how to manage company information. Employees would rather be provided with consistent guidance and procedures. This eliminates the time and effort they spend wondering whether they've made the correct decision.

- ✔ **Removing clutter:** A Records and Information Management program can reduce departmental clutter. This can be accomplished by introducing document imaging or through the proper life cycle management of paper and electronic information.

✔ **Processing improvements:** An effective Records and Information Management program should include procedures that provide employees with clear and concise instructions on how to process related functions, such as boxing records for storage, physical and electronic filing, and information destruction. In addition, significant processing improvements can be achieved through the use of automated workflow.

Although other significant benefits can be realized through the implementation of a Records and Information Management program — increased legal and regulatory compliance as well as reductions in organizational risks, for example — employees don't perceive these issues as directly benefiting them. However, with the appropriate level of employee cooperation and buy-in, it will increase the probabilities of achieving all the program objectives.

Creating a creative awareness campaign

You have two approaches to choose from when creating an awareness campaign: traditional and creative. The traditional organizational approach for introducing a new program typically involves a formal (boring) communication that informs employees of the new program and why they must comply with it. Employees understand that they must adhere to company policies and programs. However, they don't like being dictated to.

The creative approach is designed to involve employees in the new program process. The employee involvement process should begin early in the development of the Records and Information Management program. For example, you can capitalize on the opportunity to inform employees about the nature and benefits of the program and seek their feedback when you are inventorying and appraising their records.

A creative awareness campaign is as good as your creativity. You should solicit ideas from other employees involved in the program. The following methods for generating awareness have proven to be effective:

✔ **Tagline:** A tagline is a catchy phrase that communicates a central topic of your program. If effective, the tagline will cause employees to immediately associate it with the Records and Information Management program. Examples of program taglines may include "For the Record," "Find what you need, when you need it," "Managing the Information Life Cycle," and "Records Management — A Process, not a Project."

✔ **Logo:** Creating a logo gives the program an identity. Like a tagline, you want your logo to create immediate recognition of the program. Your logo may stand alone or incorporate your organization's logo.

✔ **Posters:** Fun-themed posters incorporating the program's tagline and logo can be created and placed in high-traffic areas, such as break rooms, the cafeteria, and company bulletin boards.

✔ **Newsletter/intranet:** You can draft a series of articles promoting the Records and Information Management program to be published in the organization's newsletter or posted on the intranet. In the first article, you may want to take a *mystery-theme* approach. For example, you may discuss a scenario that involves working in an environment where employees always find the information they are looking for and where no desk is cluttered, without mentioning the Records and Information Management program. This approach is used to pique the interest of the reader. Subsequent articles are used to provide more information, culminating in the unveiling of the program.

✔ **Scavenger hunt:** A fun approach for generating program awareness is to develop a virtual scavenger hunt. Usually, the company intranet is used for this purpose. The objective of the scavenger hunt is to educate employees on key points of the Records and Information Management program. It involves developing questions related to Records and Information management and distributing the questions via e-mail. The e-mail contains a link to an intranet page containing the answers. The first person to correctly answer all the questions can be recognized and awarded a prize.

✔ **Lunch and learn:** Sometimes referred to as *brown-bagging,* lunch and learn involves conducting an awareness session where employees can bring their lunch and discuss the new program. Lunch breaks can serve as an effective time to bring employees together when their schedules would not otherwise permit.

✔ **Vendors:** Records Management vendors can be a good source for communication material that promotes Records and Information management. This includes educational material, posters, and quick-reference guides.

✔ **Free stuff:** Last but not least is free stuff. Free stuff is one of the most effective ways to generate awareness. Many Records Management and Office Supply vendors are happy to provide you with trinkets and samples emblazoned with their logo. You can conduct an awareness session in a conference room or cafeteria and provide the freebies. However, it's important to announce prior to the meeting that you will have free stuff to maximize attendance — and don't forget to order the pizzas.

The Internet can be a good source for tips on generating Records and Information Management program awareness. Many academic and governmental Records Management departments have websites that you can access that provide useful information. In addition, ARMA International (www.arma. org) has Records and Information Management promotional material that can be purchased.

Developing a Training Plan

Records and Information Management training should be viewed as a continuous process and not a one-time project. A need for initial training exists when the program is first introduced to the organization, but a need also exists for periodic refresher training as well as training on new Records and Information Management requirements.

Prior to training employees, you need to plan the process. This includes determining your curriculum, figuring out how to tailor training to different audiences, and identifying additional training needs. The following sections help you examine these issues.

Deciding on the curriculum

Developing your training plan requires determining the curriculum — seeing what employees need to be trained to do. When introducing a Records and Information Management program to the organization, a need exists for comprehensive training on numerous topics. The Records and Information Management policy typically serves as an effective outline for initial training. It's recommended that your curriculum focus on the following topics:

- ✔ Vital record identification and protection
- ✔ The information hold order process
- ✔ How to use the retention schedule
- ✔ Onsite and offsite storage requirements
- ✔ Proper destruction methods
- ✔ E-mail management
- ✔ The information life cycle process
- ✔ Filing electronic information
- ✔ Records Management or Enterprise Content Management (ECM) software (if applicable)

Depending on your organization and industry, additional Records and Information Management topics may require employee training, such as how to properly safeguard HIPAA (personal health information) records and other privacy-related matters.

One size doesn't always fit all

Based on your company, employees, and their job responsibilities, it may be necessary to tailor your training approach. This involves understanding whether your training curriculum needs to be modified for different workgroups or employee categories. For example, different training plans may be developed for management employees, employees with extensive job responsibilities, and other employees who have limited processing duties.

A training plan for management employees may consist of an overview of important topics, with an emphasis on management employee responsibility for ensuring compliance. This may include areas such as information hold orders, vital record identification, and approving the destruction of records. The training plan for other nonmanagement employees may include specific procedural instructions for how to use Records and Information Management software, how to process records for offsite storage, and how to use the retention schedule.

Although training plans need to be appropriately tailored for different audiences, the reality is that most employees use, process, and handle records while performing their assigned job functions. This means that the majority of topics typically covered in the organization's Records and Information Management policy may be applicable to a large percentage of company employees. Understanding your organization's operations and employee functions can help you avoid excluding any pertinent training topics.

How refreshing

Over time, some employees transfer into different roles, some leave the company, and new employees come on board. Laws, regulations, and software upgrades create changes and new requirements. This fact of corporate life means that Records and Information Management training has to be a continuous process.

Records and Information Management Program procedures can help employees understand how to perform some of the related tasks. However, in many cases, refresher training may be a more effective tool than relying solely on procedures — especially if the procedures haven't been updated. Refresher training can consist of current or new material.

Instead of assuming what refresher training needs to be conducted, it's recommended that you review the results of compliance audits that may have been conducted or survey employees to determine areas where they feel they may be deficient and need additional training. Figure 14-1 gives you an idea of what such a survey might look like.

Records and Information Management Program

Refresher Training Survey

Name:	Jane Doe
Location:	Phoenix Division
Department :	Marketing
Phone #:	(555)555-5555

Please indicate below which areas you would like to be trained on.

Check all that apply.	Topic	Comments
	Filing (paper)	
√	Filing (electronic)	How to create an electronic folder structure.
	Record retention schedule	
	Onsite storage	
√	Offsite storage	How to prepare boxes for offsite storage.
	Destruction	
	Email management	
	Vital record identification	
	Information hold order process	
√	Records management software	How to search for records in the system.

Figure 14-1:
Refresher training survey form.

Training the Masses

Training is essential to the success of the program. Employees need and want to know the correct way to manage the organization's records and information. For small businesses, the challenge of finding time to train all employees may be minimal. However, for medium- and large-sized organizations, the challenge can be significant. Therefore, you need to look at all your training options.

The following sections examine training issues, options, and recommendations for ensuring that all employees receive the necessary Records and Information Management training they need. This includes time constraints, webinars, and the use of the company intranet.

How much time do I have?

After you select the training curriculum, you need to determine how much time is needed to adequately conduct the training. You probably will not have the luxury of conducting a three-day training seminar; it's more likely that you'll have just an hour or two. Based on this constraint, you need to make the most of the training. This means determining the key points that need to be conveyed.

Limited training time is usually a result of employees not being able to be absent from their work area for long periods. If this is the case, you may be able to schedule multiple one- or two-hour training sessions over a period of several days or weeks. This will allow you adequate time to cover multiple topics and reduce the potential of trying to cover too much at one time. Although it's important to determine how much training time will be allotted, the most important issue is ensuring that employees are adequately trained on all important aspects of the program. You should request additional training time if it's needed.

Face-time training

Training is traditionally conducted in a face-to-face conference room setting — far and away the most effective training method. This approach may be possible for organizations with one location and a manageable number of employees.

Face-to-face training works so well because it allows the trainer and the trainee to interact. The trainer is able to monitor employee body language, which helps to identify the level of interest and whether the message is sinking in. Identifying these issues allows the trainer to quickly alter the content delivery or reiterate certain points.

Face-to-face instruction can also work for a large number of employees, but will typically require conducting multiple training sessions due to lack of conference room space. Organizations that have employees scattered in multiple geographical locations may decide to conduct face-to-face training, but then they probably need to budget for related travel expenses.

Webinars

Web-based training is a good option if you need to train large numbers of employees in multiple locations, have a limited training budget, or are under training time constraints.

Advances in technology have made *webinars* (live web-based training) a viable alternative to face-to-face training. Webinars typically involve sharing your desktop PC screen with attendees and using an audio connection. This approach allows employees to visually follow the training material and ask questions through the audio or by typing questions through the webinar interface. Several vendors such as GoToMeeting and Microsoft's Live Meeting are good tools for conducting webinars.

Intranet-based training

You find two primary intranet-based training approaches. One involves posting a noninteractive copy of the training material to the intranet. Employees receive a link to the material via e-mail. This approach is not preferred. It relies on the employee to read the training material. The noninteractive method doesn't test the employee on her knowledge of the content or allow her to ask questions.

The second option is an interactive approach. This presents the training information to the employee, but also requires the employee to test his knowledge of the content as he proceeds through the material. In addition, the interactive approach allows the employee to post questions that can be answered by the trainer.

Part VI
The Part of Tens

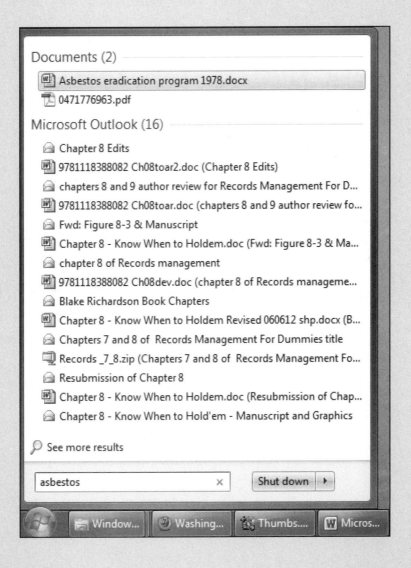

In this part . . .

This part provides you with two handy lists of ten tips. The first — Ten Simple Management Guidelines — provides you with practical, easy-to-follow recommendations that are sure to make managing records and information easier. The second — Ten Emerging Trends — examines what I'm calling trending issues. (Okay, some of them have been around for a while, but many companies are only just now taking the steps to address them; other trends are just now popping onto the scene.) Part VI gives you a sneak peek into all ten emerging trends and describes how they can potentially impact your organization.

Chapter 15

Ten Simple Management Guidelines

A Records and Information Management program has many components, processes, and principles. However, the positive thing is that all the different pieces are not that complicated; remembering to do them all is the hard part. The solution is simple: Build good Records and Information Management principles into your daily work routine. Chances are, after a while, you will not identify them as "Records and Information Management principles," but as processes that make your work life easier.

Employees should take the time to understand the tricks of the Records and Information Management trade. The investment in time will begin to immediately pay dividends as employees realize that they can find information more quickly, aren't always having to manage their e-mail quota, and don't need additional file cabinets.

This chapter provides ten guidelines guaranteed (okay, not guaranteed, but proven) to help simplify the management of records and information.

Limiting E-Mail Attachments

A great way to help manage your e-mail quota and reduce the amount of duplicate company information is to use links to access documents in an e-mail instead of sending the attachments themselves. However, remember that if you send a link to a file in your e-mail rather than an attachment, the recipient has to have access to the server and folder where the file resides.

Here's how it's done:

1. **Open your e-mail application.**
2. **Place your cursor where you want the link to appear.**
3. **Right-click in the body of the e-mail.**
4. **Choose Hyperlink from the menu that appears. (See Figure 15-1).**

   The Insert Hyperlink window appears, as shown in Figure 15-2.

5. **Click in the Text to Display box.**
6. **Type the name of the link as you would like it to appear.**
7. **Using the Look In box, navigate to the document that you want to provide access to and select it.**
8. **Click OK.**

   A link to the document is added to your e-mail. You can now send the e-mail, knowing that your e-mail recipient only has to click the link to access the document.

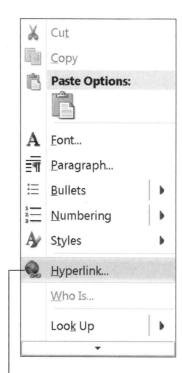

Figure 15-1: Choosing the Hyperlink option.

Hyperlink

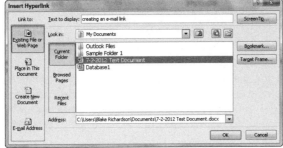

Figure 15-2:
Naming the hyperlink and establishing the link.

A link will only work if the recipients have access to the network drive and folder in which the file resides.

Knowing How to Dispose of Information

Following these simple guidelines takes the guesswork out of information destruction:

- ✔ If information is business related, it should be placed in a secure document shred bin.

- ✔ Documents that contain no business information can be placed in a secure shred or recycle bin.

All records whose retention periods have expired and are not part of an information hold order should be disposed of in a secure document shred bin. Nonrecord information that has or once had business value should also be placed in a secure document shred bin. This may include documents, spreadsheets, and presentations. Nonrecord information may still contain information of a personal, confidential, or competitive nature, requiring that it be placed in a secure document shred bin for disposal.

Information of a nonbusiness nature can be placed in a recycle bin. However, some organizations use a shred-all approach for disposing of information. This means that all information is placed in secure document shred bins.

When deleting electronic information, in many cases, it doesn't really go completely away. If you delete a file on your hard drive, it places the file in your computer's Recycle Bin. You should regularly delete all items from your Recycle Bin. When it's time to discard your computer, it should be degaussed (demagnetized), or deletion utility software should be run on the computer before it's disposed of. These methods can help ensure that no information of a personal, confidential, or competitive nature falls into the wrong hands.

Structuring Electronic Folders

Imagine opening your file cabinet drawer and inside is one large hanging folder containing various record types and date ranges. Now imagine attempting to quickly find what you need. This scenario is played out electronically every day in companies throughout the world. You open a shared network drive folder and it's full of unrelated documents, spreadsheets, presentations, image files, and PDFs that have accumulated over the years.

Creating an effective electronic folder structure can significantly improve electronic filing and retrieval. The first steps in creating a folder structure are to understand your primary business functions and to develop a folder and subfolder structure that supports it. Figure 15-3 provides an example of an Accounts Payable folder structure.

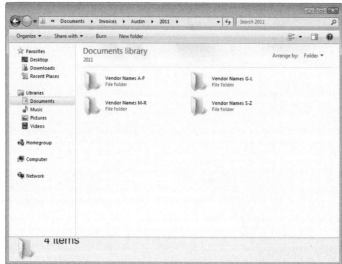

Figure 15-3:
Effective
folder
structure.

When naming folders, avoid using cryptic names, numbers (dates may be appropriate), and acronyms. Employees should be able to determine the contents of a folder or subfolder by its name.

Naming Files

So the boss needs you to send her the analysis you saved to your hard drive six months ago. Trying to find the document can be a challenge if you saved it with a name that made sense then, but doesn't seem as obvious now. You may have to open several files before you find it. Knowing how to effectively name electronic folders and files can help you to quickly find information when you need it. Following are tips for filing electronic information:

- ✔ **Hard drives:** Avoid storing company records and information of business value on your local hard drive — go for the shared network drive instead. Information that may be useful to other employees is inaccessible if it's stored on your local drive. This may include information that is useful for processing or lawsuits, audits, or governmental inquiries.

- ✔ **Naming conventions:** An effective filename allows others to determine the contents of the file without having to open it. The way files are named can be the difference between quickly being able to retrieve information or having to open several files before you find what you need. You should avoid using cryptic names, numbers (except dates as a prefix or suffix to the filename), and acronyms. Be consistent in the way that you name files. For example, if you use an employee name in the filename, always use the last name first.

- ✔ **Maintenance:** A key to efficiently finding electronic information is to maintain the repository in which it resides. If you store files to a shared network drive, you should regularly delete eligible information. This reduces the number of files that you have to scroll through or potentially review.

Managing Active and Inactive Periods

All records and information have life cycle phases that need to be managed. Two phases of the life cycle include an active and inactive period. In the active phase, records and information are used to process functions and are retrieved for inquiry purposes. During this time, physical (paper) records and information need to be readily accessible and typically are stored in departmental file cabinets. Active electronic information is stored on a server for quick retrieval.

During the inactive phase, records and information are infrequently needed. Although official company records may no longer be considered active, they may still need to be retained for legal, regulatory, and operational purposes. Inactive nonrecord information should be deleted as soon as it's no longer needed as long as it's not part of an information hold order. Inactive electronic records that must be retained are sometimes migrated to less-expensive storage media, such as optical discs or magnetic tape.

When items become inactive, it's important to remove them from active storage to minimize the amount of stuff you have to search through when looking for what you need. In addition, when file cabinets are free of inactive content, it makes filing and retrieval much easier and reduces the potential for needing more filing equipment. As soon as possible, inactive records that still need to be retained should be boxed and sent to storage.

Scheduling Destruction and Deletion

Destroying records and information in the normal course of business helps to ensure that the organization stays in compliance with laws and regulations and eliminates clutter. Destroying and deleting eligible information prevents the accumulation of unneeded information that, over time, can make it difficult to find the information you need.

This includes routinely reviewing, destroying, and deleting eligible physical and electronic information in file cabinets, in record storage boxes, and on hard and shared network drives, as well as archived data. An effective electronic information file review can eliminate or significantly reduce the need to purchase additional storage.

Before destroying or deleting company information, it's essential to ensure that the retention periods have expired and that the content is not part of any active or anticipated information hold orders.

Creating the Proper Filing System

Selecting the right filing method can enhance employee efficiency, customer service, and compliance to laws and regulations. Implementing the wrong filing system can lead to lost records, misfiles, increased labor costs, and frustration.

Understanding the types of records and information you have, as well as how they are used and requested, is the key to developing and implementing the appropriate filing system. For example, if employee files are normally requested by employee ID, you don't want to file them by last name or department.

Information growth is an important factor to consider and analyze when developing a physical (paper) filing system. Past growth can serve as an effective indicator of future growth. However, you should take into consideration new corporate initiatives such as acquisitions, new product launches, and services that may impact future volumes.

Avoiding the "Keep Everything" Syndrome

Don't be a corporate hoarder — only specific records, with long-term operational or historical value, are meant to be retained permanently. Only keep information that has active business value. When the information no longer provides benefit to your company, it should be discarded, unless the content's retention period hasn't expired or if you need the information for an active or potential lawsuit.

It is common for employees to feel the need to hang on to everything for that *just-in-case* moment — like the one that happened ten years ago when Bob in Accounting asked you for a copy of that travel invoice you had thrown out the week before. The CYA effect is another classic example and reason why employees feel the need to keep information that was eligible to be destroyed years ago. It may be appropriate in some cases to retain information for CYA purposes. However, if an issue hasn't surfaced after a reasonable amount of time, it's probably safe to destroy it.

Managing Copies

Copies of records and information are the biggest contributor to corporate clutter. This includes both electronic and physical content. Records and document management experts have estimated that over 50 percent of organizational information consists of copies that could be immediately destroyed.

Many times, it's appropriate and necessary to create a copy. However, if not properly managed, copies can increase organizational costs and risks by increasing storage and discovery costs. To properly manage copies, it's important to understand their characteristics and intended uses. Copies are meant to be

- ✔ Temporary in nature
- ✔ Not an official record
- ✔ Used for short-term or immediate reference purposes, such as meetings and reporting

A significant source of copies is system-generated reports. Many employees treat reports as official company records and retain them for long periods of time. Many organizational reports are generated on a daily, weekly, or monthly basis and lose their immediate value when the next the report is generated. For example, you may receive a weekly sales report that includes the previous week's sales figures. It may be appropriate in this case to only retain the current report and shred the previous week's information.

Employees can take the following steps to effectively manage copies:

✔ **Retention schedule:** Some retention schedules list the *department of record.* This is the department or custodian responsible for a specific record type. Other departments that possess the information should consider the item a copy and only retain it for the period of time it serves its intended business purpose.

✔ **Electronic filing:** Electronic filing practices can have a significant impact on the volume of organizational copies. The absence of an effective departmental folder structure and cryptic filenames lead to duplicate information with different names being stored throughout the organization. A good folder structure and use of proper file-naming conventions provide employees with a filing road map. After an employee locates the folder she needs to save a file to, she can determine whether the file already exists, reducing the potential for information duplication.

Using shared network drives instead of local hard drives reduces information duplication. Shared drives enable files to be accessed by multiple employees, eliminating the need for additional file copies.

✔ **Software:** The use of Records, Document, or Content Management software can significantly reduce the amount of duplicated information. The software allows you to provide multiple metadata fields to electronic content, which reduces the potential for duplicated content to exist. Many software applications alert the user when he attempts to assign metadata to a file and another file with that exact metadata already exists.

✔ **Version control:** Version control is a process that allows you to determine the most recent version of a document. If you use a Document or Content Management system, version control can happen automatically. However, versioning can also be performed manually, just by eyeballing the modification dates. (See Figure 15-4.) Knowing which file is the most recent allows you to delete prior versions or copies.

✔ **E-mail:** It's very common for employees to attach documents to an e-mail and distribute the message to multiple recipients. This creates duplicate information. Whenever possible, it's recommended that you include a link to documents in your e-mail instead of including them as attachments.

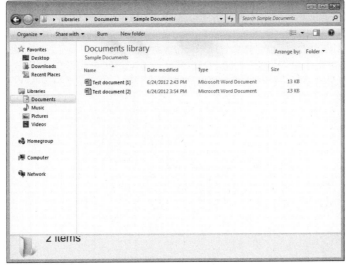

Figure 15-4:
Version
control
(manual).

Keeping It Simple

Records and information concepts and principles are simple:

- ✔ Know what you have.

- ✔ Know how long to keep what you have.

- ✔ File what you need to keep so that you can find it when you need it.

- ✔ Properly dispose of what you don't need.

Granted, this may be an oversimplification of Records and Information management, but it's not too far off. The concepts are simple; it's the volume of records and information that makes it seem such a daunting task. The good thing is that Records and Information Management processes are consistent and repeatable. The variable is volume. Volume determines how much time it will take to inventory your content, how many individual record series you have listed on your retention schedule, and how long it will take to review records and information that are eligible for destruction. Although you may have a lot of volume, the principles are simple.

When communicating Records and Information Management issues to employees, it's recommended that you keep it as simple as possible. This is not because employees aren't intelligent enough to grasp the concept — the concepts themselves are not complicated — but because Records and Information management simply isn't an employee's core function. Regardless of what new initiative or program a company is rolling out, if employees perceive it to be easy and convenient, they are more likely to comply.

Chapter 16

Ten Emerging Trends

*A*lthough Records and Information Management principles have tended to stay constant over the years, the volume of content that organizations have to manage has significantly increased. The increase in information is directly attributable to the advancements in Communication and Collaboration technologies, such as e-mail, instant messaging, Facebook, Twitter, and Microsoft SharePoint.

Product vendors, consultants, and their clients have seen the information train barreling down the track for more than a decade. Most companies have acknowledged the fact that they need to take action. However, most organizations have not implemented the appropriate steps and technologies needed to offset the effects of the information onslaught.

The objective of this chapter is to introduce and examine emerging Records and Information Management trends and to see how they can help you begin the process of addressing and resolving your challenges.

Governing Information

We know for a fact that companies are being bombarded with information from a variety of sources, such as customers, social media, employees, vendors, and regulatory agencies. The issue we're facing today is that organizations don't have the appropriate infrastructure in place to capitalize on the value of the information they possess.

Information governance is a concept born out of organizational necessity. Most companies understand that they aren't properly managing their informational assets. Information governance is a process that allows organizations to mesh technologies, processes, and people together to build an information infrastructure that will allow them to understand what information they have and how to appropriately use it.

The overarching principles of information governance are control and accountability. Typically, information governance takes the form of a committee comprised of employees from key organizational areas such as Records Management, Legal, Compliance, IT, and Information Security. The employees who serve on the committee should be in a decision-making capacity.

The committee provides oversight on all information-related areas and is specifically tasked with formulating the organization's information strategy. Such a strategy would address the following:

✔ How information is to be accessed and used

✔ Security of information

✔ Quality and integrity of information

✔ Management and disposal of information

Computing in the Clouds

Cloud computing is a term that many are familiar with at this point, but aside from a catchy name, what is it? Ask five people what cloud computing is and you'll likely get five different answers. In layman's terms, *cloud computing* describes a situation where you'd use a vendor's software (and store any associated data) on a vendor's computers and servers located in its data center via the Internet. It's software as a service (rather than as a product or application) that you load on your own computer.

It's important to understand the premise that supports cloud computing. Cloud providers (such as Amazon, IBM, and CSC) have data centers full of state-of-the-art computer equipment. All the vendor's clients share the computing power of the equipment. Think of it as the electrical grid in your city. When a customer needs more power, it's there for the taking, and in most cases, you pay only for what you use.

Cloud computing can provide significant benefits. It reduces the amount of computer equipment, software, storage, and supplies that have to be purchased and maintained by any single organization. However, some organizations are still reluctant to use it on a large-scale basis due to the following concerns:

- ✔ **Availability:** A major cloud concern centers around potential downtime. The vendor's cloud must be available to organizations whenever needed.

- ✔ **Performance:** Organizations are concerned that an Internet-based computing approach will result in diminished processing time.

- ✔ **Security:** Security is a major concern to companies. Organizations continue to be reluctant to transmit and retrieve their sensitive data via the Internet, as well as to store this type of information in a vendor's data center whose equipment is used by other clients.

- ✔ **Disaster recovery:** Companies need assurance that their information is being appropriately backed up. Storing information in a cloud data center eliminates the control that IT departments had in ensuring that proper backups were conducted.

- ✔ **Information ownership:** Organizations must be sure to include contractual language that establishes their ownership of the data that they store in the cloud.

If your organization is considering a move to the cloud, it's important to conduct an extensive vendor evaluation that includes the issues mentioned here, as well as to ensure that your information can be retained for the appropriate retention periods and that you have the ability to remove your data from the vendor's cloud in the event that you terminate the relationship. In addition, you should establish a Service Level Agreement (SLA) with the cloud provider that documents performance and availability expectations. The SLA should provide remedies for actual results that don't meet your requirements. Remedies need to be specified. Usually they include a reduction in the monthly fees you are contractually required to pay.

Big Data

Big data, the big brother to data mining and analytics, is a new concept that's starting to gain some traction in large private and governmental organizations that have huge amounts (petabytes and exabytes) of structured and unstructured data. The objective of big data is content analysis, or trying to identify repeatable business trends and patterns in an effort to make better-informed business decisions. Many organizations feel that hidden within their repositories of data are gems that could provide significant competitive advantages and operational knowledge.

The problem with big data is that the volumes are so vast that you just can't dump the information into a Microsoft Access database and run some queries against it. It requires exceptional computing horsepower — what is being referred to as Big Data technologies. Large cloud providers and their extensive computing framework can be a good option for Big Data processing.

Social Media

Who would have thought something like social media would affect businesses, let alone that it would impact the management of organizational policies, records, and information?

Most folks are familiar with Facebook, Twitter, and the many other social media sites that continue to spring up. They're now a regular part of how businesses and customers stay in touch. Many companies have departments dedicated to social media interaction. Companies use social media sites to post special deals, upcoming events, and coupons. In turn, customers are able to post reviews and comments about the organization.

Social media has an impact on Records and Information management. Many of the communications between organizations and the public qualify as official records. For example, if a company provides coupons or offers product discounts on its Facebook page, it constitutes a promise to honor the deal. The record of the offer should be retained in accordance with the company's retention schedule in the event of a customer dispute. In addition, customer inquiries and employee responses can also be records of the company. It is recommended that all organizations using social media for external communication purposes analyze the record types that are created and assign appropriate retention periods to them.

Organizations using social media tools are discovering the need to develop social media usage policies. Similar to e-mail usage policies, social media policies address the proper usage of social media by employees both during work and during nonwork hours. The intent of the policy is not to stifle employee creativity and opinions, but to ensure the integrity and reputation of the organization.

Companies don't want employees using social media sites to disparage the company or co-workers or divulge personal and confidential information about its customers. Therefore, many organizations have included some of the following topics in their policies:

- ✔ **Access:** In some organizations, only certain job roles may need access to social media sites. It's important to ensure that corporate oversight exists when it comes to who is actually granted access.

- ✔ **Confidentiality:** The policy should include language that instructs employees not to disclose any information of a personal, confidential, or competitive nature.

- ✔ **Accuracy:** Employees should be instructed to ensure that all information they post on social media sites is accurate.

- ✔ **Appropriate conduct:** Employees shouldn't post any content that is of an inappropriate or offensive nature.

- ✔ **Transparency:** When appropriate, employees should clearly identify themselves in their postings and specify their role within the organization.

Putting Some Structure to It

Traditionally, Records and Information Management has addressed physical content such as paper accounting, Human Resources records, and unstructured content (images, word processing documents, spreadsheets, and PDF documents). However, the need to manage structured data has recently started to receive a lot of attention.

Structured data is information found in database table fields, such as the information you'd find in an Accounting or HR software application. Just like unstructured information, structured data can accumulate significantly over time if not properly managed. Most organizational Record and Information retention schedules don't address the retention of structured application data. This is primarily due to the challenge of managing data fields as records.

For example, in an Accounting database, vendor invoice information may reside in multiple fields such as vendor name, vendor number, street address, city, state, and zip code. (See Figure 16-1 for an example.)

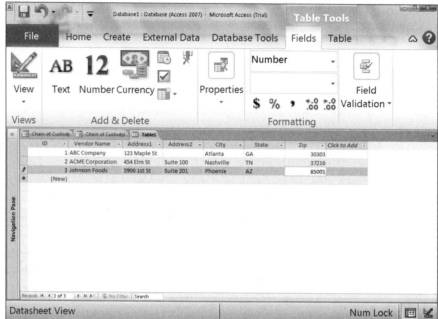

Figure 16-1:
Database
table.

When the underlying software brings these fields together, you end up with a viewable invoice. However, viewing each field separately doesn't have much meaning. So the question is, should individual fields be considered records? The answer is yes — but. The *but* in this case is due to data fields being used for other purposes. In the previous example, the vendor name is used for invoice purposes, which may need to be retained for seven years. However, the Vendor Name field may also be used for tax form purposes, which may have a different retention period. Therefore, it's important to understand the connection between fields and tables in the application.

Let's Collaborate

Organizations understand the importance of project *collaboration*. Collaboration is defined simply as working with others to achieve a goal. This may involve initiatives such as the development of a new product, the implementation of a software application, or the review of existing company policies.

Vendors have created software tools to assist employees (and, in some cases, entities outside the organization) to collaborate on projects. One such application is Microsoft SharePoint. SharePoint is now commonly used by quite a number of companies for collaboration purposes.

SharePoint has provided significant benefits to organizations, but it has also created Records and Information Management challenges. The issues aren't typically software related but are due to a lack of organizational control and governance. In many companies, employees can create a SharePoint site without having to obtain approval. This approach leads to numerous SharePoint sites that contain official company records that aren't appropriately accounted for and managed. In addition, when the project collaboration ends, the content remains on the site, which is no longer actively used.

Organizations should provide oversight and guidance to employees who need to use SharePoint. This includes a review, approval, and periodic follow-up process for anyone wanting to establish a SharePoint site. This approach helps to ensure that only valid needs are approved and that sites are regularly audited to properly account for company records. Some Records and Enterprise Content Management systems offer SharePoint integration tools. This provides the ability to ensure that record content is unalterable and that the retention periods are managed.

Generally Accepted Recordkeeping Principles

ARMA, a not-for-profit professional association and the authority on managing records and information, has published its Generally Accepted Recordkeeping Principles (GARP). GARP was developed to bring awareness to records management principles and standards.

GARP is comprised of the following eight principles:

- ✔ **Accountability:** An organization shall assign a senior executive who will oversee a recordkeeping program and delegate program responsibility to appropriate individuals, adopt policies and procedures to guide personnel, and ensure program auditability.

- ✔ **Integrity:** A recordkeeping program shall be constructed so that the records and information generated or managed by or for the organization have a reasonable and suitable guarantee of authenticity and reliability.

✔ **Protection:** A recordkeeping program shall be constructed to ensure a reasonable level of protection to records and information that are private, confidential, privileged, secret, or essential to business continuity.

✔ **Compliance:** The recordkeeping program shall be constructed to comply with applicable laws and other binding authorities as well as the organization's policies.

✔ **Availability:** An organization shall maintain records in a manner that ensures timely, efficient, and accurate retrieval of needed information.

✔ **Retention:** An organization shall maintain its records and information for an appropriate time, taking into account legal, regulatory, fiscal, operational, and historical requirements.

✔ **Disposition:** An organization shall provide secure and appropriate disposition for records that are no longer required to be maintained by applicable laws and the organization's policies.

✔ **Transparency:** The processes and activities of an organization's recordkeeping program shall be documented in an understandable manner and be available to all personnel and appropriate interested parties.

ARMA also provides the GARP Maturity Model. The model serves as a reference tool that allows an organization to determine the state of its Records and Information Management program. The GARP Maturity Model can be found in the online appendix for this book, available for download at www. dummies.com/go/recordsmanagefd.

Mapping Your Data

Most organizations are finding it difficult to manage the explosion of electronic information. Most large companies have hundreds of data repositories and software applications in use. It's important to know where your information is located, its purpose, and who owns it. Determining these factors is known as *data mapping*. Data mapping is a time-consuming process. However, many companies have decided to undertake the initiative in an effort to be better positioned to meet the electronically stored information (ESI) requirements that were introduced in the updated Federal Rules of Civil Procedure (FRCP 2006).

To comply with the FRCP, parties to a lawsuit have to provide each other with a copy or description, by category and location, of all documents and electronically stored information that each side has that supports its case.

Data mapping involves conducting an inventory of the company's electronic applications and repositories to document the name, location, and purpose of each application and repository, including what type of information it contains, the retention periods of the data, and the department or operational owner. Some organizations make the decision not to data-map all ESI, but only data they deem to be more of a risk to the organization. The process of data mapping is similar to the inventory and appraisal approach used for paper and unstructured data. Like an inventory or appraisal, it's important to remember that a maintenance factor is involved. New applications and repositories are added over time and will need to be documented.

 Many organizations that have tried to complete a data map themselves have found that the project is too big to do alone. Vendors provide software designed to assist in the mapping process. In addition, consultants are available that specialize in electronic records and information management that provide data-mapping services.

Enterprise Searching

When using the Search feature on your computer to locate a file, you usually end up entering all or part of the filename or a phrase of text in the body of the document, as well as the specific drive you need to search. For example, if you search your hard drive first, but don't find what you are looking for, you then can specify another drive location if you are connected to a network. The point is that you have to search each repository individually. *Enterprise search* eliminates this issue.

Enterprise search software allows you to search for content in multiple network repositories at the same time by using a query as long as you have access to the repositories. Think of it as an internal Google, Bing, or Yahoo! search. Enterprise search allows you to search for structured and unstructured data located on shared drives, e-mail servers, databases, intranets, extranets, external-facing websites, and other network repositories.

Enterprise search engines work by first indexing all content in specified repositories through the use of a *crawler*. The crawler wanders through each repository, database, and website, collecting information to form a searchable index of the content. It's important to remember that an enterprise search engine crawler has to be provided authentication rights to enter a repository or application. Without the proper permissions, the crawler will skip the repository.

Using enterprise search to find organizational content provides the look and feel of an Internet search, including the format of the search results. Many of the enterprise search engines will sort the results in order of relevance based on the search criteria.

Don't Get Duped

It's been estimated that over 50 percent of organizational information is duplicates. Duplicates exist in paper and electronic formats. So why is there so much duplication of information? Duplication of information can exist for valid reasons, such as needing to print a copy of an e-mail to review at a meeting, or if multiple departments need the same information to process different functions. Duplicate information should be properly disposed of as soon as it has served its business purpose.

However, the duplication and ongoing retention of electronic information are often the result of improper folder and file naming. Folders and files that are named in a cryptic manner make it difficult for other employees to know whether the file they're saving already exists. In addition, e-mail attachments are a significant source of duplicate information.

Don't despair; once again, technology has come to the rescue. *Deduplication* software tools can help organizations identify and delete duplicate and potentially duplicate content. Deduplication works by comparing chunks of data and looking for duplication. Deduplication uses two primary approaches:

- ✔ **Postprocess:** Postprocess deduplication allows new data to be entered in the application or repository throughout the workday without interruption. Then at a later time, the deduplication process will run to determine whether any duplicate information exists.

- ✔ **In-line:** The In-line deduplication process is working at all times in an effort to detect duplicate information. When duplicate or potentially duplicate information is entered in the application, the employee is notified of the issue.

Deduplication can provide several significant benefits. It shrinks the volume of information that needs to be backed up, reduces the volume of information during eDiscovery, and can improve system performance.

Appendix

Sample Forms and Vendor Listings

. . . .

. . . .

*N*o offense intended to the feline lovers out there, but there's usually more than one way to skin a cat — Records and Information management is no exception. Although the objective is creating an effective and compliant Records and Information Management program, how you choose to achieve the goal can vary. In this appendix, you find different form templates that give you options for documenting a Records and Information inventory and appraisal, as well as different retention schedule formats.

If you think that software may be appropriate for your business, the appendix provides a listing of Records, Document, and Enterprise Content Management applications for organizations of all sizes, as well as vendor contact information.

Sample Forms

In the following sections, you find different form options for conducting and documenting Records and Information inventories, appraisals, and format options for your retention schedule. (See Figures AA-1 through AA-10.) This includes templates for full-blown Records and Information inventories, as well as forms that you can use for an interview or questionnaire approach.

Inventory and appraisal forms

RECORDS INVENTORY WORKSHEET

1. Department	2. Division / Section	3. Location of Records

4. Record Series Title	5. Records Retention Schedule Number (if known)

6. Record Series Description. Include contents (e.g., reports, applications, correspondence) and purpose.

7. ☐ Original File ☐ Duplicate File	8. If duplicate, list location of original file.

9. Storage Media (check all that apply)	10. Data Privacy Classifications (list statute number or date of temporary classification)

☐ Paper   ☐ X-Rays
☐ Microfilm (not   ☐ Other (list)
COM)   _____
☐ Computer Output   _____
  Microfilm (COM)   _____
☐ Electronic   _____
☐ Photographs   _____
☐ Slides   _____
☐ Computer Cards
	☐ Public _____
	☐ Private (individuals) _____
	☐ Confidential (individuals)
	  _____
	☐ Private (decedents) _____
	☐ Confidential (decedents)
	  _____
	☐ Nonpublic _____
	☐ Protected Nonpublic _____

11. Retention Requirements (check all that apply and list citations)

☐ Federal Law _____
☐ State Law _____
☐ Statute of Limitations _____
☐ Audit Period _____
☐ Administrative Needs _____

12. Recommended Retention Periods A. Department _____ B. Onsite Storage _____ C. Offsite Storage _____ D. Total Retention (A + B + C) _____	13. A vital record is essential to the continuation or resumption of your operations after a disaster. A. Are any documents in this records series considered vital? ☐ Yes ☐ No B. If yes, which are vital and why?

14. Inventory Completed By	15. Title	16. Phone	17. Date

Figure AA-1:
A Records
Inventory
worksheet.

Records Inventory and Analysis Form

<table>
<tr><td rowspan="5" style="writing-mode: vertical">D E P A R T M E N T</td><td>

1. Department: _____

2. Address: _____

3. Account Number: _____ 4. Phone: _____

5. Name and Title of Records Contact: _____

</td></tr>
</table>

D E P A R T M E N T

1. Department: _____

2. Address: _____

3. Account Number: _____ 4. Phone: _____

5. Name and Title of Records Contact: _____

C L A S S I F I C A T I O N

6. Records Series Title: _____

7. Purpose of Records: _____

_____

8. Description of Records Type: (Summary of contents, include form numbers and titles if any, attach sample and additional sheets if needed)

_____

_____

_____

_____

_____

C U R R E N T   S I T U A T I O N

9. File Arrangement: ☐ Alphabetical   ☐ Numerical   ☐ Other: _____

10. Current Volume in cubic feet: Active: _____ Inactive: _____

11. Date Range from _____ to _____

12. Annual Accumulative Rate (cu. ft.): _____

13. Current Format: ☐ Paper ☐ Magnetic ☐ Microfilm ☐ Other: _____

Figure AA-2: A Records Inventory and Analysis form — page 1.

14. Are the records: ☐ Vital   ☐ Confidential

15. Are the records: ☐ Original   ☐ Duplicate (Originals maintained where?):
_____

V
A   16. Records Value (check all that apply: ☐ Administrative   ☐ Historical
L   (Archival)
U   ☐ Legal (If legal, cite statute or regulation below)
E

_____

17. Are records subject to fiscal audit? ☐ Yes   ☐ No
      If so, check which box applies: ☐ Federal   ☐ State   ☐ Both

D   18. Media Recommendations:
I   Maintain records in: ☐ Current Format   ☐ Microfilm
S
P   19. Recommended Disposition:
O   The files are to be cut off at the end of each: ☐ Calendar Year ☐ Fiscal
S   Year
I
T   ☐ Maintain in office _____ year(s); then
I   ☐ Transfer to Records Center; hold _____ year(s); then
O   ☐ Destroy
N   ☐ Transfer to Archives

A
P   20. _____
P
R   Name of Person Taking Inventory   Date
O
V
A   21. _____
L
              Department Head   Date

R   22. Records Code:
e   _____
c
o   23. Records Series Title:
r   _____
d
s
         24. Retention Period: Department: _____   Storage: _____
M   _____
a   mos/yrs
n   mos/yrs
a   Other (Explain): _____ _____
g   _____
e   mos/yrs
m   Total yrs
e   25. Disposition:
n   _____
t

U   26. _____
S
E   Manager, Records Management Department   Date

O
N
L
Y

Figure AA-3:
A Records
Inventory
and
Analysis
form —
page 2.

RECORDS INVENTORY WORKSHEET

1. DEPARTMENT/AGENCY NAME AND DIVISION	
2. DEPARTMENT/SECTION/UNIT	3. LOCATION OF RECORDS
4. NAME AND TITLE OF PERSON RESPONSIBLE FOR MAINTAINING RECORDS	5. TELEPHONE

RECORD SERIES IDENTIFICATION

6. WORKING RECORDS SERIES TITLE

7. DESCRIPTION (Summary of contents; function of records; form numbers, if any.

8. STATUS RECORD COPY CONVENIENCE COPY	9. RECORD MEDIUM PAPER (SPECIFY SIZE) _____ MICROFORM-SPECIFY _____ ELECTRONIC-SPECIFY _____ MAPS, DRAWINGS _____ COMPUTER PRINTOUT	10. ARRANGEMENT ALPHABETICAL NUMERIC ALPHA-NUMERIC OTHER _____
11. VOLUME (IN CUBIC FEET) CURRENT TOTAL _____ ANNUAL ACCUMULATION RATE _____	12. ESTIMATED ACTIVITY PER FILE DRAWER FOR HOW LONG? HIGH (DAILY) _____ MEDIUM(WEEKLY TO MONTHLY) _____ LOW(LESS THAN ONCE A MONTH) _____	13. RESTRICTIONS LEGAL VITAL (ESSENTIAL) CONFIDENTIAL ARCHIVAL SUBJECT TO AUDIT
14. STORAGE FILING CABINET BOXED SHELVING OTHER	15. CURRENT RETENTION PERIOD ACTIVE INACTIVE (IN OFFICE) (IN STORAGE)	16. INCLUSIVE DATES FROM _____ TO _____
17. INFORMATION MAINTAINED ON MORE THAN ONE MEDIUM		
18. INFORMATION DUPLICATED ELSEWHERE		
19. INFORMATION SUMMARIZED ELSEWHERE		
20. NAME AND TELEPHONE NUMBER OF PERSON TAKING INVENTORY		21. DATE OF INVENTORY

Figure AA-4: Another Records Inventory worksheet.

Records Inventory Form

Office or Department	Location/Building	Date

Street Address ▒▒▒▒▒▒▒▒ City ▒▒▒▒▒ State ▒▒▒ Country ▒▒▒▒ Zip/Postal Code ▒▒▒▒	Contact Person	Telephone No. / E-mail Address

Title of Record	What Department Calls Record

Description of Record

Location of Record

Purpose of Record	Is Record Still Created? ☐ Yes ☐ No ☐ Unknown

Type of Record Original – Location of Duplicates ▒▒▒▒▒▒▒▒ Duplicate – Location of Original ▒▒▒▒▒▒▒▒	Is Record Imaged? ☐ Yes ☐ No

Record Format
☐ Letter ☐ Plans/Drawings ☐ Printout ☐ Magnetic Media (indicate type) ▒▒▒▒ ☐ Form # ▒▒▒▒
☐ Legal ☐ Video/Audio Tape ☐ Microfilm ☐ Publication/Books ☐ Binder
☐ Other ▒▒▒▒▒▒▒▒

Filing Method
☐ Alphabetic ☐ Numeric ☐ Chronologic ☐ Subject ☐ Alphanumeric
☐ Geographic ☐ Calendar Year ☐ Fiscal Year ☐ Other ▒▒▒▒▒▒▒▒

Record Characteristics ☐ Vital ☐ Confidential ☐ Restricted ☐ Important ☐ Useful	Type of Equipment Use code - see back

Range of Records (e.g. 1/1/98 – 6/30/01, Li – Ru, 200 – 550) ▒▒▒▒ through ▒▒▒▒	Does Record Have Historical/Archival Value? ☐ Yes ☐ No ☐ Unknown	Volume of Records ▒▒ Filing Inches ▒▒ Cubic Feet	Accumulation Per Yr. ▒▒ Filing Inches ▒▒ Cubic Feet

Reference Rate ▒▒ times ☐ Daily ☐ Weekly ☐ Monthly ☐ Yearly ☐ Other ▒▒	Federal Funds? ☐ Yes ☐ No	External Audit Required? ☐ Yes ☐ No

File Break/Cutoff
☐ Month ☐ Calendar Year ☐ Fiscal Year ☐ Academic Year ☐ Other ▒▒▒▒▒▒▒▒

Department or Office Recommendations (Check all that apply)
☐ Destroy immediately after cutoff.
☐ Destroy ▒▒ month(s) or ▒▒ year(s) after cutoff.
☐ Hold in active file area ▒▒ month(s) or ▒▒ year(s).
☐ Transfer to ▒▒▒▒ department after ▒▒ month(s) or ▒▒ year(s).
☐ Transfer to Records Center after ▒▒ year(s).
☐ Transfer to Archives for permanent retention.
☐ Microfilm for permanent retention after ▒▒ month(s) or ▒▒ year(s).

Justification for Department or Office Recommendations

Note: Attach Sample Copy of Record/Form

Figure AA-5:
A Records Inventory form.

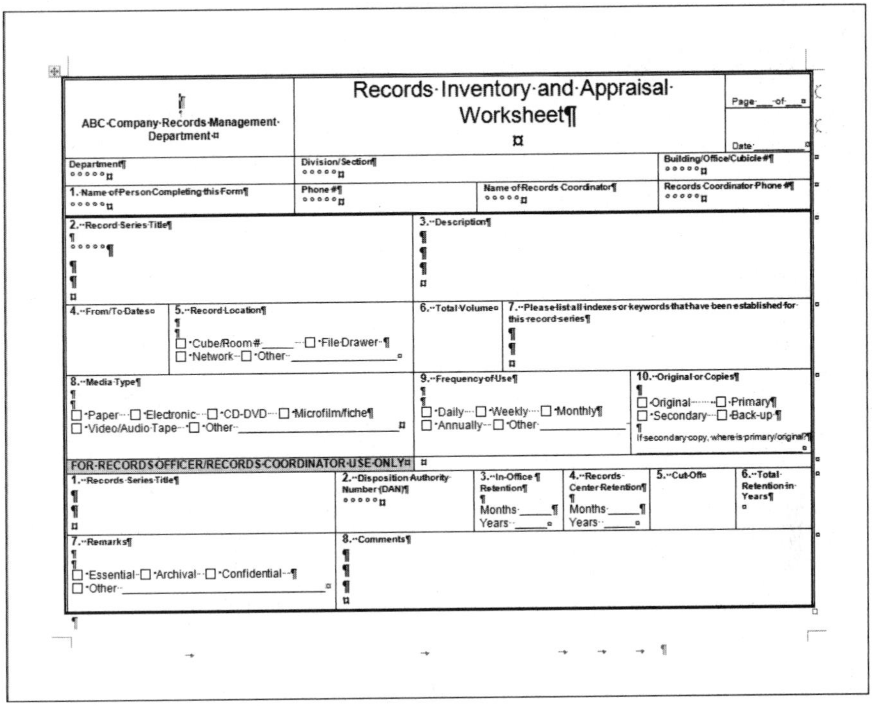
ABC Company Records Management Department

Records Inventory and Appraisal Worksheet

Page ___ of ___

Date: ________

Department

Division/Section

Building/Office/Cubicle #

1. Name of Person Completing this Form

Phone #

Name of Records Coordinator

Records Coordinator Phone #

2. Record Series Title

3. Description

4. From/To Dates

5. Record Location
☐ Cube/Room # ______ ☐ File Drawer
☐ Network ☐ Other ________________

6. Total Volume

7. Please list all indexes or keywords that have been established for this record series

8. Media Type
☐ Paper ☐ Electronic ☐ CD-DVD ☐ Microfilm/fiche
☐ Video/Audio Tape ☐ Other ________________

9. Frequency of Use
☐ Daily ☐ Weekly ☐ Monthly
☐ Annually ☐ Other ____________

10. Original or Copies
☐ Original ☐ Primary
☐ Secondary ☐ Back-up
If secondary copy, where is primary/original?

FOR RECORDS OFFICER/RECORDS COORDINATOR USE ONLY

1. Records Series Title

2. Disposition Authority Number (DAN)

3. In-Office Retention
Months ______
Years ______

4. Records Center Retention
Months ______
Years ______

5. Cut-Off

6. Total Retention in Years

7. Remarks
☐ Essential ☐ Archival ☐ Confidential
☐ Other ________________

8. Comments

Figure AA-6: A Records Inventory and Appraisal worksheet.

ABC Company

Records Inventory Questionnaire Form

Division:	
Location:	
Department :	
Contact Name:	
Email Address:	
Phone #:	

Describe departmental responsibilities:	

Record Name	Record Description	How is Record Used	Date Ranges of the Record	Is the Record a Duplicate Y/N	How Frequently is the Record Referenced	How Long is the Record Currently Retained	Is the Retention of the Record Governed by an Outside Entity - Specify

Figure AA-7:
A Records
Inventory
Question-
naire form.

Retention schedule forms

ABC Company

Record Series Retention Schedule

Department: General & Administrative

Record Name	Record Description	Record Series Code	Start Code	Retention Period (years)*	Media Format	Vital Y/N	Citation
Articles of Incorporation	Documentation that establishes legal existence of the company.	GENA0001	PERM	PERM	Paper and Electronic	Y	
Board of Director's Meeting Minutes	Detailed transcription of meeting topics and responses during Board of Director meetings.	GENA0002	PERM	PERM	Paper and electronic	Y	
Bylaws	Rules adopted by the company.	GENA0003	PERM	PERM	Paper and Electronic	Y	
Capital Stock Certificates - Canceled	Canceled stock certificates.	GENA0004	Current Month (CMO)	7	Electronic	N	SEC ####
Capital Stock Certificates - Outstanding	Outstanding stock Certificates.	GENA0005	PERM	PERM	Electronic	Y	SEC ####
Mergers	Merger and due diligence information.	GENA0006	Active (ACT)	20	Paper and Electronic	N	IRS ####
Governmental Filings	Securities and Exchange Commission filings.	GENA0007	Current Month (CMO)	10	Electronic	N	SEC ####

*Sample retention periods.

Figure AA-8: A Sample Departmental Retention Schedule form.

ABC Company

Functional Retention Schedule

Accounting

Functional Series	Record Function	Description	Department of Record	Retention Period*
050	Accounts Payable	Invoices, purchase orders, Pcards, shipping and receiving records	General Accounting	7 Years
055	Accounts Receivable	Billing and edit sheets	General Accounting	7 Years
060	Banking	Reconciliations, deposits and transfers	Banking	7 Years
065	Budget	Operating, project and fiscal budgets, working papers and memos	Financial Planning	7 Years

*Sample retention periods.

Figure AA-9:
A Sample
Big Bucket
Retention
Schedule
form.

Software Applications and Vendor Contact Information

Due to the amount of records and information that most companies create and receive, it may no longer be feasible to try to manage them with multiple sets of fast hands and ever-vigilant eyes. Records, Document, and Enterprise Content Management applications have become a necessity for ensuring that records and information are managed in an efficient and compliant manner.

The Records and Information software market is full of vendor applications designed to meet the needs of small to global organizations. Table A-1 lists vendors, their applications, and their website addresses to help you in your research and evaluation.

Table A-1   Software Vendors and Applications

Vendor Name	Software Name	Type of Software	Website
Alfresco	Alfresco Enterprise 4	ECM, Records and Document Management	http://www.alfresco.com/
Archive Systems	OmniRIM/Virtual File Room	Records and Document Management	http://www.archivesystems.com/
ASG Software Solutions	ASG ViewDirect/ ASG Records Manager	ECM, Records (electronic) and Document Management	http://www.asg.com/
Docuware	Docuware 5	ECM, Records and Document Management	http://www.docuware.com/
Eloquent-Systems Inc.	Eloquent Records	Physical and Electronic Records Management	http://www.eloquent-systems.com/
EMC Corporation	Documentum/ ApplicationXtender	Documentum - ECM, Records and Document Management; ApplicationXtender - Document Management	http://www.emc.com/domains/documentum/index.htm
EVER TEAM	EverSuite	ECM, Records and Document Management	http://www.ever-team.com/
Fabasoft	Fabasoft Folio	ECM, Records and Document Management	http://www.fabasoft.com/
File Trail Inc.	File Trail RM	Physical Records Management	http://www.filetrail.com/FT_Home/Index.asp?gclid=
HP	Autonomy Content Management/TRIM	Autonomy - ECM, Records and Document Management; TRIM Physical and Electronic Records Management	http://www.autonomy.com/ http://protect.autonomy.com/products/records-management/trim/index.htm
Hyland Software	OnBase	ECM, Records and Document Management	http://www.hyland.com/onbase-and-ecm.aspx
IBM	FileNet/InfoSphere	ECM, Records and Document Management	http://www-01.ibm.com/software/ecm/filenet/
Infolinx	Infolinx	Physical Records Management	http://www.infolinx.com/
Iron Mountain	Accutrac	Physical Records Management	http://www.ironmountain.com/Services/Records-Management-And-Storage/Records-Management-Software.aspx
Knowledgeone Corporation	RecFind 6	ECM, Records (electronic) and Document Management	http://www.knowledgeonecorp.com/

Laserfiche	Laserfiche Rio/ Laserfiche Avante	ECM, Records (physical records manage-ment provided through an integration with Infolinx) and Document Management	http://www.laserfiche.com/en-us
Lexmark/ Perceptive Software	ImageNow/ Retention Policy Manager	ECM, Records and Document Management	http://www.perceptivesoftware.com/
Marex Group	FileBound	Document Management	http://www.filebound.com/
Microsoft	SharePoint	ECM, Records and Document Management	http://sharepoint.microsoft.com/en-us/Pages/default.aspx
Newgen Software Technology	ECM Suite	ECM, Records and Document Management	http://www.newgensoft.com/homepage
Objective	Enterprise Content Management	ECM, Records and Document Management	http://www.objective.com/anz/index.html
Open Text Corporation	Open Text ECM Suite	ECM, Records and Document Management	http://www.opentext.com/2/global.htm
ORACLE	Universal Content Manager (UCM)/ Universal Records Manager (URM)	ECM, Records and Document Management	http://www.oracle.com/index.html
Paper Tiger	Digital Tiger/Paper Tiger	Physical and Electronic Records Management	http://thepapertiger.com/
Saperion			
Triadd Software Corporation	Enterprise Content Management	ECM, Records and Document Management	http://www.saperion.com/en/
Xerox	GAIN RM	Physical and Electronic Records Management	http://www.triaddsoftware.com/
Zasio Enterprises, Inc.	DocuShare	Physical and Electronic Records Management	http://docushare.xerox.com/
	Versatile (Enterprise, Professional and Express)	Physical and Electronic Records Management	http://www.zasio.com/

Index

● **F** ●